The Campus History Series

HOOD COLLEGE

ON THE FRONT COVER: The Woman's College of Frederick class of 1900 poses for its graduation photograph. (Courtesy of the Hood College Archives.)

BACKGROUND: The four columns of Alumnae Hall, Hood's administration building, are emblematic of the ideals of the college. Each column is named for one of those ideals: Hope, Opportunity, Obligation, and Democracy. (Courtesy of the Hood College Archives.)

The Campus History Series

HOOD COLLEGE

THE STAFF AND VOLUNTEERS OF THE HOOD COLLEGE ARCHIVES
FOREWORD BY RONALD J. VOLPE, PRESIDENT OF HOOD COLLEGE

ARCADIA PUBLISHING

ISBN 978-0-7385-9802-4

Published by Arcadia Publishing
Charleston, South Carolina

Printed in the United States of America

Library of Congress Catalog Card Number: 2012944314

For all general information, please contact Arcadia Publishing:
Telephone 843-853-2070
Fax 843-853-0044
E-mail sales@arcadiapublishing.com
For customer service and orders:
Toll-Free 1-888-313-2665

Visit us on the Internet at www.arcadiapublishing.com

This book is dedicated to all—past and present—who have touched, and been touched by, Hood College. May it be inspiration for those who will create its future.

Contents

FOREWORD

It has been my distinct privilege to serve as president of this treasured institution since 2001. During my tenure as Hood's 10th president, I have had the pleasure of traveling the country meeting and speaking with many Hood alumni, donors, and friends. And while I was quick to "tell the Hood story," including our vision and plans for the future, those conversations also addressed Hood's formative years.

The inspiring story of Hood College through more than 100 years is told here in photography and short writings. It is the authors' hope that this collection of images and words takes readers back through Hood's humble beginnings to today's transformative coeducational institution.

Ralph Waldo Emerson said, "The history of an institution is but the lengthened shadows of one man." While there is truth to this, especially considering Hood's first and longest-serving president, Joseph Henry Apple, the authors rightfully present the many men and women whose lengthy shadows have held sway for over a century.

Navigating this history, from presidents Truxal to Church, the college continued to flourish. Not without challenges, Hood weathered all storms, thanks largely to those "lengthy shadows" (Brodbeck, Coblentz, Hodson, Meyran, Shriner, and Whitaker to name a very few) who served as its protectors. You will meet them along with students and great teachers in these pages.

I can only imagine what my predecessors might say if they had the opportunity to see Hood today. Change has been the centerpiece of our rich history, but our core values, identity, and mission are as steadfast as ever.

After 12 years as president, I continue to marvel at how, each semester, Hood repeats its extraordinary cycle of teaching, learning, and discovery to fulfill its mission of educating its graduates for lives of responsibility, leadership, and service. This is made possible in part by the vision of those giants of the past. I feel great pride to know that new giants, casting new shadows, will emerge in the future, a future that will make us so proud. But for now, enjoy this memorable journey into the past.

Warmest Regards,
Ronald J. Volpe, PhD
President

Acknowledgments

Like Hood College's history itself, this book came about as the result of the efforts of many people. The authors would like to express our sincere thanks to Lissie Cain, our editor, for early lessons in style sheets and keeping us focused; thanks to Hood's president, Dr. Ronald J. Volpe, not only for his foreword but also for his infectious enthusiasm for anything and everything associated with Hood College; thanks to Dr. Katherine Conway-Turner, Hood's provost, who saw the value in this project and gave it her eager stamp of approval; thanks to Hood's Office of Marketing and Communications, which assisted us with accessing archival photographs; thanks to Toby Peterson, image scanner par excellence; thanks to friends, spouses, and coworkers, who exercised patience and forgiveness when our attention was focused on the book to the exclusion of other important things; thanks to the late Nancy Nolf Carl (1976), whose wide-ranging research on Hood's history for its centennial celebration informed us all as we wrote the later chapters; and thanks to the late Dr. Sydney Silverman, professor of biology at Hood from 1979 to 1989, whose embryonic, unpublished history of the college provided countless facts about, and insights into, the earlier years of Hood's past.

Finally, we need to recognize all of the individuals, groups, events, and traditions that we could not include in these pages, for they have also made Hood and its history what they are, and this snapshot of our treasured institution would have been very different without them.

All images are courtesy of the Hood College archives.

All years in parentheses, unless otherwise noted, reflect a graduation date from Hood College.

INTRODUCTION

Hood College traces its earliest history to Hiram Winchester's idea that girls should be educated. His vision was a grander one than he could promote by himself, however, and he sold the idea of a female seminary to the Maryland Legislature, which officially chartered Winchester's school in 1840. The Frederick Female Seminary offered a primary through secondary curriculum, educating girls, as well as boys of primary school age, for nearly 50 years. A second strand was woven into this history by the Reformed Church. Precisely at the moment that the Frederick Female Seminary was contemplating shutting its doors, the Potomac Synod of the Reformed Church wanted to relocate the "female department" of its Mercersburg (Pennsylvania) College to a location below the Mason-Dixon Line. The hard times of the Frederick Female Seminary became the good fortune of the Reformed Church, for in it they had found a complete educational institution in a suitable location. The trustees of the Frederick Female Seminary leased the seminary buildings to the Potomac Synod under the condition that the synod would continue to fulfill the provisions of the seminary's charter; that is, they would continue to educate women.

The historical focus then turned to another determined man with a vision. Joseph Henry Apple, a high school teacher, was hired by the Potomac Synod to take on the formation of the Woman's College of Frederick. He had some latitude in building the institution, limited by the existing facilities and a modest budget, and was empowered by his endless capacity for difficult work and vision for what the college could become. He hired faculty, reorganized offices, classrooms, and dormitory rooms, wrote advertising copy, and recruited students. He taught at least seven different subjects. He did it all, and he kept at it for 41 years, aided by faculty and administrators who shared the vision and rolled up their sleeves. Later in life, he wrote that if he had known at the outset what the task would entail, he might not have accepted the presidency and the challenges that came with it.

But Dr. Apple had taken on the responsibilities and had set the Woman's College—and Hood College—on a course with a clear trajectory of educational excellence and collegiate tradition to be built upon by nine additional presidents over the ensuing decades. The first years of the new millennium presented their own set of challenges to the most recent of those presidents, Dr. Ronald Volpe. Following in the tradition of Hiram Winchester and Joseph Henry Apple, he met the challenges head-on, strengthening the college by pursuing the difficult decision to make the transition to coeducation. The vision and optimism, dogged determination, and sheer hard work he has applied during his tenure, with the assistance and dedication of faculty, staff, and alumni, have brought a fresh luster to the college, evident in the new buildings and facilities on campus, the vibrant new programs, and in the record numbers of students attending Hood College today.

One

Our Precursor
The Frederick Female Seminary, 1840–1893

Hiram Winchester, a New England Yankee, moved to Frederick, Maryland, in 1838. He was a public-minded citizen, involved in the Presbyterian Church, and an advocate for a public water system. Before coming to Frederick, he ran a girls' school in Baltimore, and he intended to establish a similar institution in his newly adopted city.

He opened a school on East Patrick Street before moving to larger quarters on North Market Street. The school thrived, and Winchester decided to launch an even larger school. Working with the Maryland Legislature, he secured a charter for his school for "the promotion and advancement of female education and the cultivation and diffusion of literature and science." He conducted a lottery to raise funds for land and construct a new building for the enterprise. A suitable property was located on East Church Street, and ground was broken in 1843. The edifice, styled after a Greek temple, was designed by Winchester himself.

The Frederick Female Seminary opened in 1845. The term *seminary* was used at the time to describe a girls' school. The faculty of seven teachers taught at three levels—collegiate, preparatory, and juvenile—with subjects running the gamut from spelling and penmanship to languages, music, algebra, astronomy, and "fine needlework."

The seminary's enrollment grew, and in 1856 work began on a new building. The second building was identical to the first, and the two were connected by a three-story corridor. Those buildings, known today as Winchester Hall, now house Frederick County government. After the bloody Battle of Antietam in September 1862, West Hall, as the new building was called, was used as a hospital for wounded soldiers.

The Civil War disrupted classes, and the school closed for over a year, reopening in 1864. Hiram Winchester, in failing health, retired in 1865. Rev. Thomas Cann became president and added classes in pedagogy for students wanting to become teachers. Three additional presidents succeeded Cann between 1873 and 1885. When the last of these, William Henry Purnell, resigned his post in 1893, the Frederick Female Seminary, after half a century, ceased operations.

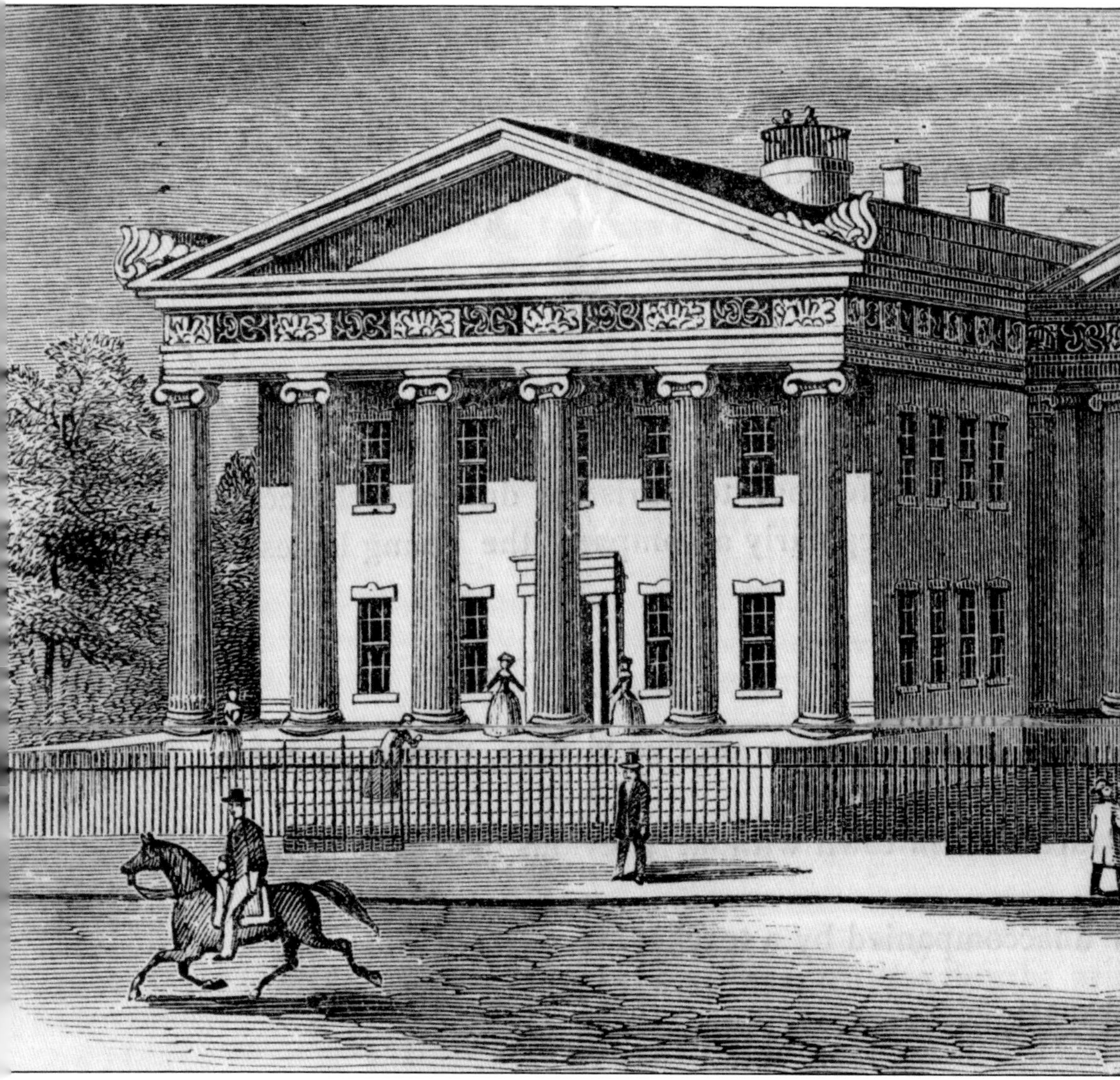

This lithograph of the Frederick Female Seminary, dating from the mid-19th century, shows the twin buildings that were designed by Hiram Winchester, president of the seminary. He clearly had an artistic bent, as he personally prepared the matrices for the decorative cornices and ornamental woodwork that adorn the buildings. Ground was broken for the first of the two buildings, East Hall, in 1843, and it was ready for occupancy in 1845. The seminary grew

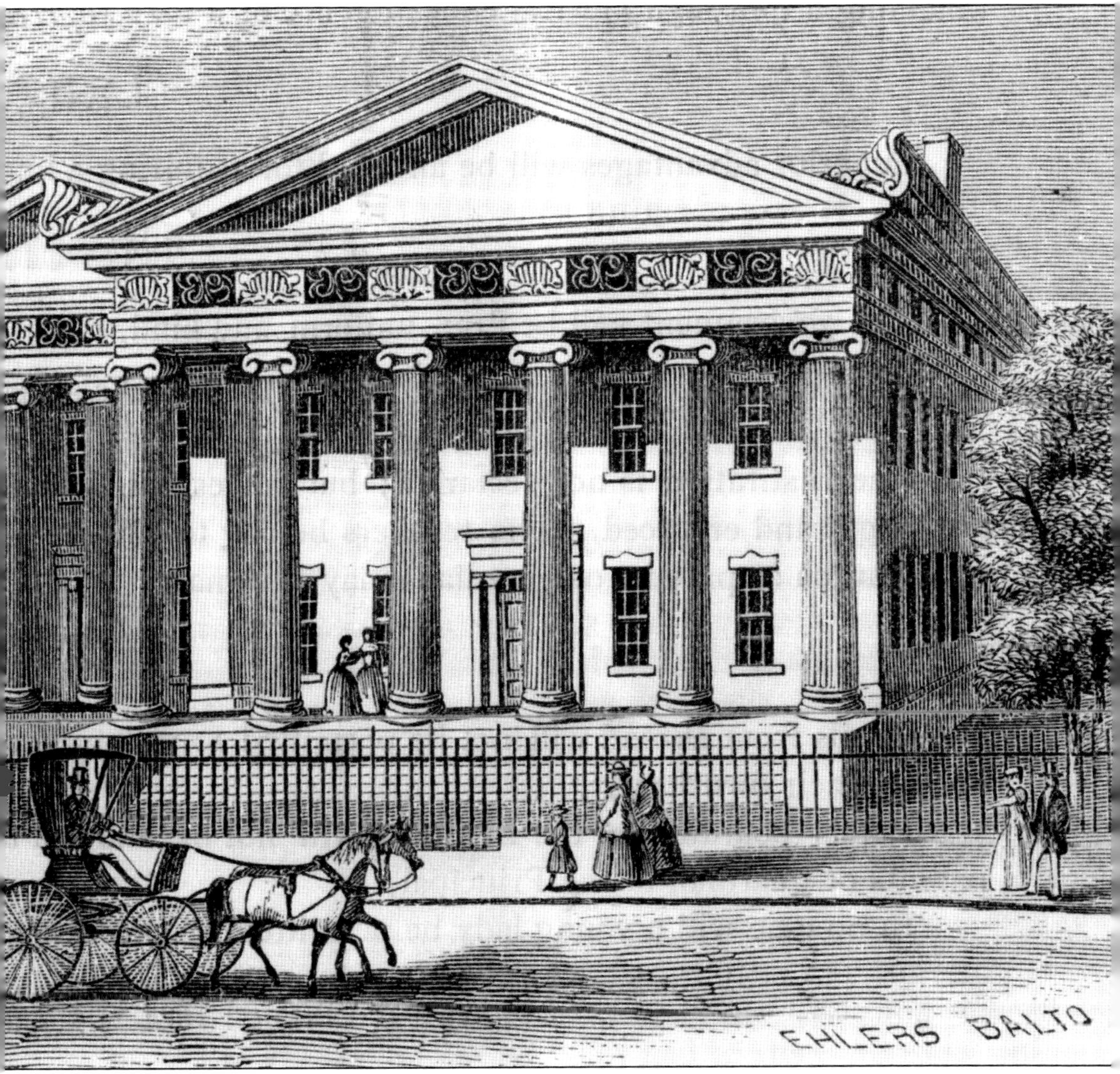

quickly, and in 1856 West Hall was added. The Ionic columns on the facades represent one of the college's first traditions, as this motif is reflected in many structures on the current campus, including its first building, Alumnae Hall. The columns of Alumnae Hall—named Hope, Opportunity, Obligation, and Democracy for the college's values—were dedicated by the classes of 1915, 1916, 1917, and 1918.

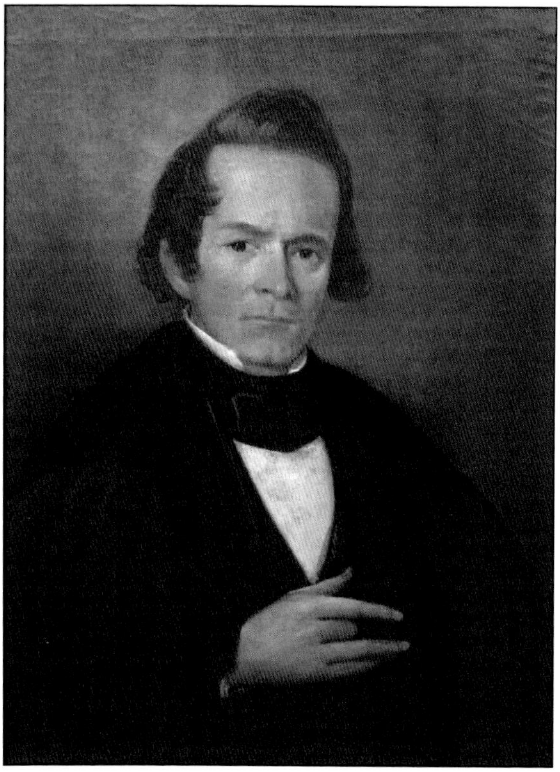

Hiram Winchester was born in Massachusetts in 1803. He married Juliette Kirkham in 1831, and the couple had five children, only two of whom survived to adulthood. The family arrived in Frederick in 1838 after Winchester directed a school in Baltimore. He must have been a very busy man, as he served not only as the president of the Frederick Female Seminary but also taught numerous subjects.

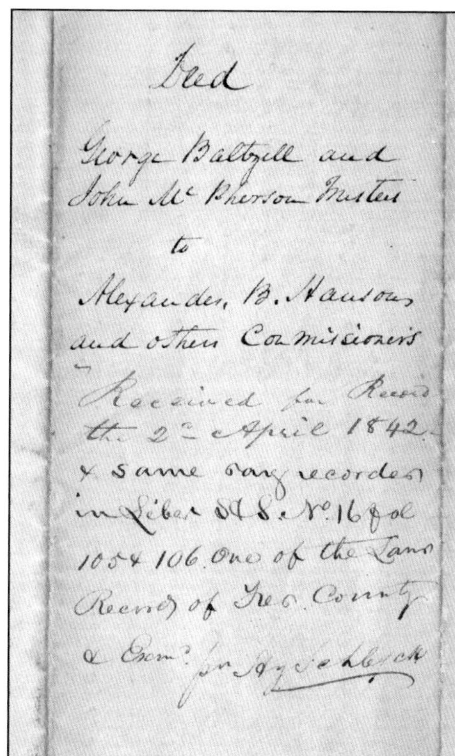

Deed

George Baltzell and John McPherson Trustees

to

Alexander B. Hanson and others Commissioners

Received for Record the 2nd April 1842 & same day recorded in Liber HS No. 16 fol 105 & 106 One of the Land Records of Fred. County & Exam. per H. Schley Clk

The deed to the Frederick Female Seminary property is dated April 2, 1842, and signed by clerk Henry Schley. It records a detailed description of the property and the sale by George Baltzell and John McPherson to the commissioners of the seminary: Alexander B. Hanson, David Boyd, Gideon Bantz, Albert Ritchie, and John Brunner. The names Schley, Hanson, Bantz, and Brunner appear frequently in Frederick history.

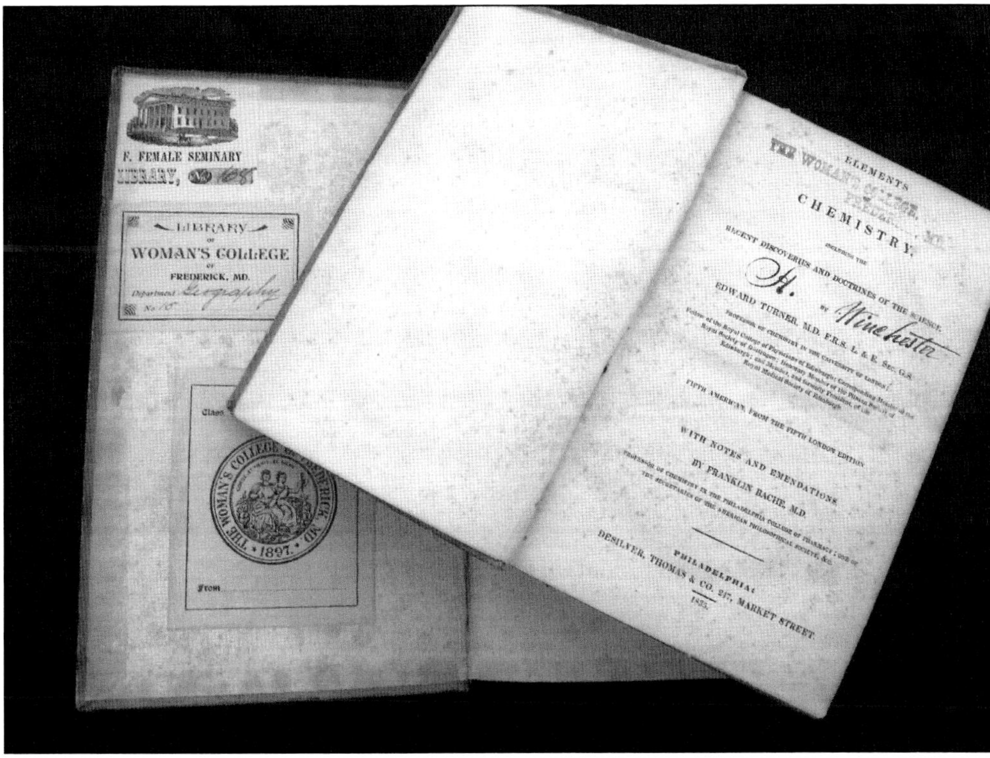

A few books from the seminary library survive, as shown by the bookplate on the left and Hiram Winchester's signature on the right. The presence of a chemistry book suggests that ideas regarding women's education were evolving. The 1850 catalog states that the seminary "was intended to be an institution where all may have their daughters instructed in the branches of science and literature adapted to the female mind."

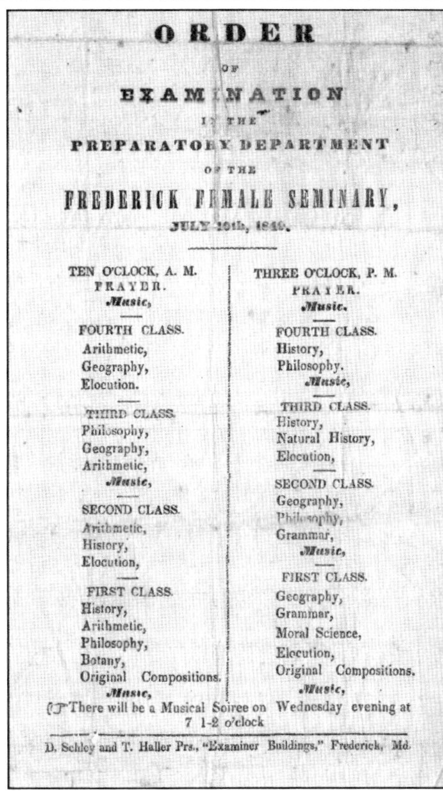

ORDER
OF
EXAMINATION
IN THE
PREPARATORY DEPARTMENT
OF THE
FREDERICK FEMALE SEMINARY,
JULY [illegible].

TEN O'CLOCK, A. M.
PRAYER.
Music,

FOURTH CLASS.
Arithmetic,
Geography,
Elocution.

THIRD CLASS.
Philosophy,
Geography,
Arithmetic,
Music,

SECOND CLASS.
Arithmetic,
History,
Elocution,

FIRST CLASS.
History,
Arithmetic,
Philosophy,
Botany,
Original Compositions.
Music,

THREE O'CLOCK, P. M.
PRAYER.
Music.

FOURTH CLASS.
History,
Philosophy.
Music,

THIRD CLASS.
History,
Natural History,
Elocution,

SECOND CLASS.
Geography,
Philosophy,
Grammar,
Music,

FIRST CLASS.
Geography,
Grammar,
Moral Science,
Elocution,
Original Compositions.
Music,

☞ There will be a Musical Soiree on Wednesday evening at 7 1-2 o'clock

D. Schley and T. Haller Prs., "Examiner Buildings," Frederick, Md.

The announcement of the "Order of Examination" for the Frederick Female Seminary Preparatory Department provides an example of the curriculum. Margaret Scholl (later wife of James Mifflin Hood) would have sat for these very examinations before she graduated from the seminary in 1849. Probably much to the dismay of the students, these oral examinations were open to the public.

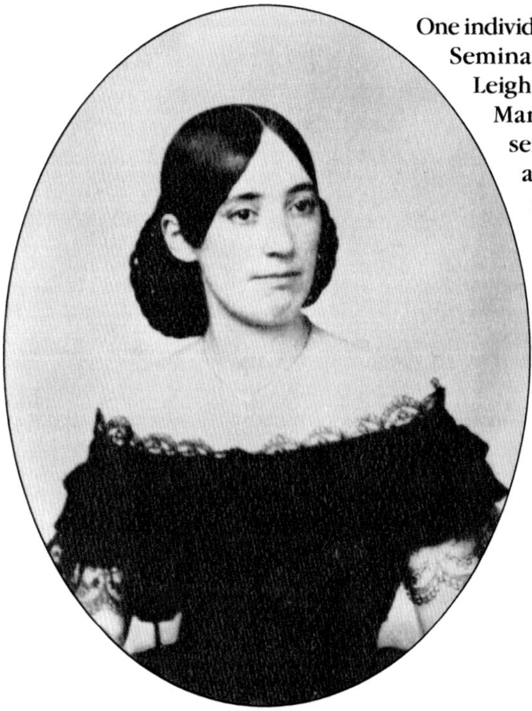

One individual who graduated from the Frederick Female Seminary in 1849 with Margaret Scholl was Lucy Leigh Gardiner, who served as the principal of St. Mary's Female Seminary in St. Mary's City. This seminary, which was established in 1846 just after the Frederick Female Seminary and also financed by a lottery, was the predecessor of St. Mary's College of Maryland.

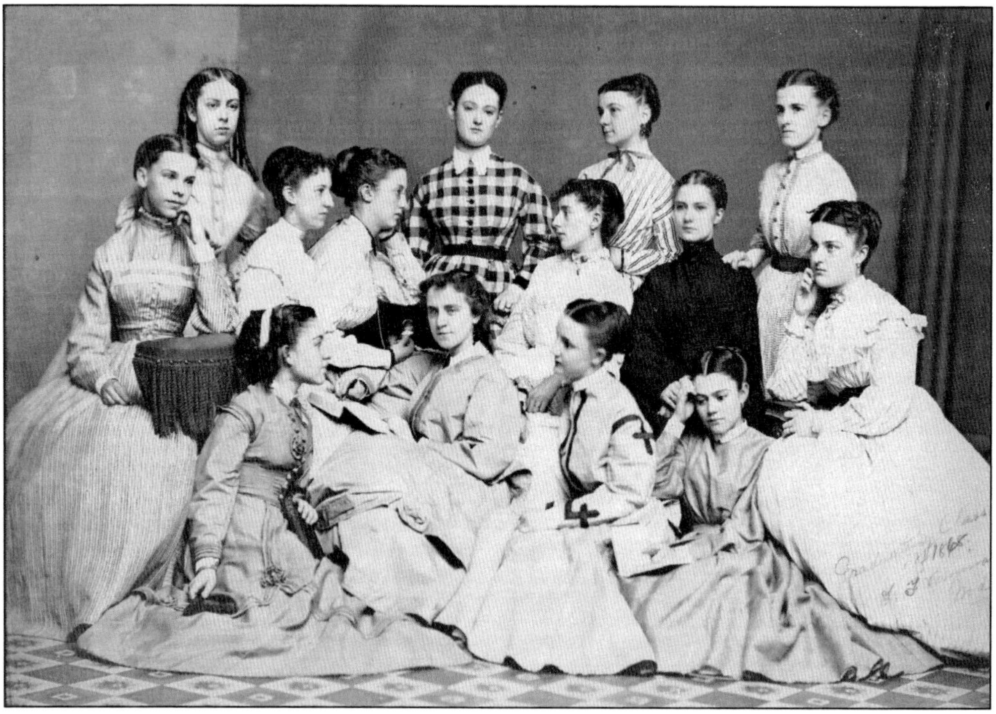

After the Civil War was over, the Frederick Female Seminary reopened under the direction of Rev. Thomas Cann. The young ladies in this photograph of the 1868 graduating class no doubt studied under him. One of them, May, is Cann's daughter. Another, Florence Doub, went on to teach art at the Woman's College of Frederick, later renamed Hood College.

James Hackleton followed Cann as president of the Frederick Female Seminary in 1873. He and his wife administered a female seminary in Memphis, Tennessee, before coming to Frederick. When her husband died in 1877, Maria Hackleton assumed the office of president. Apparently, the transition was smooth, and little changed in the running of the institution. She served until 1885, when she was hired as coprincipal of the Media (Pennsylvania) Seminary.

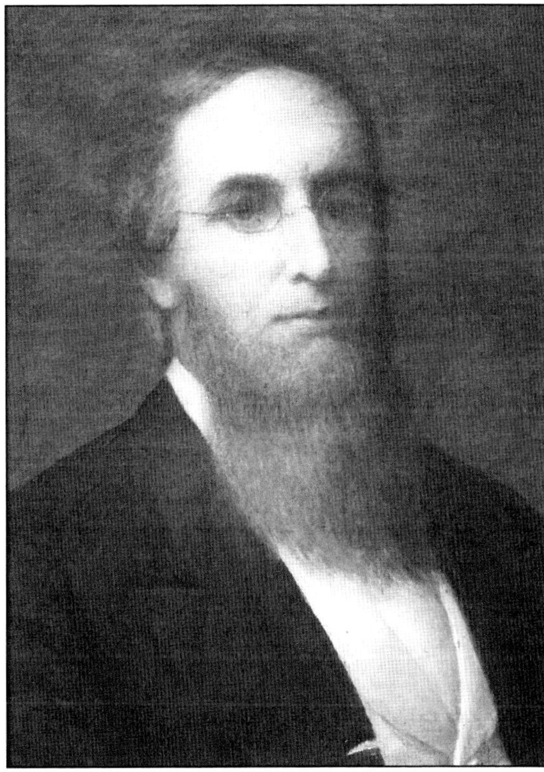

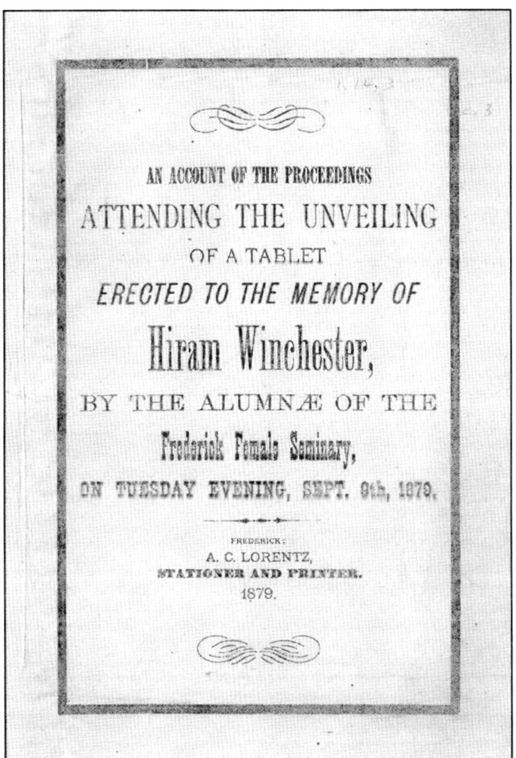

AN ACCOUNT OF THE PROCEEDINGS

ATTENDING THE UNVEILING

OF A TABLET

ERECTED TO THE MEMORY OF

Hiram Winchester,

BY THE ALUMNÆ OF THE

Frederick Female Seminary,

ON TUESDAY EVENING, SEPT. 9th, 1879.

FREDERICK:

A. C. LORENTZ,

STATIONER AND PRINTER.

1879.

Due to poor health, Hiram Winchester retired to Cambridge, Maryland, when the Frederick Female Seminary suspended operations during the Civil War. He died in Cambridge on July 5, 1876. His contributions were recognized by appreciative alumnae, who commissioned a large plaque for Collegiate Hall. It can still be viewed today in downtown Frederick at Winchester Hall, formerly known as Collegiate Hall.

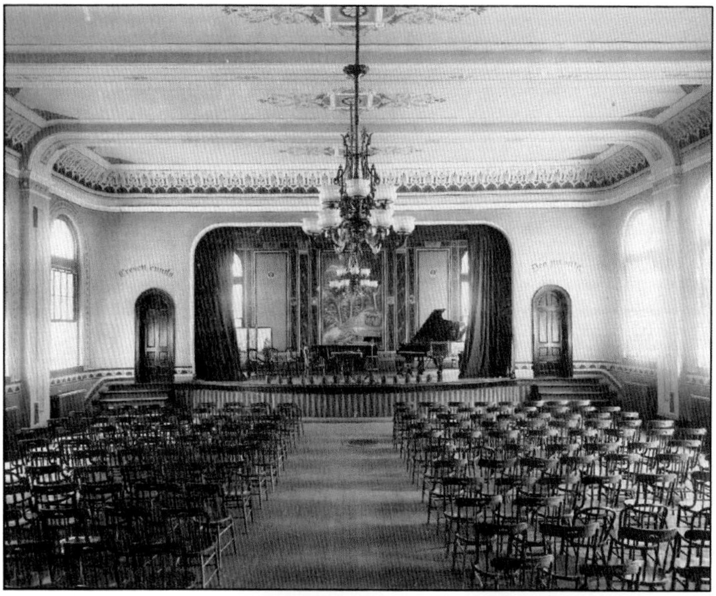

The auditorium of West Hall provided a space for frequent soirees and other entertainments. The motto on the walls flanking the stage, reading, "*Crescit eundo, Deo juvante*," means "In going, it grows, with God's help" and is an expansion of a phrase the Roman poet Lucretius used when he described an arcing lightning bolt. Perhaps, used here, it refers to the accretive nature of education.

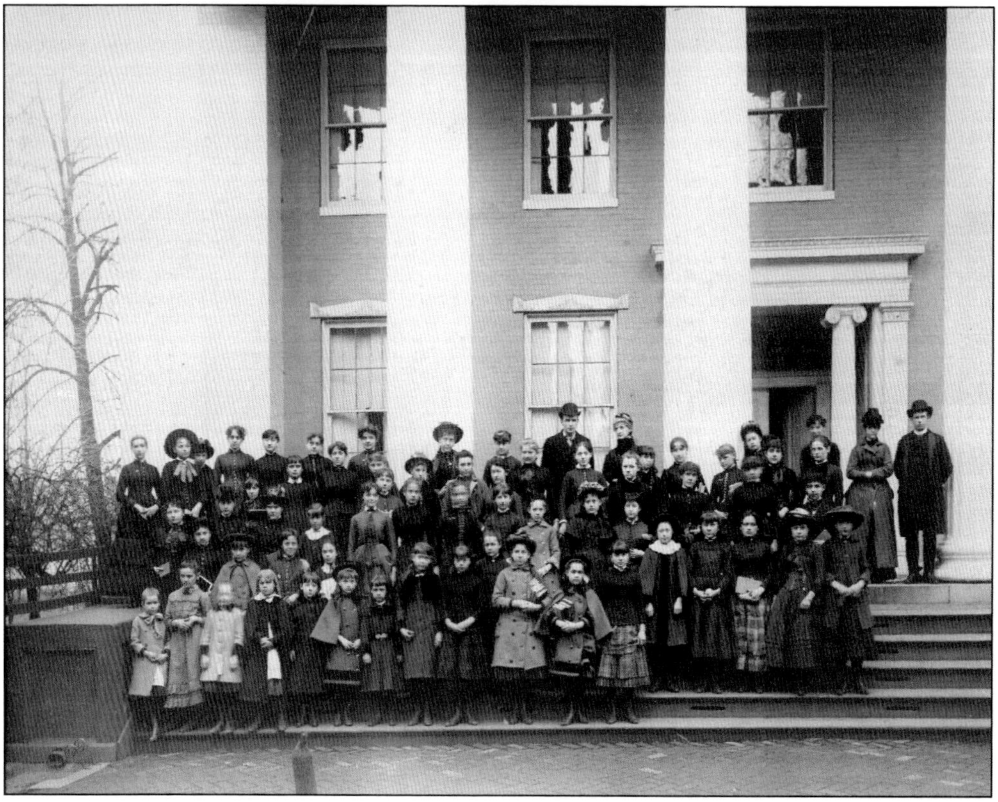

The students and faculty of the Frederick Female Seminary are shown in this photograph from 1885. The seminary offered elementary, preparatory, and collegiate curricula, which explains the age range of the students pictured here. In the 1884 catalog, the board of visitors "recommends the Frederick Female Seminary as eminently deserving the confidence and patronage of those who have daughters or wards to educate."

Two

Our Founding
The Woman's College of Frederick, 1893–1912

The fact that the Woman's College was founded in Frederick resulted from a simple coincidence. The Frederick Female Seminary was having financial difficulties at the same time that the Potomac Synod of the Reformed Church was trying to move the "woman's department" of Mercersburg College in Pennsylvania to a location south of the Mason-Dixon Line. The synod had considered several locations, but the availability of an entire educational institution, complete with prospective students and even some faculty, made it an easy decision. The seminary trustees, with assurances from the synod that they would carry out the educational mission of the seminary's charter, agreed to lease the buildings to the synod in May 1893. Joseph Henry Apple, a high school mathematics teacher, agreed to become president of the new institution, while his wife, Mary Rankin Apple, also an educator, was named vice president.

President Apple immediately brought drive and enthusiasm to the development of the college, recruiting students, hiring additional faculty (for a total of 12), and organizing the refurbishment of classrooms, as well as developing a curriculum. Classes began on September 12, 1893, with 83 students. The first two graduating classes in 1895 and 1896 received certificates, and in 1897 the college was incorporated by the State of Maryland and began awarding degrees.

By 1898, it was apparent that East and West Halls did not afford sufficient space for the growing institution, and over the next several years the college occupied an additional seven buildings in downtown Frederick. In 1897, Margaret Scholl Hood enabled the college to acquire farmland on the west side of town, and Dr. Apple began to dream of a "Greater Woman's College" in that location.

Meanwhile, the student body and faculty grew. By 1912, the curriculum included biology, chemistry, geology, physics, astronomy, economics and sociology, two modern and two ancient languages, philosophy, English language and literature, and mathematics, including calculus; in short, a rigorous liberal arts course of study. The Music Conservatory, School of Art, School of Expression, and School of Home Economics offered separate curricula.

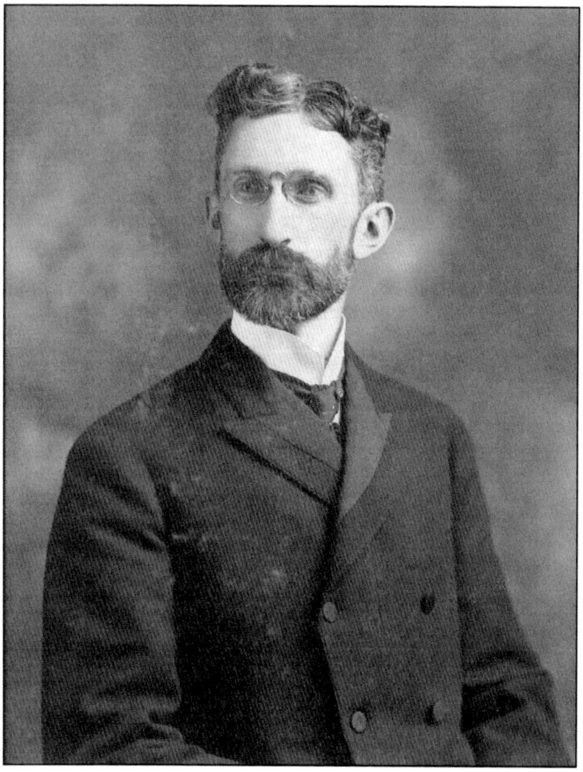

Joseph Henry Apple began his presidency at the Woman's College as a 28-year-old, clean-shaven man. Because he wanted to present himself to the students as an authoritative figure, he decided to grow a beard in order to make himself look older. He reported that when he decided to shave it off some years later, his wife did not recognize him.

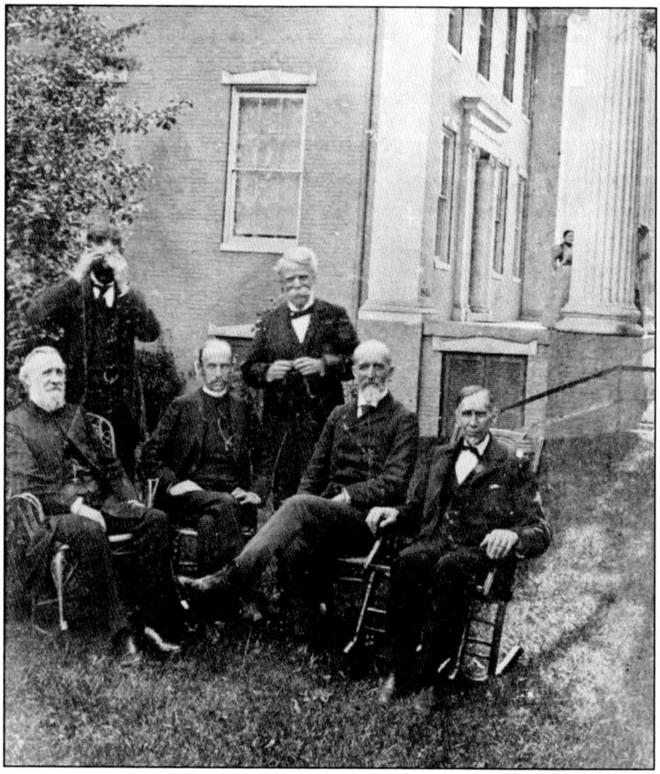

The first meeting of Joseph Henry Apple and the board of directors of the Woman's College took place on the lawn beside East Hall in 1893. President Apple has his hands over his eyes, while treasurer A.C. McCardell stands beside him. Seated from left to right are Rev. E.R. Eschbach, president; Rev. C.S. Slagle, secretary; Gen. John E. Roller; and William H. Lakin.

Marie Diehl was an 1872 graduate of the Frederick Female Seminary. This is, presumably, her graduation photograph. She taught piano at the seminary until it closed and then became one of the inaugural faculty members of the Woman's College, retiring in 1910. She was loved by students, colleagues, and members of the Frederick community and was a founder of the Frederick Society for the Prevention of Cruelty to Animals.

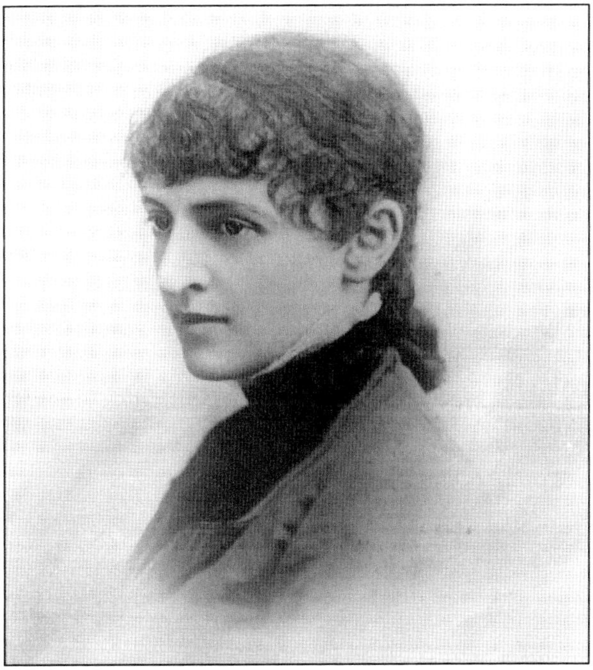

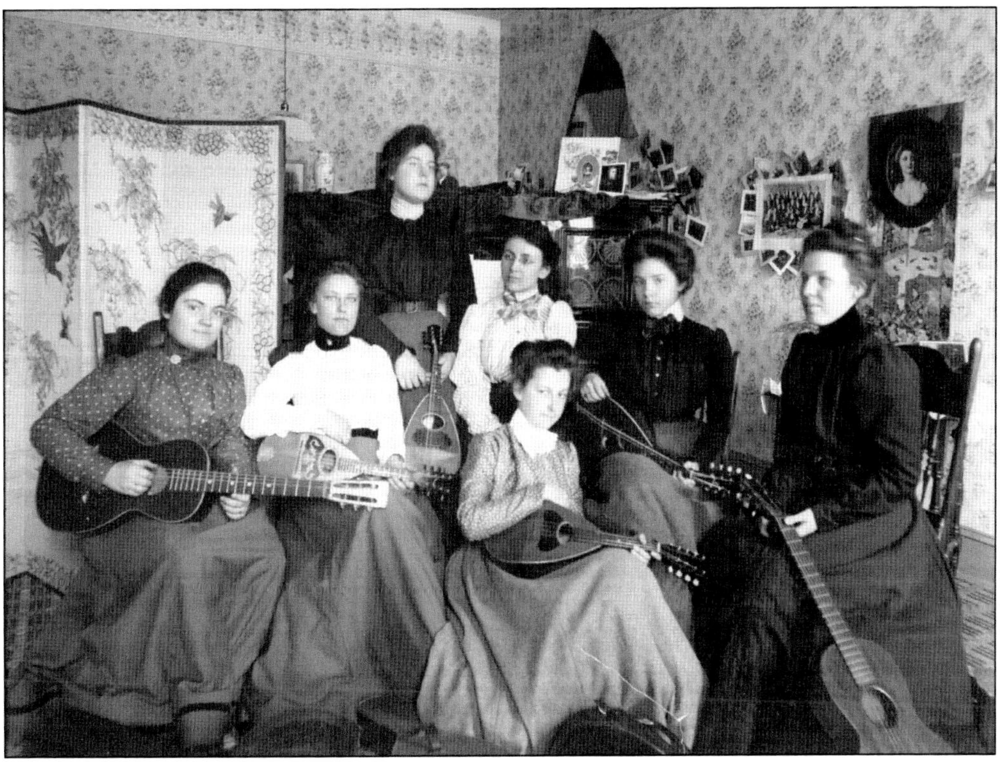

The mandolin club met in Marie Diehl's studio for this 1895 photograph. At the time, a mandolin craze was sweeping the United States, initiated by a group of Spanish musicians who toured America in 1880. Their music caught on, and mandolin groups sprang up everywhere, including at the Woman's College of Frederick.

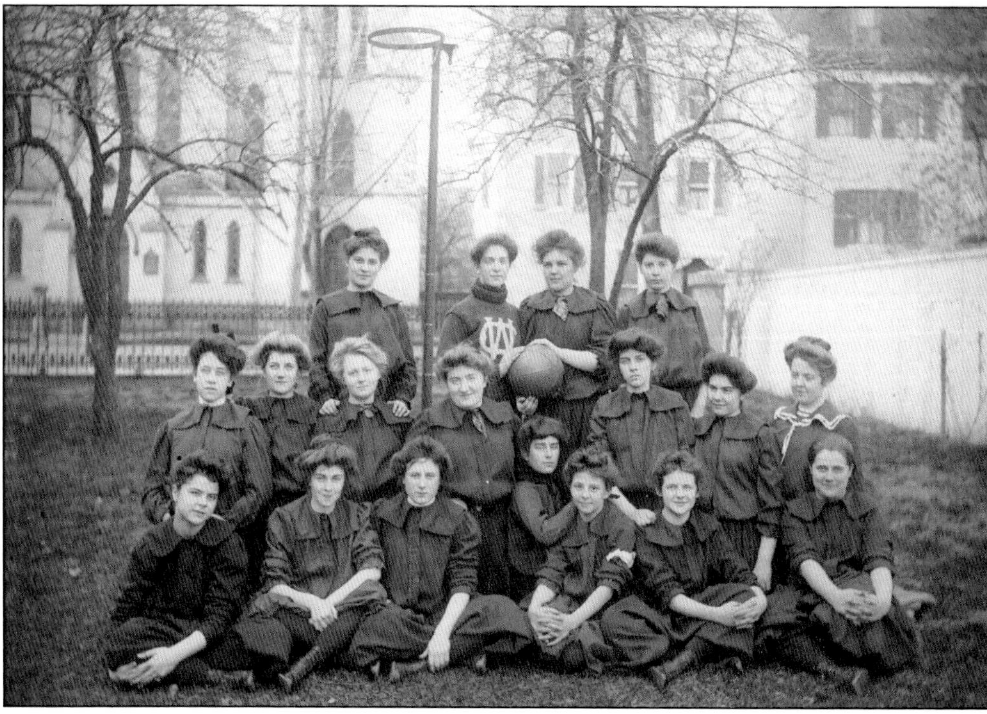

President Apple was a great proponent of physical culture, not only for men but for women as well. From the beginning, exercise and sports were an integral part of life at the Woman's College. As this 1893 photograph demonstrates, students played basketball during the first semester of the college's existence.

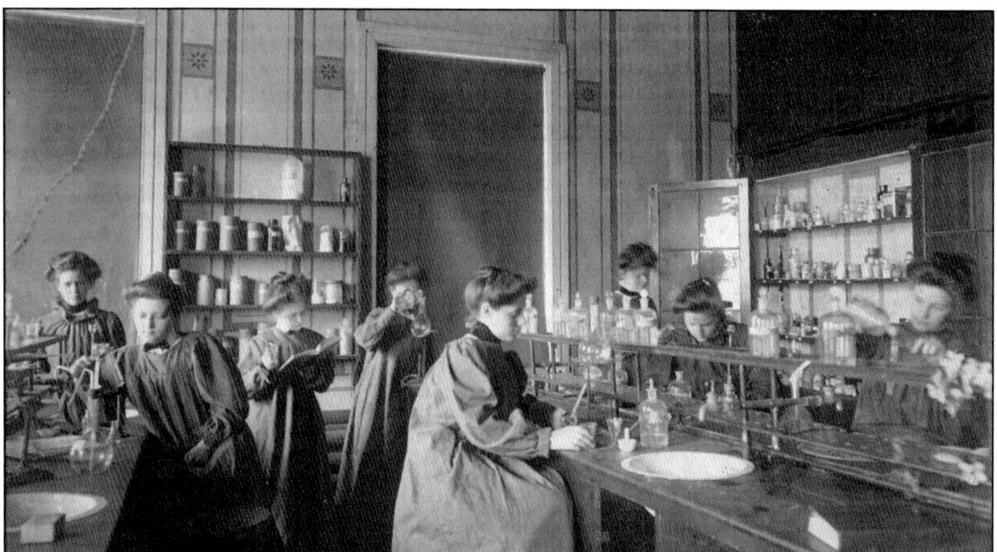

The late 19th century was an exciting period in the history of chemistry, and as this 1895 photograph shows, students worked in a fully equipped chemistry lab. Using a gift from Margaret Scholl Hood, the college retrofitted rooms in West Hall and "converted [them] into a Scientific Laboratory. . . . All the apparatus and appliances for the equipment of a modern, working laboratory have been secured, including a dark room for photograph[s]."

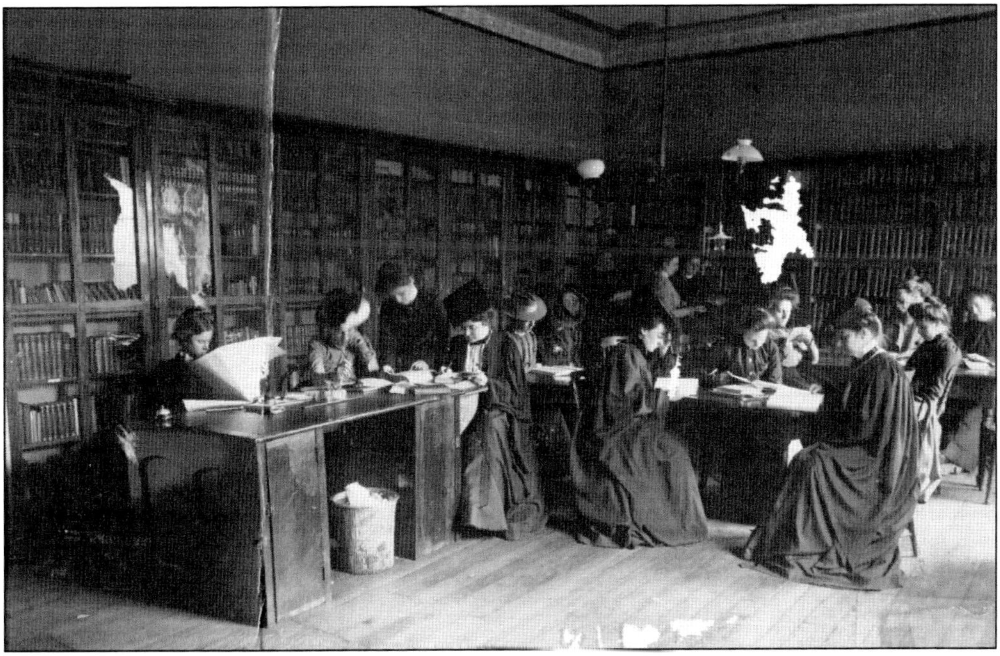

West Hall housed the college's library. Some of the books pictured here have survived and are now found in the Woman's College Collection of the Beneficial-Hodson Library. The Frederick Female Seminary's collection numbered about 1,500 volumes, and by 1895 another 600 or so had been purchased, mostly through donations. A "regular librarian," according to the 1895–1896 catalog, was in charge. The library subscribed to 25 periodicals, including three newspapers.

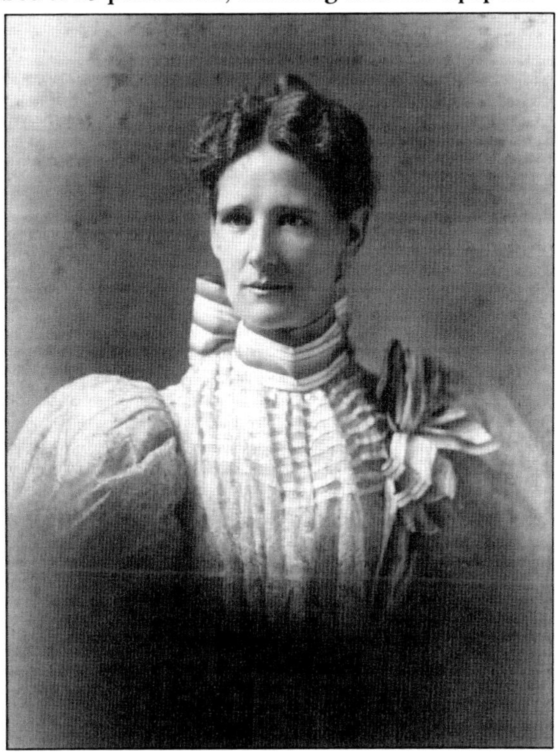

President Apple appointed Anna Froehlich, shown here in 1899, from the Clarion (Pennsylvania) Normal School, to teach in the preparatory department of the Woman's College. She was one of the eight original faculty members. While the focus was on college-level teaching, the Woman's College continued the preparatory instruction of the Frederick Female Seminary. When the college moved across town, the seminary stayed downtown, continuing in Winchester Hall.

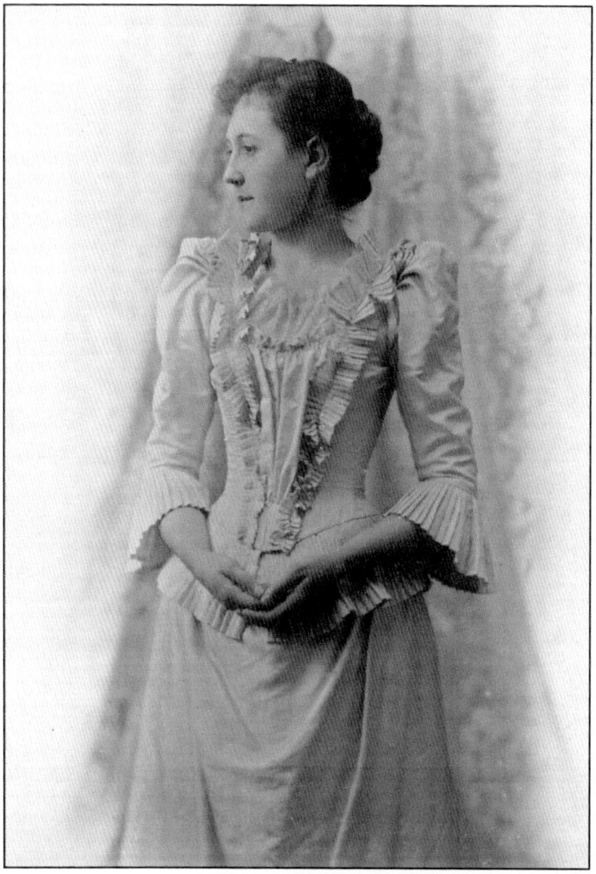

Gertrude Harner, seen in her high school graduation photograph, joined the faculty as an English teacher in 1895. She was the founder of the college's first literary magazine but is best known as President Apple's second wife; the couple married in 1898. Dr. Apple's first wife, Mary Rankin Apple, once vice president of the Woman's College, died of tuberculosis in 1896.

Dr. Apple (right) presides over the 1896 commencement exercises. Graduates received certificates of completion, not diplomas or degrees, as the college was not yet recognized by Maryland as a degree-granting institution. The students are, from left to right, Nora Miller, Alice Kase, Emily Smith, Emma Newman, Mary Noss, and Caroline Smiley; the latter two later taught briefly at the college.

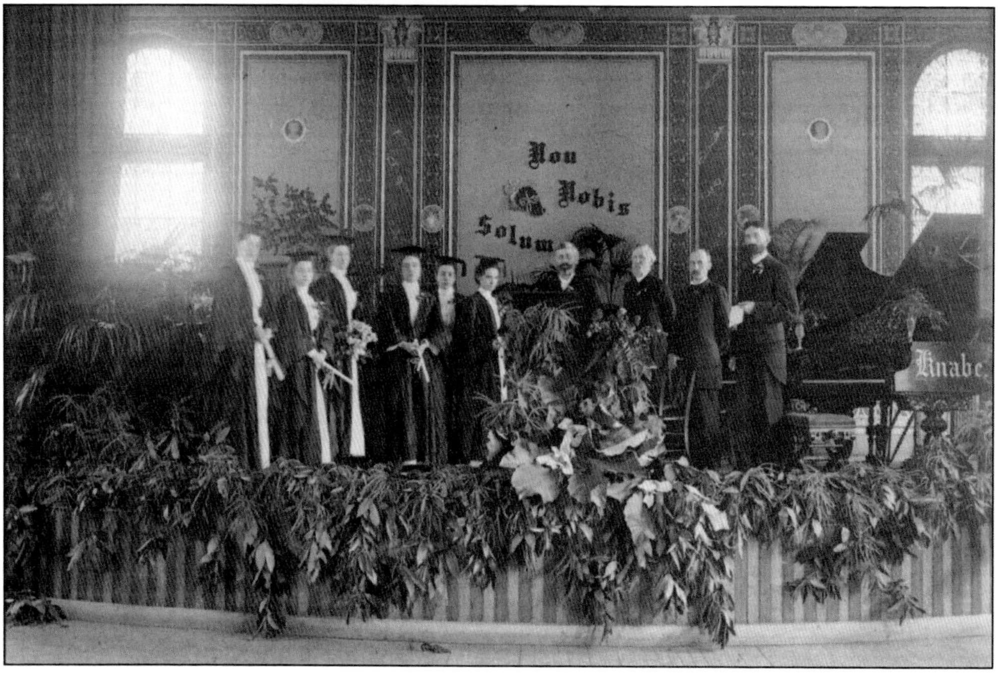

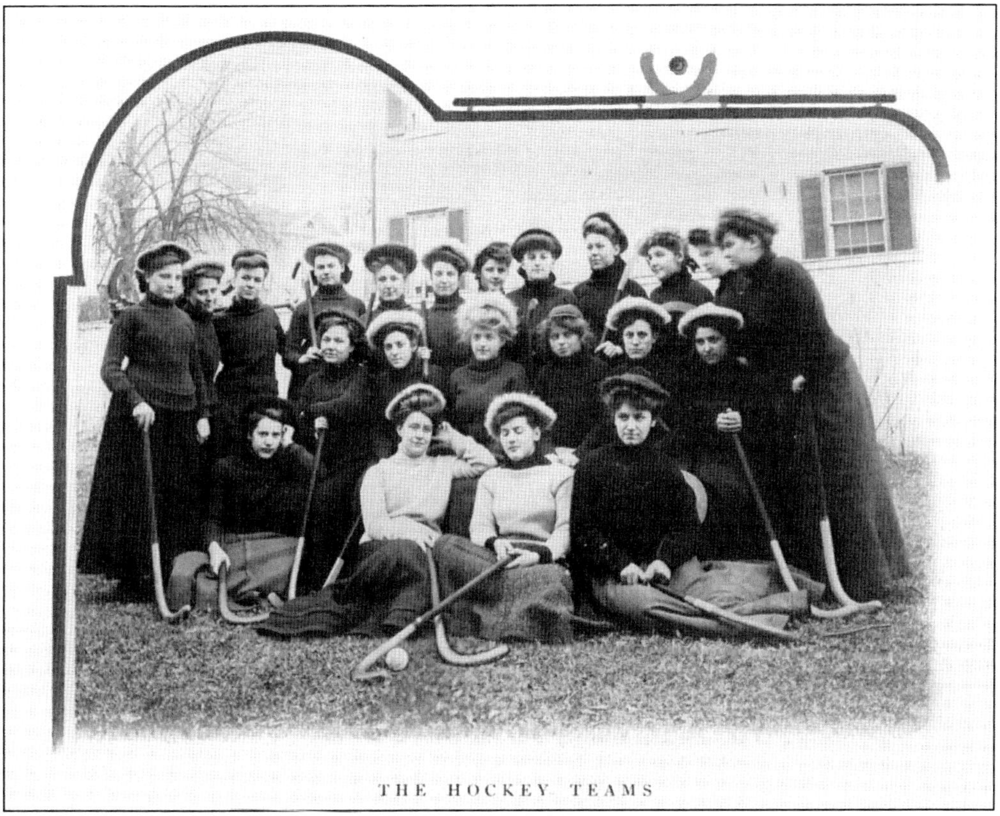

President Apple was always on the lookout for "appropriate" sports for women, and in 1902, while on a trip to England, he encountered field hockey. Shortly after his return to Maryland, he ordered sticks and balls, and soon students were playing the new game. The college was one of the first in the country to adopt the game. This c. 1905 photograph shows 22 pioneering hockey players.

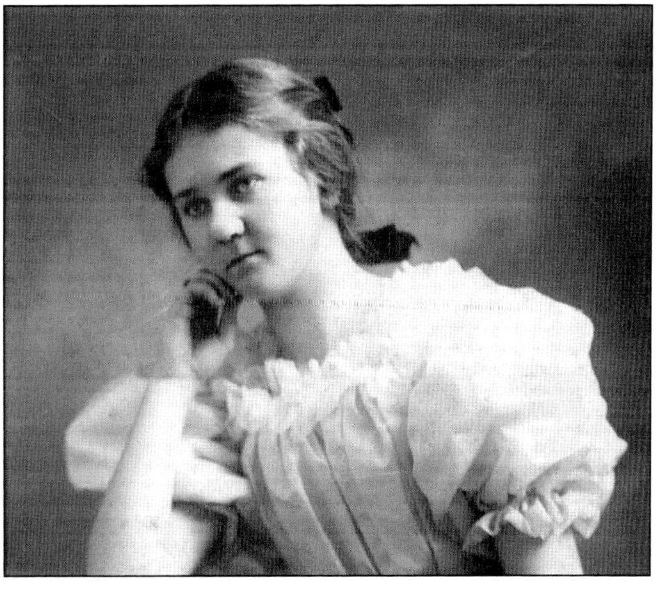

This is an 1898 photograph of student Estelle Brodbeck, who graduated in 1899. Her father was US representative Andrew Brodbeck of Pennsylvania, a friend of the college and an ardent supporter of education. The original structure on the new college land west of Frederick was named for him in 1923. Brodbeck Music Hall, as it is known today, underwent a face lift in 2012.

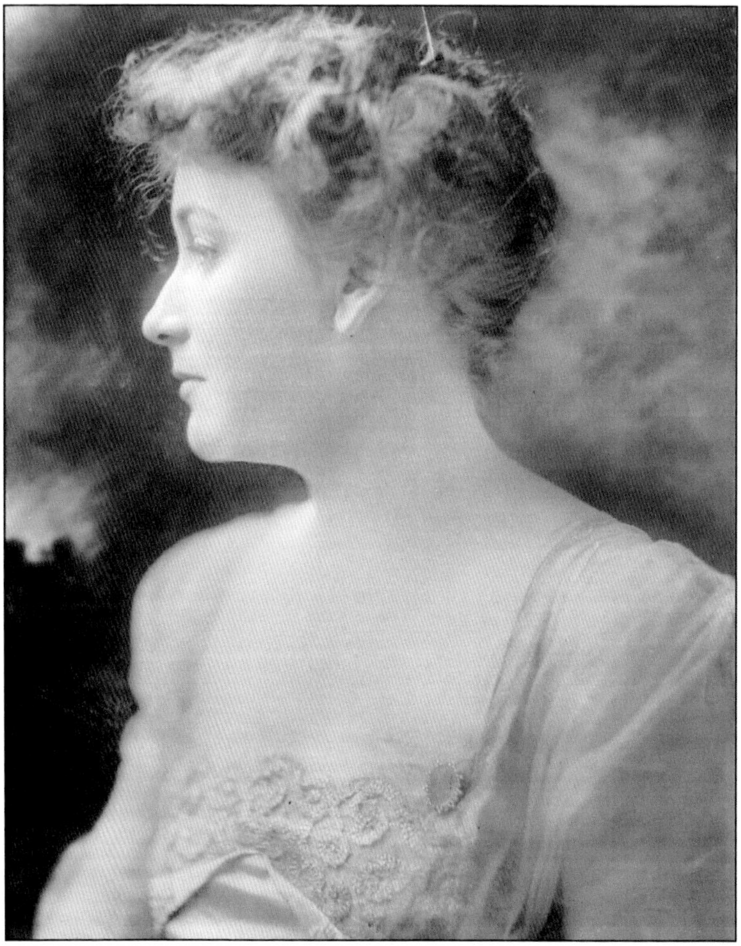

One of the more illustrious graduates of the Woman's College was Sophie Kerr of the class of 1898, seen here in this publicity photograph taken about 1915. She was a writer and magazine editor, penning hundreds of short stories, 23 novels, and a Broadway play. She is also remembered for the literary prize that she endowed at Washington College, located near her home on Maryland's Eastern shore.

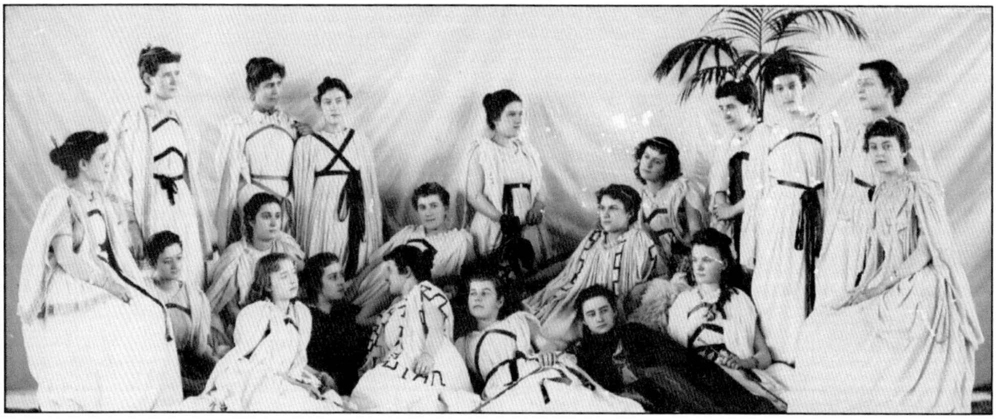

One college program that was outside of the liberal arts curriculum was the School of Expression. Students studied, among other things, dramatics, elocution, gesture, and "Shakespearean grammar." The *tableau vivant* was a popular entertainment form where costumed actors posed to represent perhaps a painting or a scene from mythology. Presumably, this photograph from 1890 depicts such a tableau. The college's literary magazine praised their "recitations, posings, and pantomime."

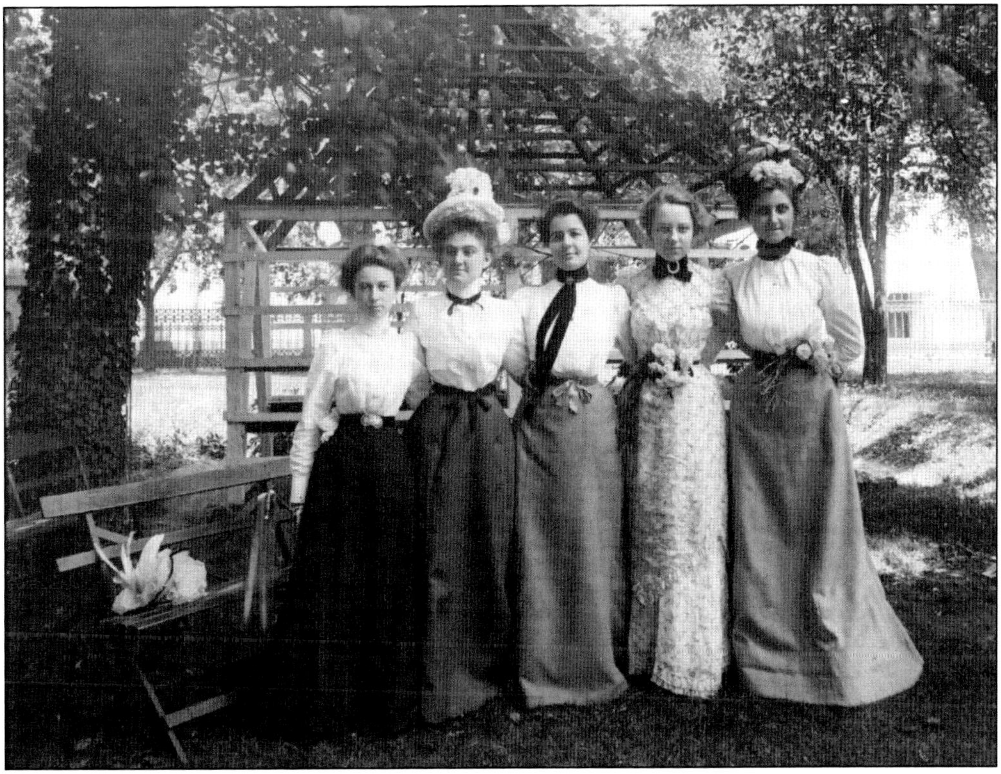

Sally Conrad Fauntleroy (center), director of the School of Expression, poses with graduates of the school in front of the pergola around 1900. As a garden structure, the pergola was popular in the 19th century and has been a part of the college's landscape since its founding; the current one is associated with some of the college's most beloved traditions.

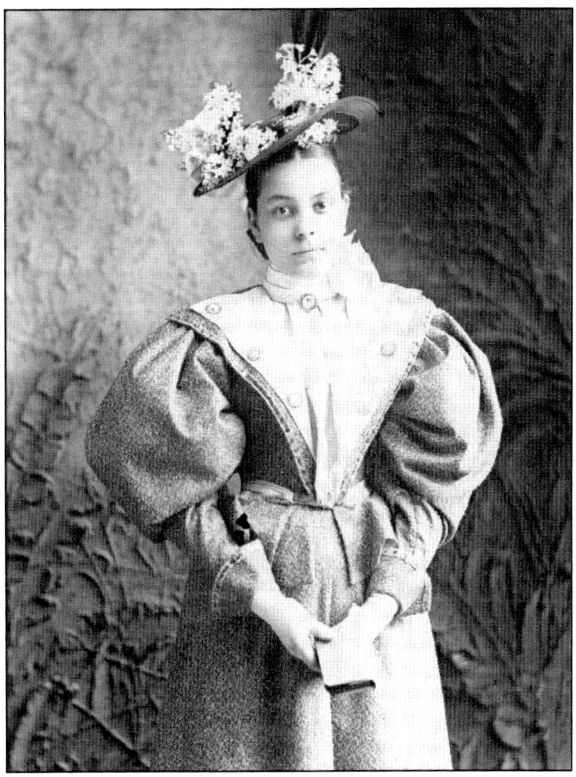

Lena Kepler (1896), as the note on the photograph reads, is "dressed for church." When the Woman's College was administered by the Reformed Church, chapel attendance was mandatory, but students attended Sunday services at the church of their parents' choice in Frederick. Hood College retains its historical relationship with the United Church of Christ, successor to the Reformed Church, but is now considered independent.

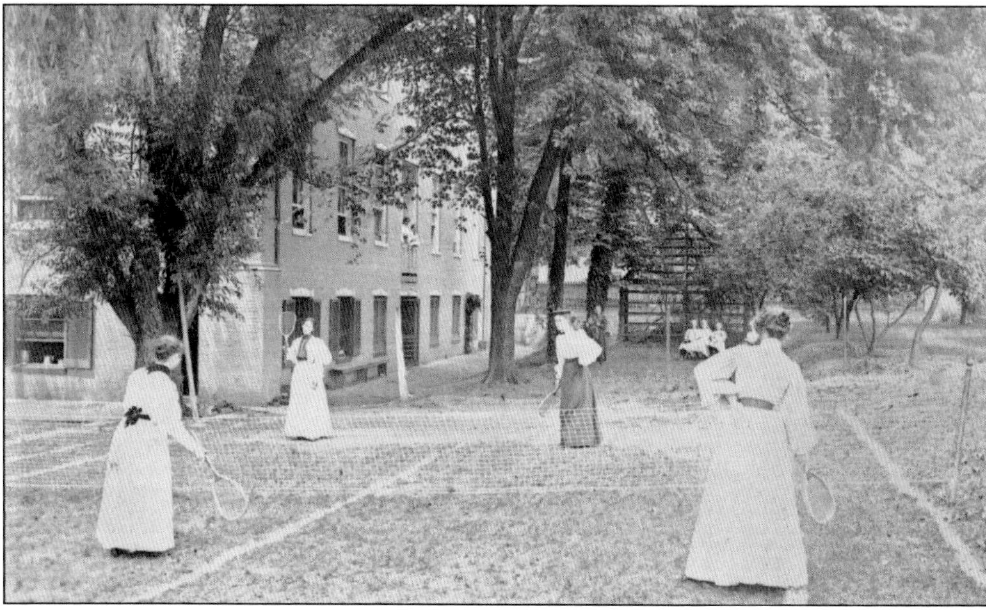

Tennis, another sport that Dr. Apple deemed appropriate for women, was one of the first to be played at the Woman's College. This c. 1894 photograph shows four students dressed in long skirts on the lawn behind East Hall, racquets poised, while three others observe the game. With tennis costumes such as these, the play must have been rather sedate.

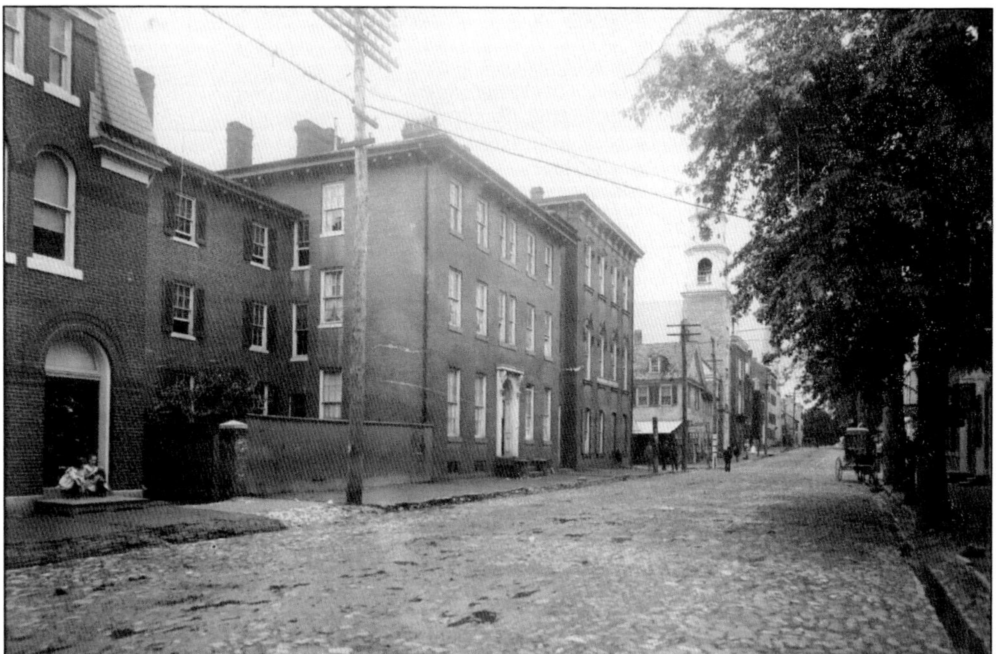

This view, looking west along East Church Street, shows some of the buildings that the college rented. The building with the arched door on the left was the president's home, and perhaps the two girls on the doorstep are his daughters. The next two structures are the conservatory building and Kemp Hall. Kemp Hall was the site of an extraordinary 1861 meeting of the Maryland Legislature where secession from the Union was discussed.

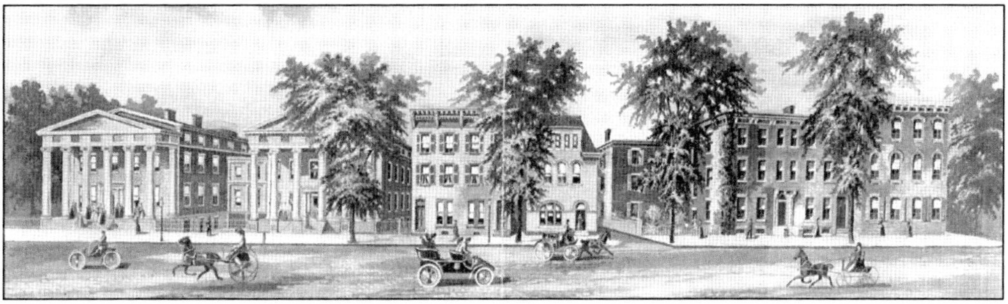

This artist's rendering of East Church Street around 1900 offers a rather fanciful impression of a broad thoroughfare. It does accurately show the relationships of the main college buildings, from left to right East Hall, West Hall, the president's home, the conservatory, and Kemp Hall, which is still owned by the Reformed Church. Note the automobiles interspersed with the horse-drawn vehicles.

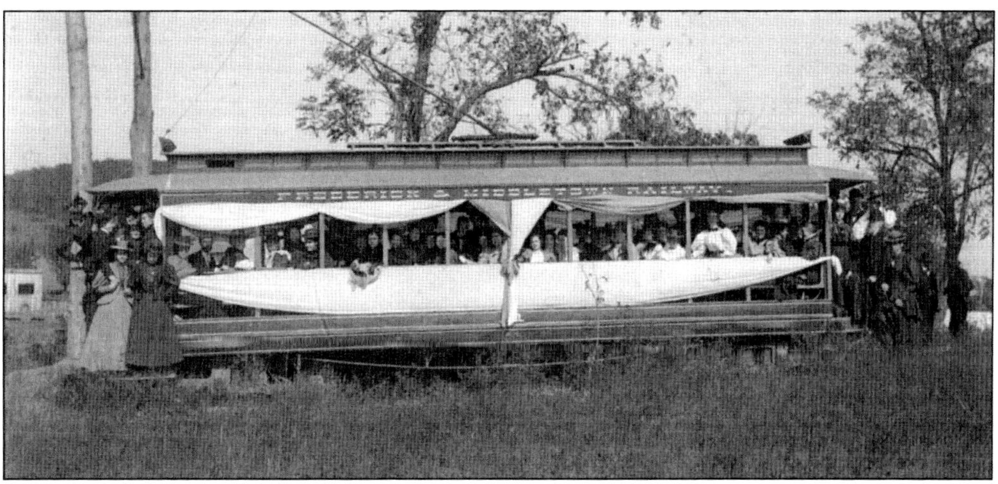

The annual trolley trip to Braddock Heights for the Braddock picnic was a popular autumn event. The railway company ran a special car for students and their chaperones the six miles from Frederick up Braddock Mountain to the little resort community. In this 1897 photograph, President Apple and Gertrude Harner, his future wife, can be seen inside the gaily decorated car at the far left end.

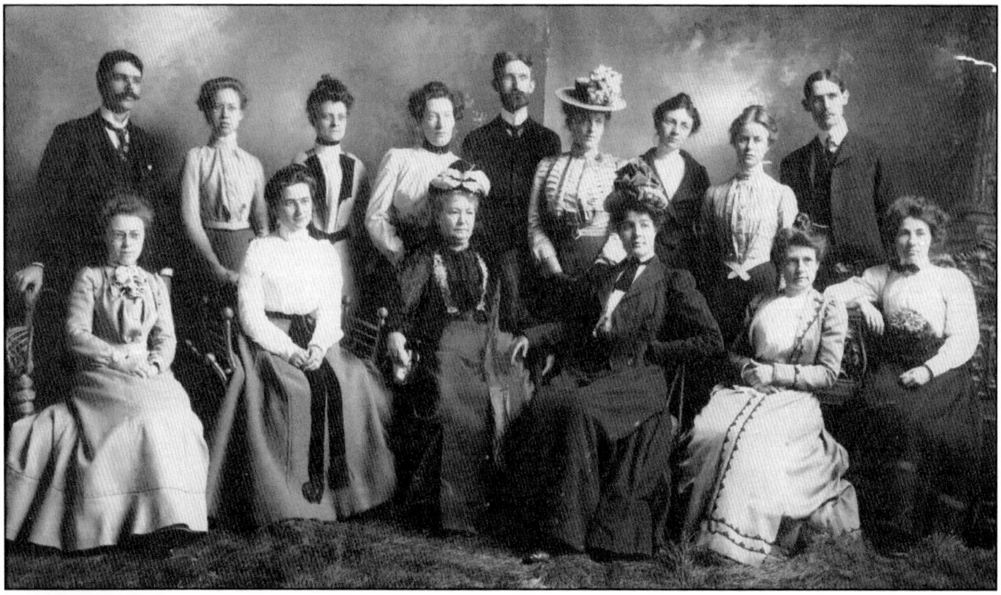

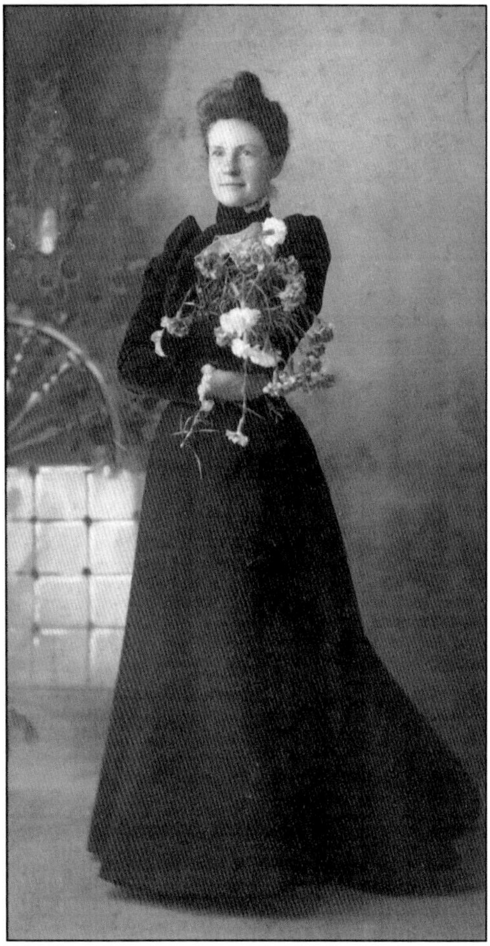

The faculty of the Woman's College gathered for this photograph in the late 1890s. They include, from left to right, (front row) unidentified, Marie Diehl (music), Martha McClelland (matron), Sally Conrad Fauntleroy (expression), Anna Froehlich (English), and unidentified; (back row) Maurice Beckwith (music), two unidentified, Caroline Smiley (science), President Apple, Gertrude Harner (English), Susan Garrot (librarian), unidentified, and Glenn Heller (mathematics and Greek).

Willie Augusta Lantz began her career at the Woman's College in 1894 and left in 1919 after 25 years of service, working first as a science teacher, school photographer, and photography instructor and later doing double duty teaching and taking on the role of registrar. She was a close associate of Margaret Scholl Hood while she resided at the college and was frequently her traveling companion.

Martha McClelland, one of the college matrons, or housekeepers, was well known for toting all of the college room keys around in the signature basket pictured on her lap. As head of the dining room, she was responsible for the cooking and used wine to flavor her dishes; she also introduced plum pudding with brandy to the college boarders.

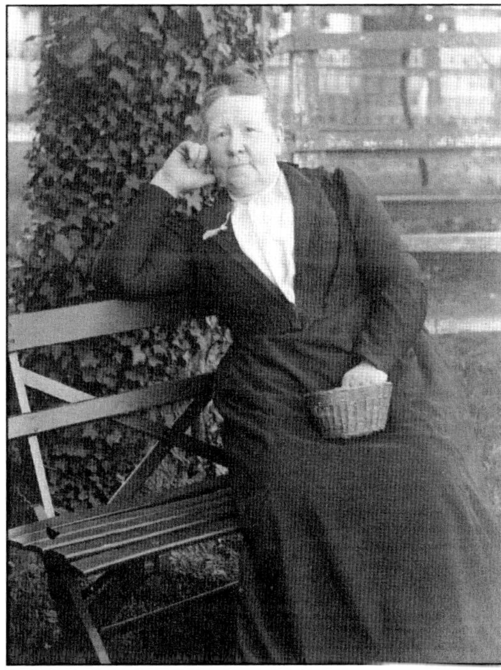

Students pictured here enjoy tea in a dormitory room. The 1903–1904 catalog describes the rooms: "Students' rooms are of fairly good size . . . are all nicely furnished, with a single bed for each student, dresser stand, table . . . and wardrobe, neatly papered and carpeted with Brussels carpet. The average room has one good-sized window for ventilation. All but a few rooms have sanitary bath-rooms on the same floor."

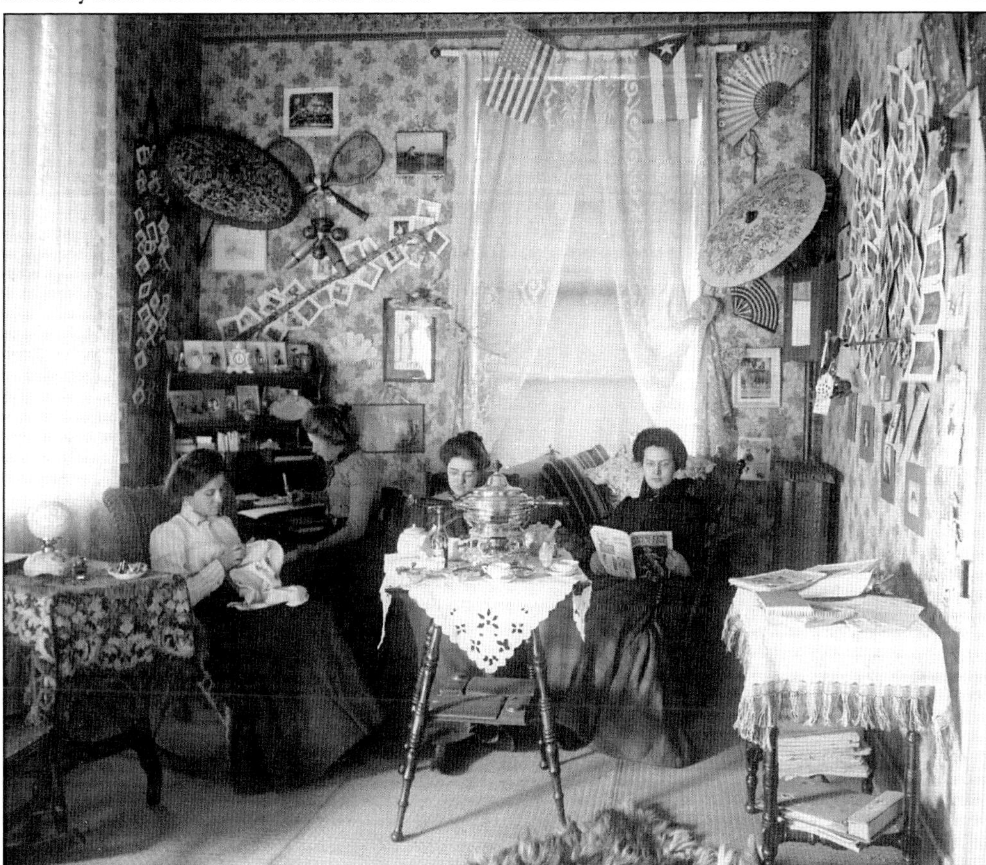

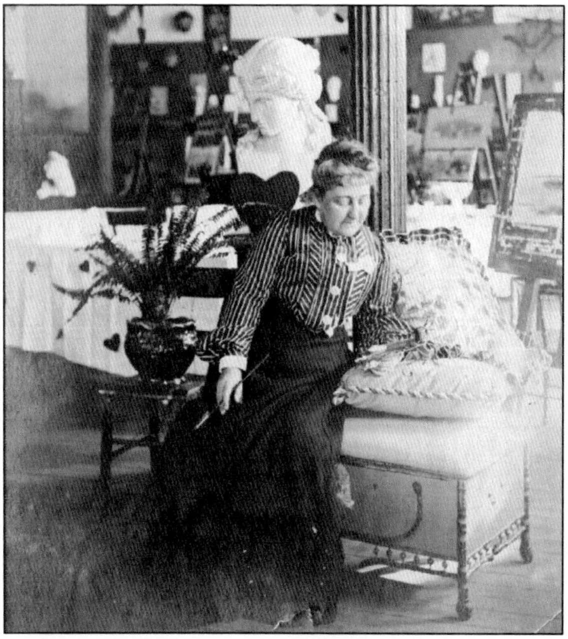

Florence Doub, an 1868 graduate of the Frederick Female Seminary, had her art studio at Kemp Hall in 1905. She was a well-respected artist in Frederick. It was reported that her students' work took many prizes at the Great Frederick Fair. She was hard of hearing and used an ear trumpet to gather sound. She also taught at the Maryland School for the Deaf in Frederick.

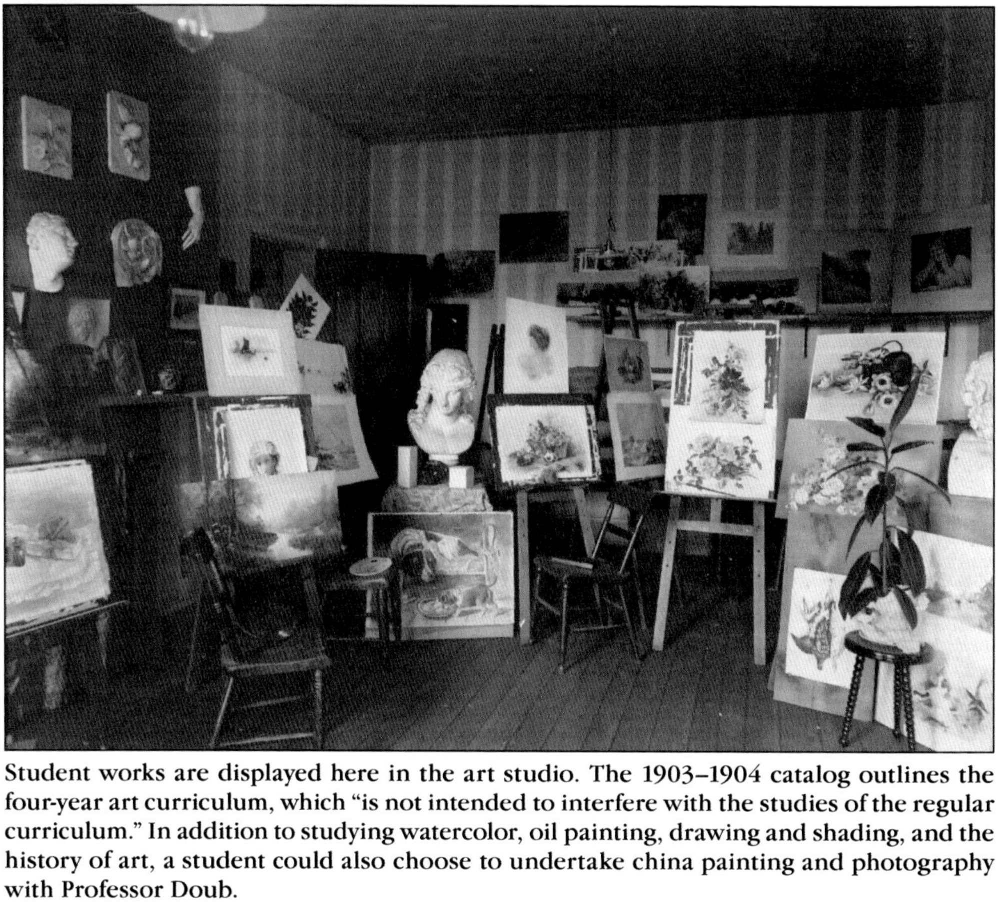

Student works are displayed here in the art studio. The 1903–1904 catalog outlines the four-year art curriculum, which "is not intended to interfere with the studies of the regular curriculum." In addition to studying watercolor, oil painting, drawing and shading, and the history of art, a student could also choose to undertake china painting and photography with Professor Doub.

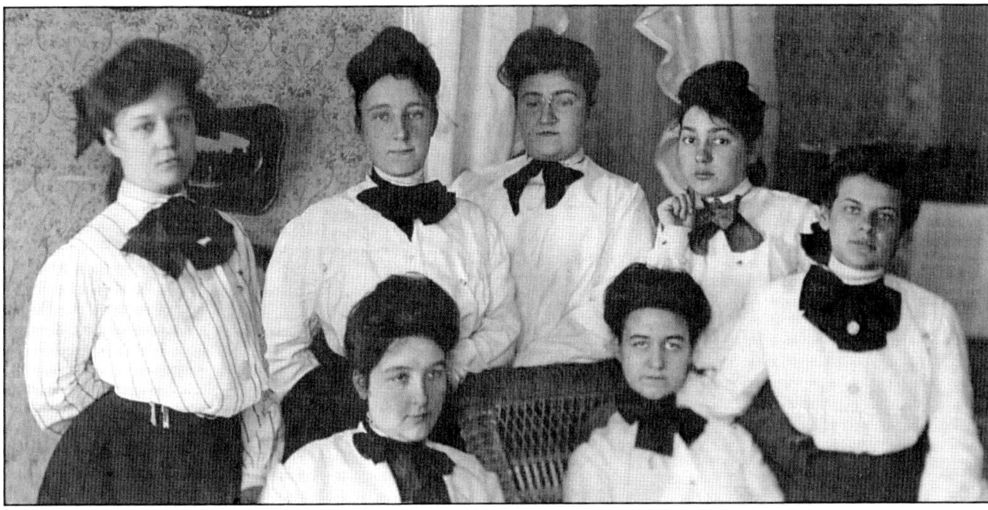

The Young Women's Christian Association was organized at the Woman's College in 1903 in order to support an alumna who was a missionary in Sendai, Japan. The 1906 YWCA student officers are shown here. The "Y" members sponsored a reception in the fall for freshmen, as well as putting on any number of parties, lectures, and socials. It was instrumental in making the college a friendly place.

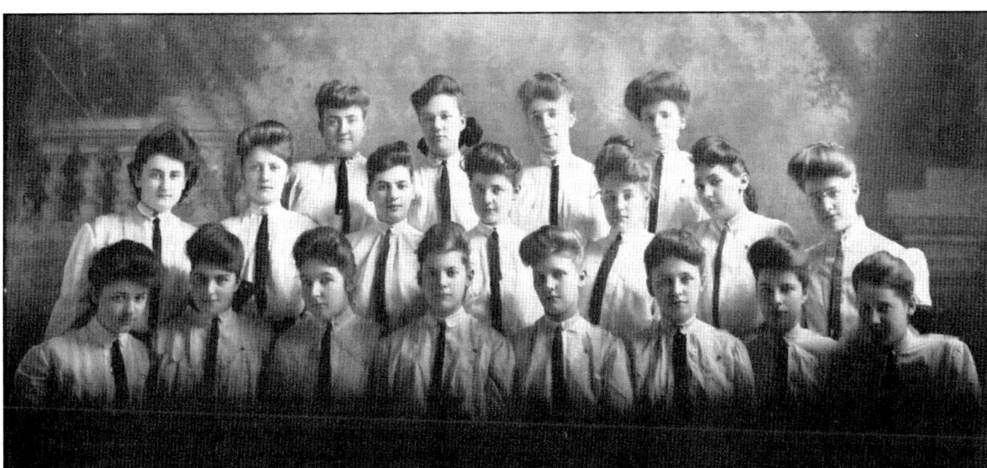

Members of Phi Mu Theta are pictured here in 1904. The Phi Mu Theta Society was one of two Greek fraternities at the college, neither of which appears to have been very active. In 1907, the faculty declared that it was "unqualifiedly opposed" to social fraternities on campus. That seems to have been the last word, and to this day there are no social fraternities at Hood.

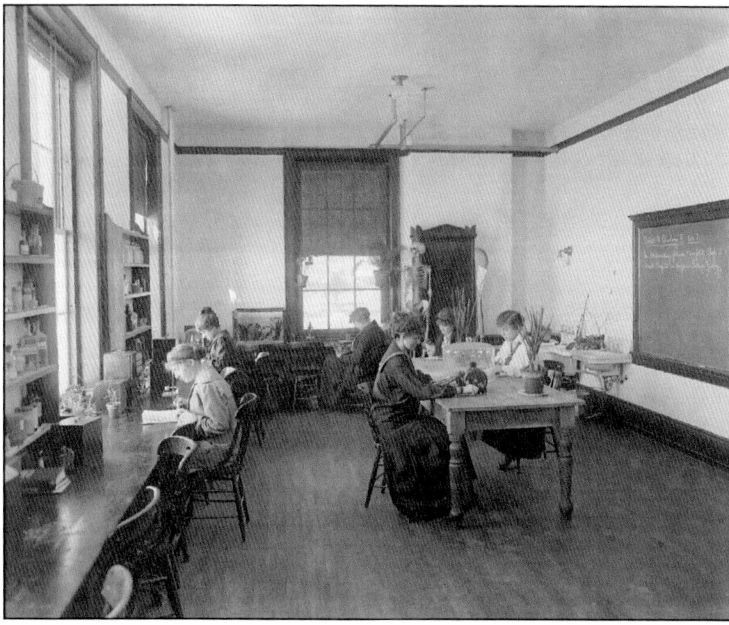

Students work in the botany laboratory about 1910. Botany, a required course for graduation, was taught by Professor Lantz until she went to Germany in 1907 to study developments in the field of chemistry for a year. Prof. Nellie Blanchard then took over biology and botany instruction, leaving Professor Lantz to teach only the physical sciences when she returned from Europe.

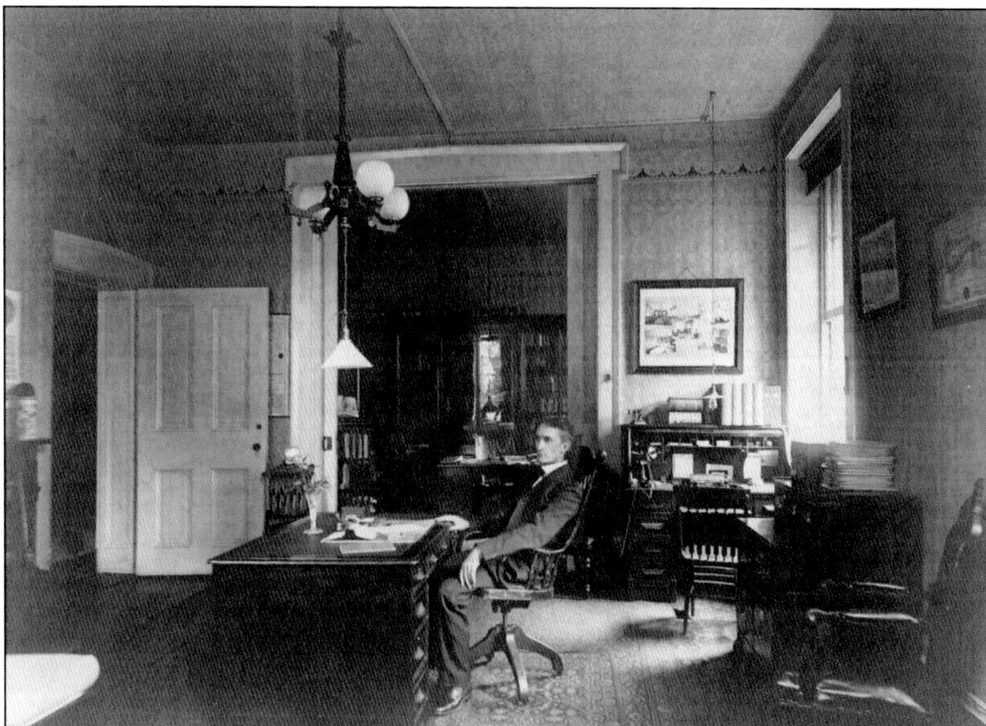

Dr. Apple sits in his office in 1905. By this time, students had begun lobbying him for a role in their own governance. Previously, the college's role was to protect students and keep them from "going astray," regulating all aspects of college life. After five years of negotiation between the students and faculty, experimental student self-government went into effect in 1910, marking the birth of Hood's Honor System.

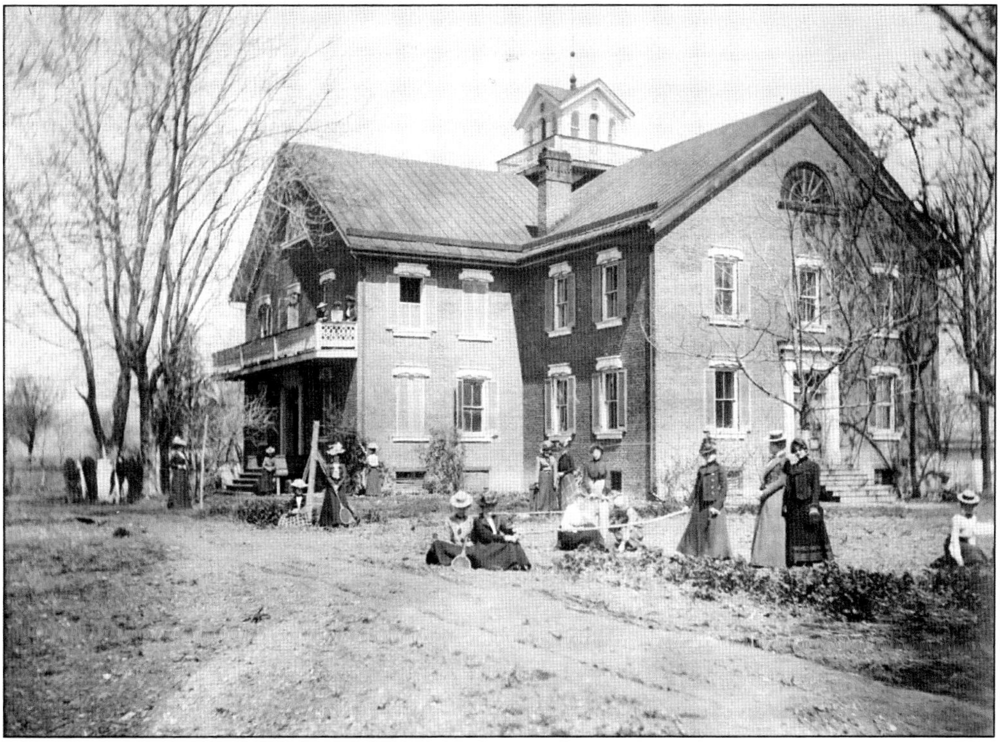

This building, now called Brodbeck Music Hall, was the only structure on what was known as West Campus, when the land was acquired in 1897. For over a decade, it was used as a haunted house venue for Halloween. The land outside provided additional space for sports, including field hockey and tennis (note the racquets). Some of the land was leased to a farmer during this time as well.

Pres. Joseph Henry and Mrs. Gertrude Apple, one of their daughters, and A.C. McCardell, a member of the board of directors, plant and dedicate a tree on West Campus. Note Brodbeck Music Hall in the background. By this time, about 1910, President Apple was actively making plans for a new college campus at this location.

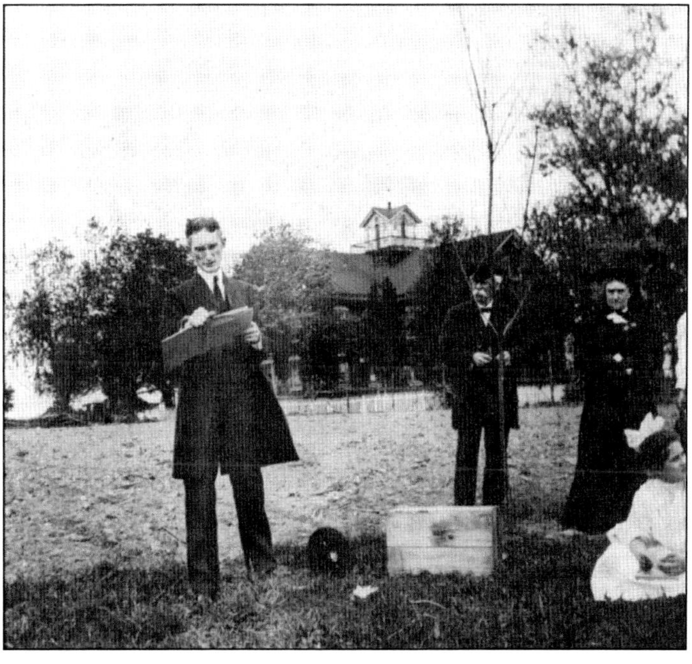

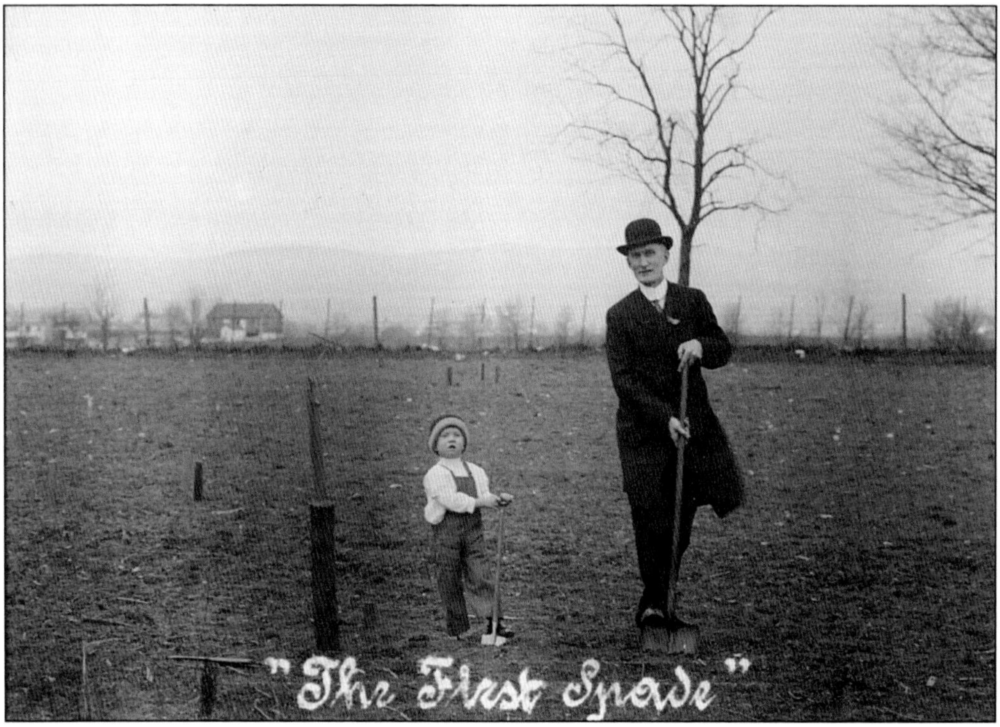

President Apple and his son Joseph Henry III participate in the ground-breaking for Alumnae Hall on April 2, 1914. For President Apple, everything had come together. In 1913, the name of the college had been changed to Hood College in recognition of Margaret Scholl Hood's generosity, and several buildings for West Campus were on the drawing board. The "Greater Woman's College" would be a reality.

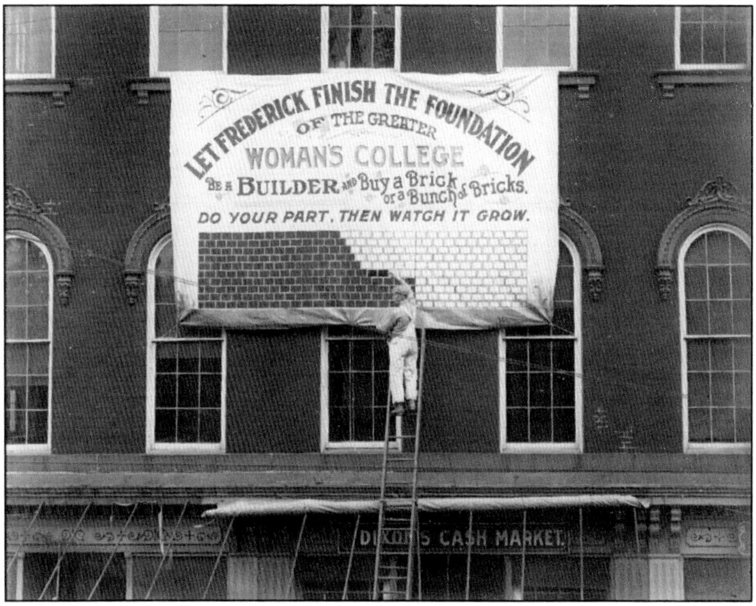

President Apple's plans for the college on the farm property included involving the community in raising funds for the first new building, which eventually became Alumnae Hall. The fundraising effort went well and was augmented by a $20,000 bequest from Margaret Scholl Hood after her death in January 1913.

Three

Our Visionary Mother
Margaret Scholl Hood

Margaret Elizabeth Scholl was born July 7, 1833, the only child of Daniel and Maria Susan Thomas Scholl. She lived most of her life at Manchester Farm on New Design Road in Frederick County. Margaret began her education at an early school operated by Hiram Winchester in Frederick City before attending Thorndale, a boarding school in Carroll County, Maryland. From 1847 to 1849, she was a student at the Frederick Female Seminary in Frederick, excelling in mathematics, and graduating in 1849 at age 16. After graduation, she lived with her parents, helping with household and farm activities and enjoying an active social life.

On October 21, 1873, she married James Mifflin Hood, who operated a carriage-making firm, Hane and Hood. James had three children by his first wife, Sarah Ann Boggs, who had had died in 1869. James and Margaret had no children; he died in 1894.

Margaret was a friend of Joseph Henry Apple, who, as president of the Woman's College of Frederick, dreamed of establishing a new campus on the outskirts of town. In 1897, thanks to a gift from her, the college acquired farmland at the northwestern edge of the city. She established the institution's first endowment in memory of her husband. In 1913, the college was renamed Hood College in her honor.

She was active in her church, now the Evangelical Reformed Church, United Church of Christ, and in community organizations, including the Frederick Art Club, the Historical Society of Frederick County, the Home for the Aged (now the Record Street Home), C. Burr Artz Library, and the Frederick City Hospital. She was generous in supporting educational institutions, specifically Hood, Franklin and Marshall College, Mercersburg (Pennsylvania) Academy, and Lancaster Theological Seminary.

When not traveling, Margaret lived at the Frederick Hotel and at Manchester Farm. During her last six years, she spent winters at the Woman's College at the invitation of Dr. Apple. She died on January 12, 1913, and is buried with her husband and parents in Mount Olivet Cemetery in Frederick.

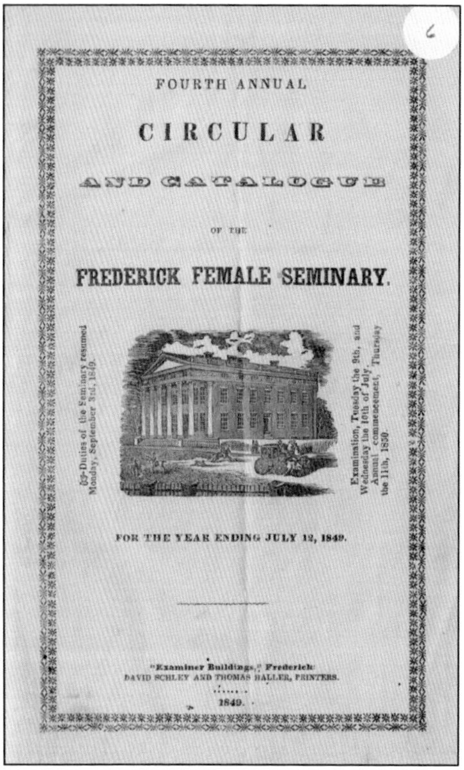
FOURTH ANNUAL

CIRCULAR

AND CATALOGUE

OF THE

FREDERICK FEMALE SEMINARY.

☞Duties of the Seminary resumed Monday, September 3rd, 1849.

Examination, Tuesday the 9th, and Wednesday the 10th of July. Annual commencement, Thursday the 11th, 1850.

FOR THE YEAR ENDING JULY 12, 1849.

"Examiner Buildings," Frederick:
DAVID SCHLEY AND THOMAS HALLER, PRINTERS.

1849.

The circular of the Frederick Female Seminary describes the courses of study, as well as the amenities offered at the institution. Margaret Scholl was 16 when she graduated in 1849, the year this circular was published. Among the courses she might have taken were chemistry, algebra, French, and Grecian history. Tuition, room, and board were $200 annually, with extra charges for music, foreign language, and painting and drawing lessons.

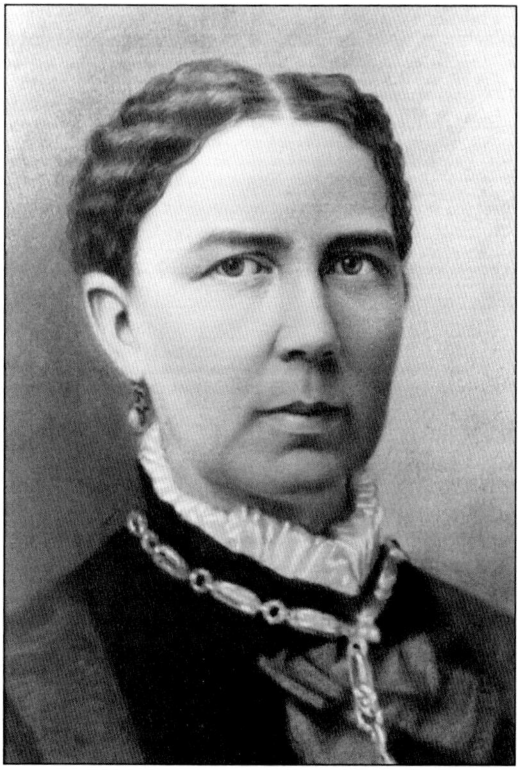

Photographs of Margaret Scholl are rare. This picture was probably taken around the time of her wedding in 1873. It is known, from her published diaries written between 1851 and 1861, that she was a popular young woman who enjoyed outings and social events with many friends. Her life was also one of routine, as she, the dutiful only child, remained with her parents and helped them manage their farm.

Margaret Scholl graduated from the Frederick Female Seminary on July 12, 1849, participating in exercises conducted in the Evangelical Lutheran Church across the street from the seminary. She became an active member of the Pioneer Club, the seminary's alumnae association. It was one of the oldest chartered women's clubs in Maryland.

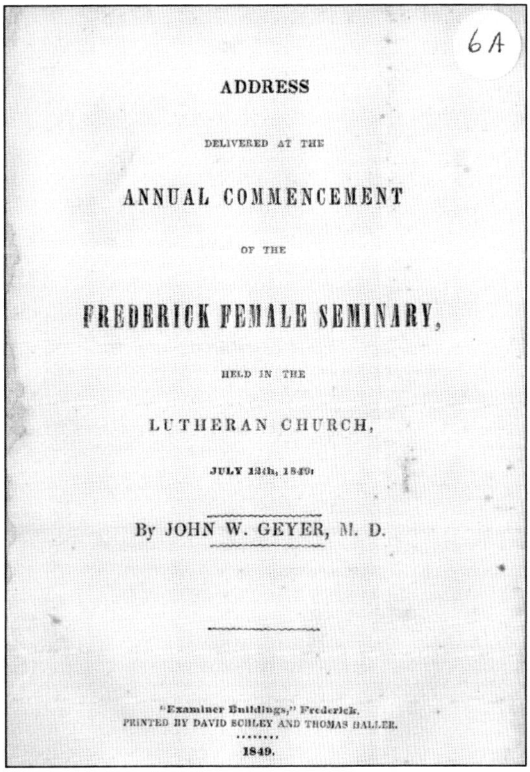

6A

ADDRESS

DELIVERED AT THE

ANNUAL COMMENCEMENT

OF THE

FREDERICK FEMALE SEMINARY,

HELD IN THE

LUTHERAN CHURCH,

JULY 12th, 1849:

By JOHN W. GEYER, M. D.

"Examiner Buildings," Frederick.
PRINTED BY DAVID SCHLEY AND THOMAS HALLER.

1849.

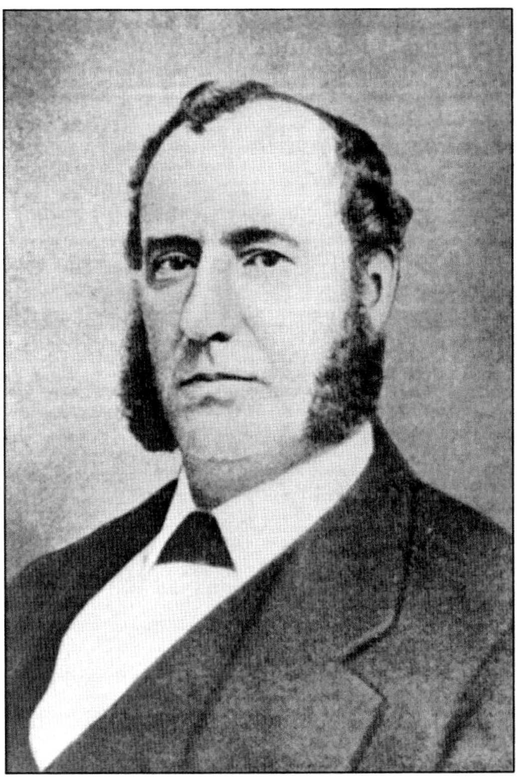

James Mifflin Hood was 12 years older than Margaret Scholl, his second wife. He was born and raised in Baltimore and moved to Frederick as a young man. Hood owned a carriage-making business that enjoyed a national reputation. He was a well-read man and shared his wife's interest in philanthropy. Urged to run for statewide office, he declined, preferring to remain active within his home community.

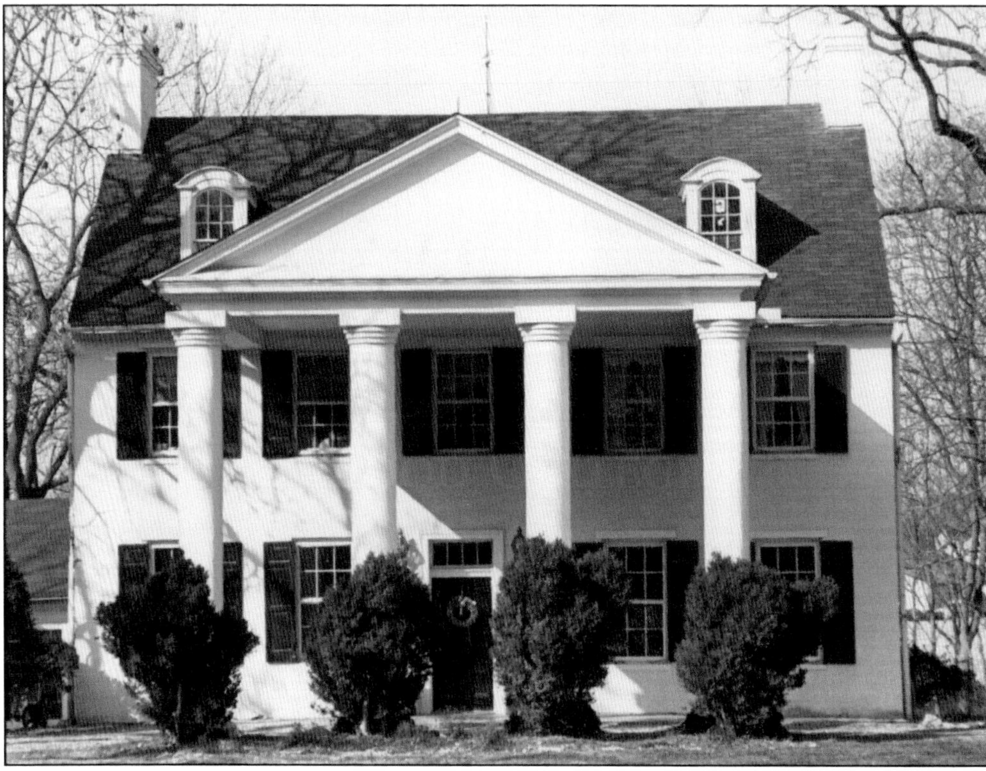

The house at Manchester Farm, about a mile south of Frederick, was erected around 1795. Margaret Scholl was raised on the farm and in this house and remained here to care for her parents as their health declined. Many changes were made to the house over time, including the addition in the 1920s or 1930s of the columned portico pictured. (Used by permission of C. Kurt Holter [1976], photographer.)

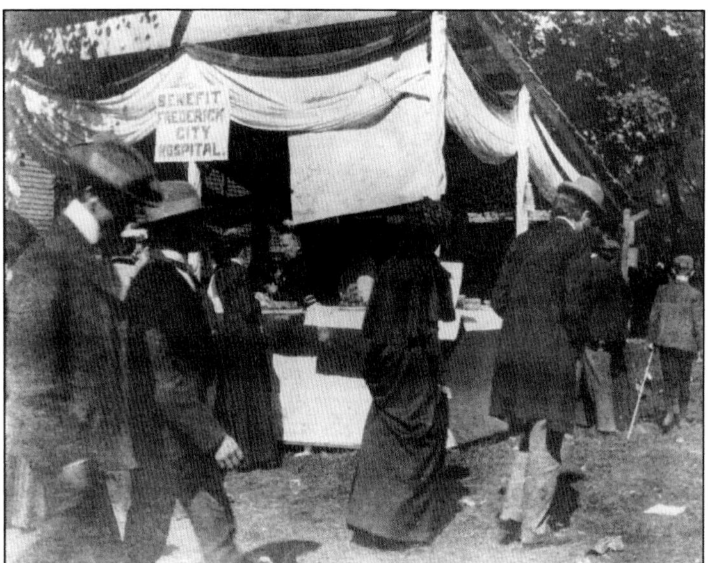

Margaret Scholl Hood stands behind the counter of a booth at the Great Frederick Fair where she was working on a fundraiser for the Frederick City Hospital. She was very involved in the establishment and management of the hospital, serving on its board for many years. She donated money to the cause, as well as gifts such as fruit, yard goods, and a gallon of vinegar for the hospital larder.

This photograph of Margaret Scholl Hood was probably taken in the 1890s. She gave her time, talent, and treasure to many organizations, and Hood College could not have become what it is today without her generosity. Between 1897 and 1913, she made major gifts to the college, totaling over $65,000. Today, that would equate to over $1.5 million.

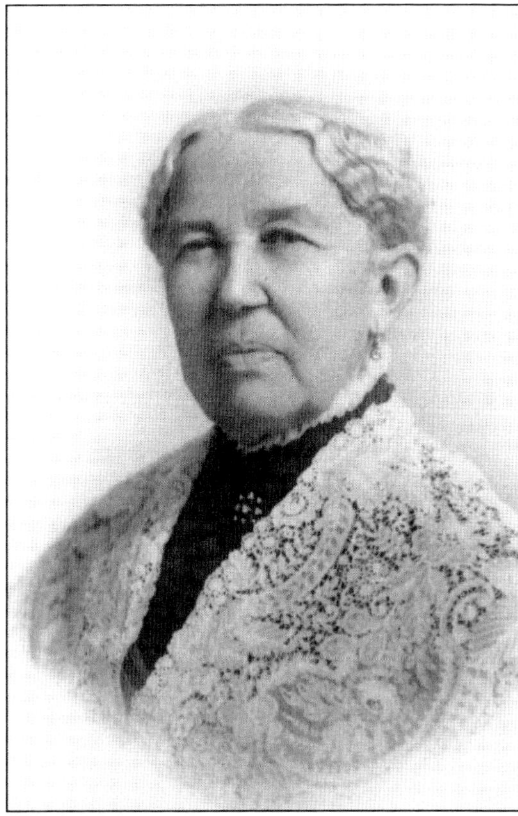

A number of items belonging to Margaret Scholl Hood are on display in the Hood College History Museum and Archives: her signature lace shawl (pictured), her pince-nez glasses, and a faded calling card. One can just barely see the words "Mrs. James M. Hood" hand-written among all of the flourishes. She was very much a Victorian lady, schooled in the social graces and observant of an unpretentious decorum.

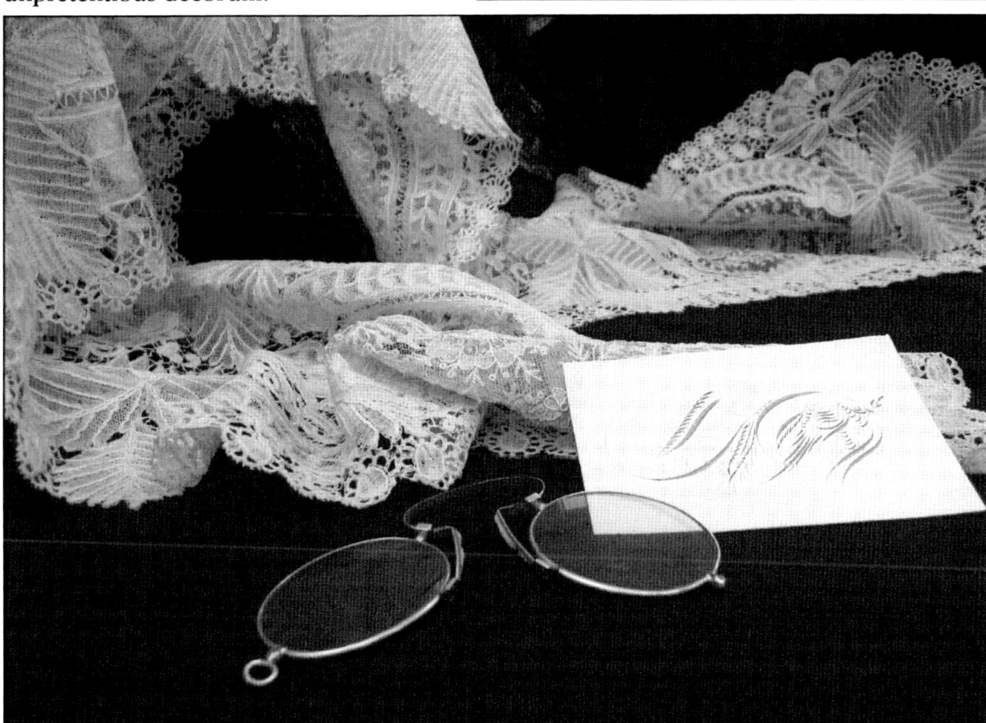

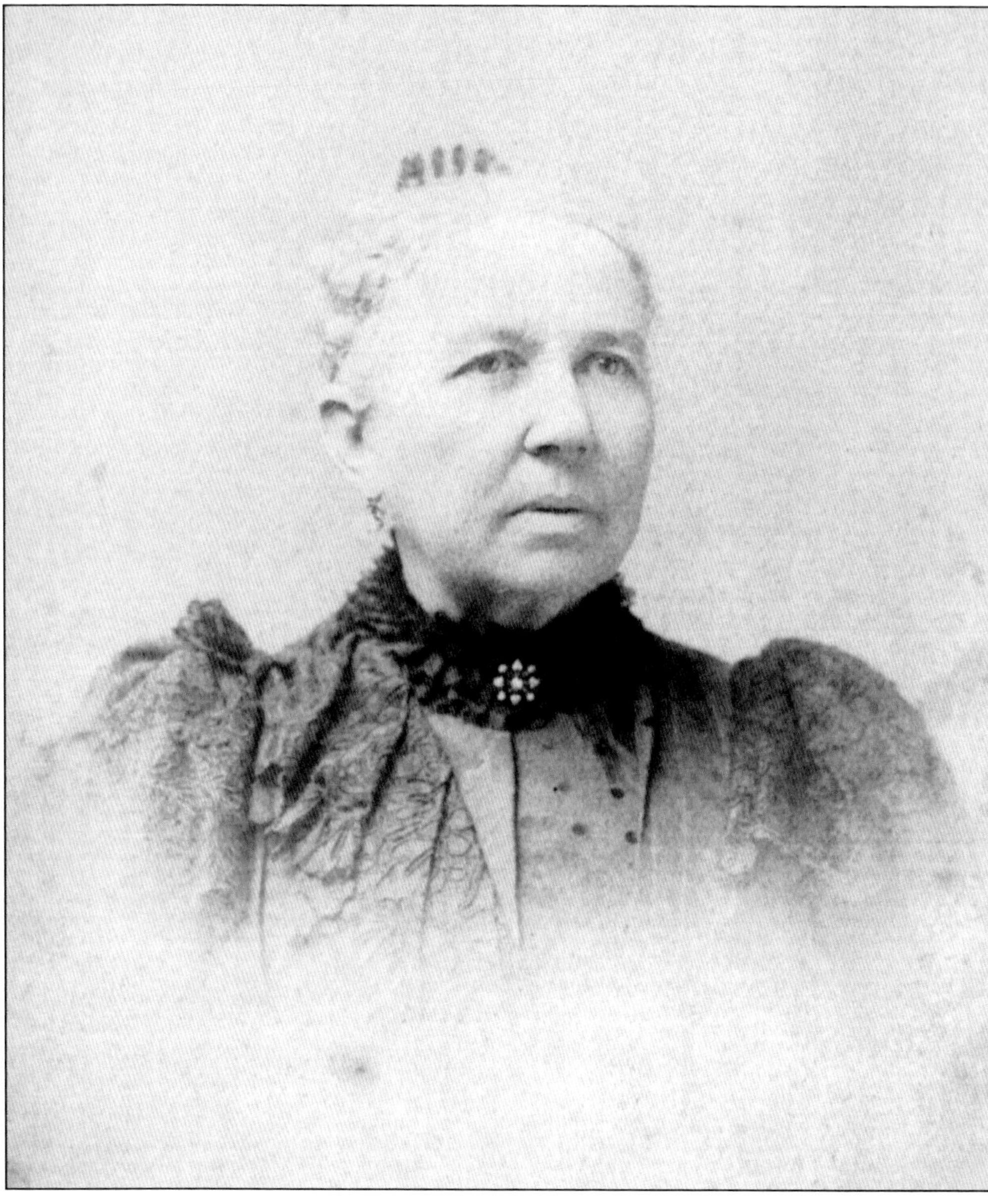

This may be the last portrait photograph of Margaret Scholl Hood in existence, probably taken around 1910. By this time, she was spending the colder months in residence at the Woman's College, attending most of the college's important events. The students admired her great enthusiasm and energy, which was surprising to them because, by then, she was well into her seventies. Throughout her lifetime, she was a staunch supporter of many organizations. One favorite charity was the Home for the Aged, organized in 1892 and known today as the Record Street Home. The home is one of Frederick's treasured gems; at any given time, it houses 25 elderly ladies, regardless of their ability to pay. The endowment that Margaret Scholl Hood helped establish makes that possible. Many of her other causes have thrived in the century since her death, including the C. Burr Artz Library, flagship of the Frederick County Public Libraries; City Hospital, now the Frederick Memorial Health System; the Frederick Art Club; and the Historical Society of Frederick County.

Four

Our New Name Hood College of Frederick, 1913–1934

Margaret Hood had been generous in her support of the Woman's College, and in 1912 the Potomac Synod of the Reformed Church authorized the renaming of the college for her. Margaret, flattered, gave her blessing, and the change was announced on October 31, 1912. The honoree died just weeks later. In May 1913, the college charter was amended to reflect the new name.

Thanks to Margaret's gifts, Dr. Apple could plan for the Greater Woman's College on West Campus. Thus far, the farm had been used for field hockey and Halloween revelry. Now, plans were being made for Alumnae Hall (the administration building) and the first dormitory, which was named Shriner Hall in recognition of Edward Derr Shriner, another generous donor, in memory of his parents. Both Alumnae and Shriner Halls were occupied in 1915. Students split their time, depending upon classes and activities, between the campuses. By 1922, all college classes were being offered on the new campus, while the Hood Seminary (the preparatory school) remained in town. Winchester Hall, as the seminary buildings were now known, was still used as a dormitory.

In 1920, the Apples moved from their East Church Street home to the new president's house (today's Alumnae House). Other structures rose: Strawn Cottage (the home economics house, built in 1918); a second dormitory, Coblentz Hall (1922); the Williams Observatory (1924); the infirmary (1925), later known as Martz Hall and since demolished; and Meyran Hall, the third dormitory (1930). With the opening of Meyran, the college sold Winchester Hall to Frederick County, and today it houses the county government.

A lively campus scene developed. Clubs, new sports teams, and honorary societies sprang up. Student government and a yearbook, the ***Touchstone***, made their appearance. New traditions such as May Day, the White Sweater Girl, and Class Day, took their places with the Alumnae Hall columns and a new pergola for the new campus.

Despite falling enrollments resulting from the Great Depression, Hood endured; still, change was afoot. Dr. Apple retired in 1934 at age 69.

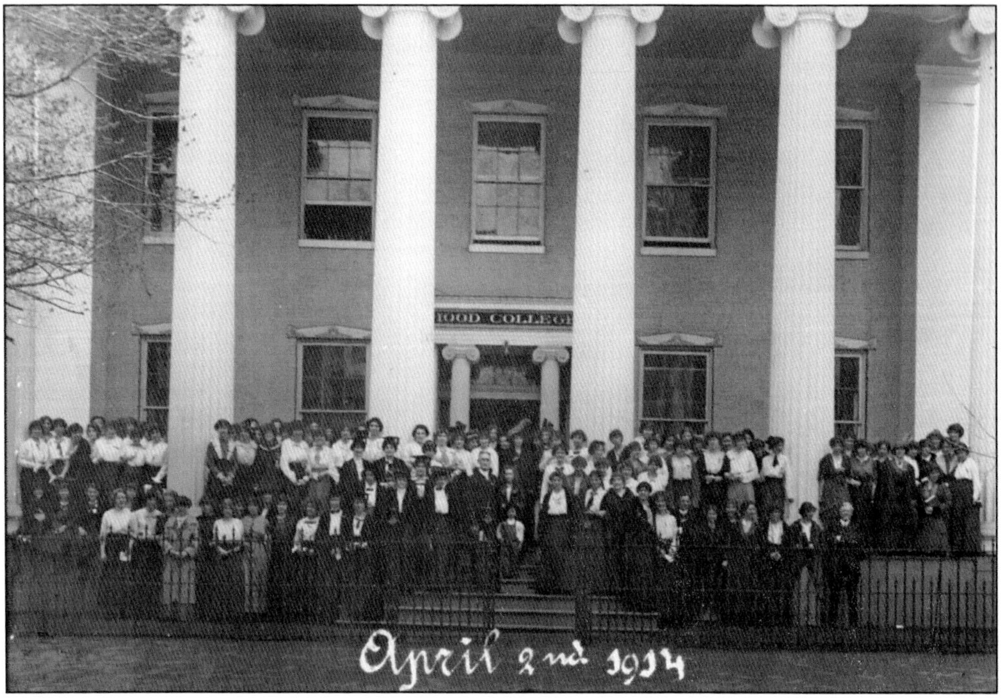

In April 1914, Collegiate Hall, situated on East Church Street, sported a sign with the college's new name. Some of the downtown buildings were home to the college for several more decades, but a new campus was eventually built, which must have been exciting for these students and faculty posing in front of the main college buildings downtown.

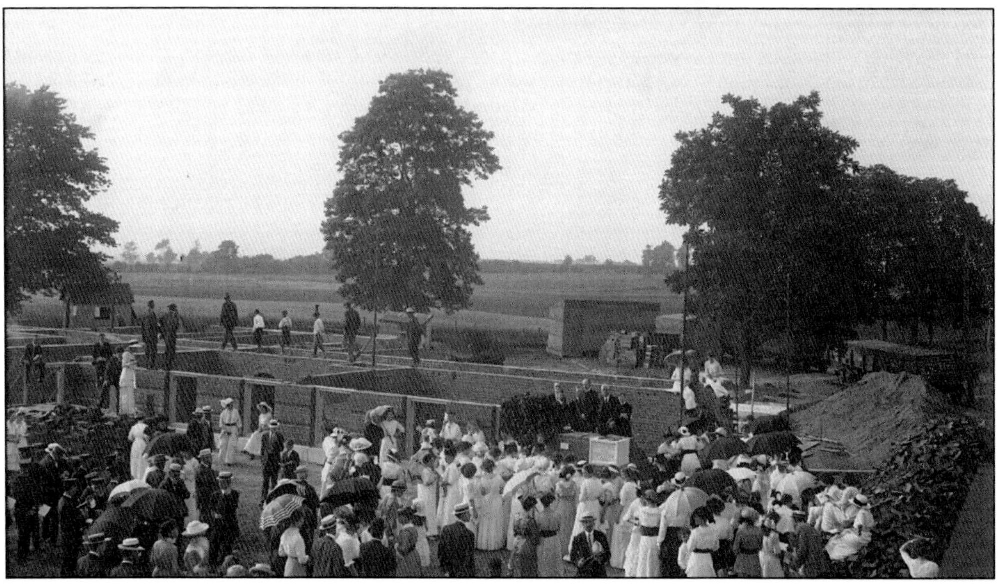

The foundations were laid, and the cornerstone of Alumnae Hall was placed on June 9, 1914. Two hundred students sang to celebrate the occasion, and the president of the Potomac Synod of the Reformed Church offered a stirring speech, full of congratulations and praise for the college and President Apple. Students planted ivy beside the rising walls, a class tradition that continued for decades.

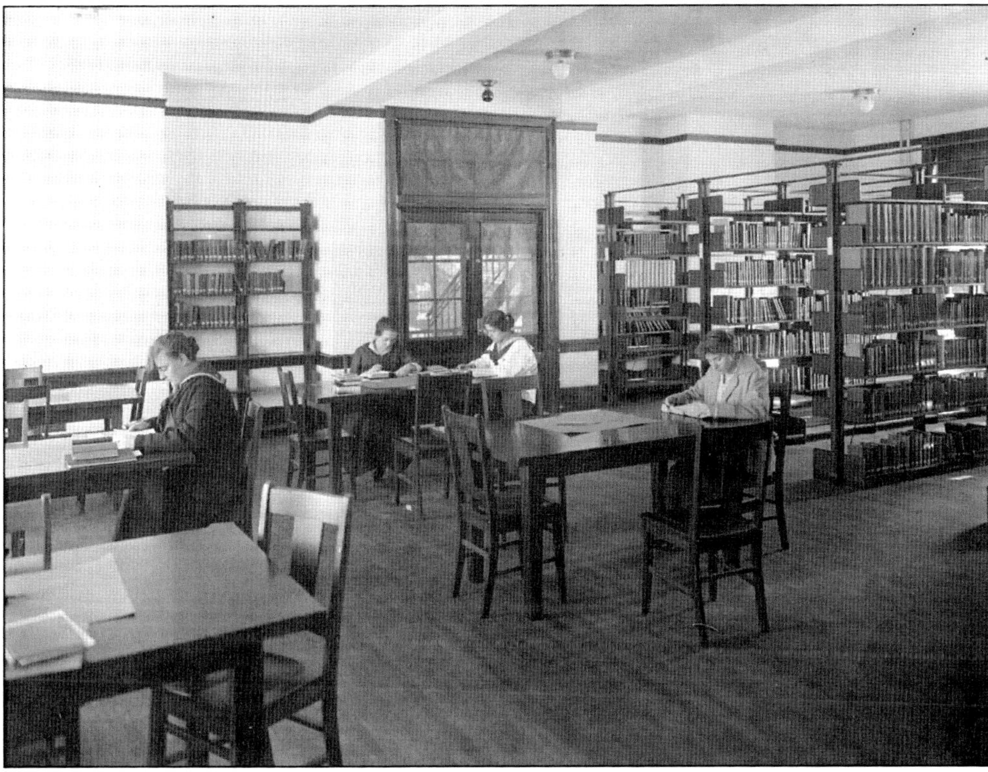

The library occupied a spacious room in Alumnae Hall. Miriam Rankin Apple, Dr. Apple's oldest daughter, graduated from Hood in 1914 and immediately became the librarian. She took a library course at Simmons College in Boston in order to enhance her knowledge of library work. She was active in college and community causes and served as Hood's librarian until her untimely death in 1950 at age 57.

Dr. Charles Wehler was vice president of the Woman's College and Hood from the early 1910s into the mid-1920s. He is pictured here with a history class around 1920 in Alumnae Hall. As with most employees of the college, he did double duty, teaching history, political science, and the Bible. Dr. Wehler's two daughters, Katherine (1916) and Margaret (1918), were active Hood alumnae.

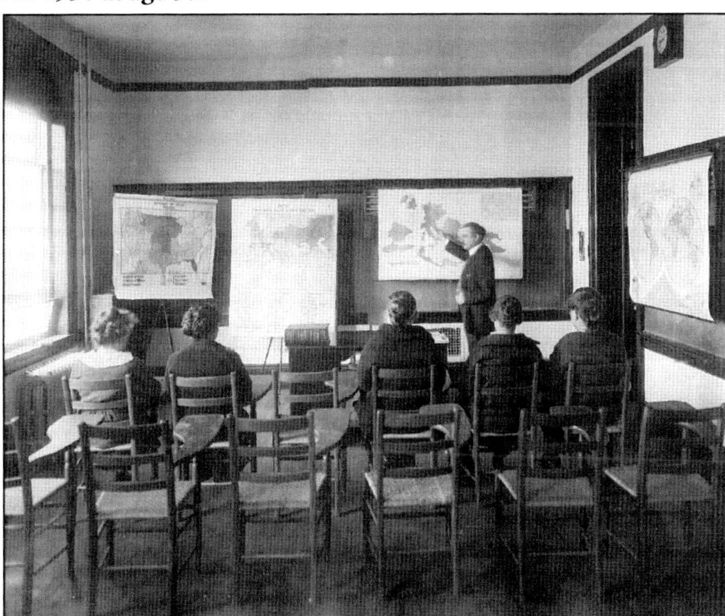

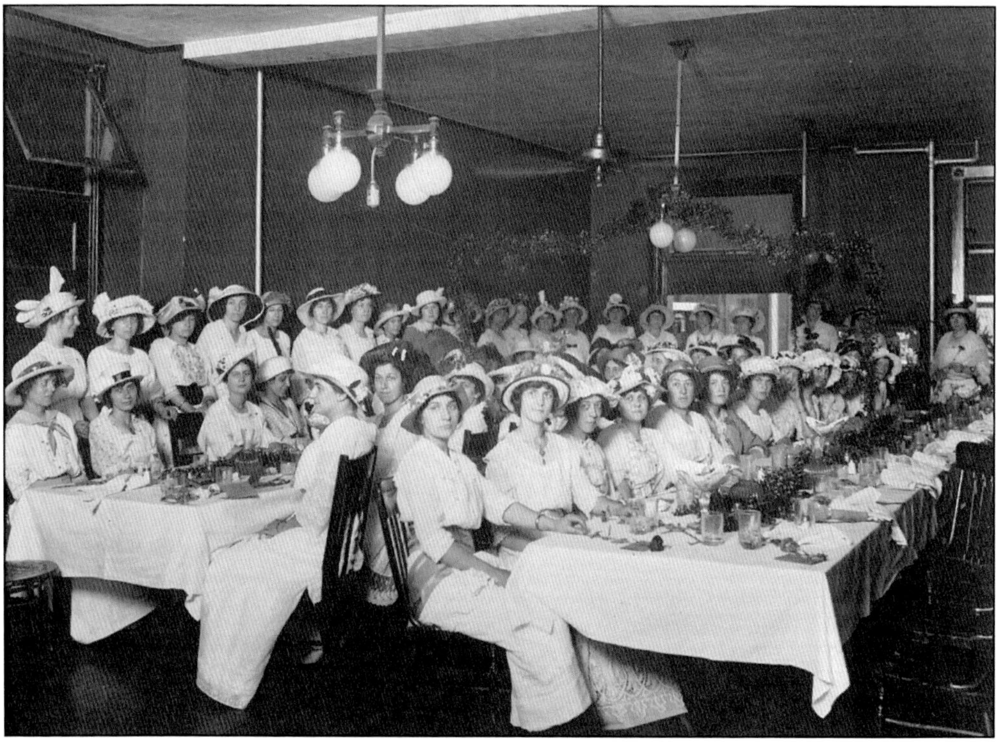

Students in the Shriner Hall dining room enjoy Strawberry Breakfast on May Day 1916. Strawberry Breakfast, a cherished Hood tradition, is now held the morning of commencement and again during Reunion Weekend. The menu includes strawberries, ice cream, and sticky cinnamon buns, made outrageously popular by Helen Little, the college dietician from 1948 to 1966.

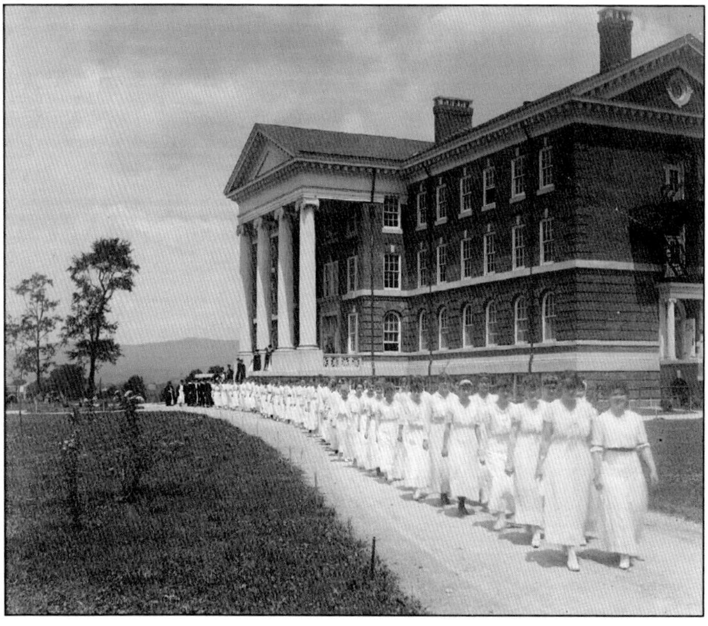

Alumnae Hall provided an impressive setting for this commencement procession in May 1916. The seniors are at the back of the line in their commencement regalia, while the rest of the student body in the front are dressed in white. A white dress for special occasions was a must-have for each student.

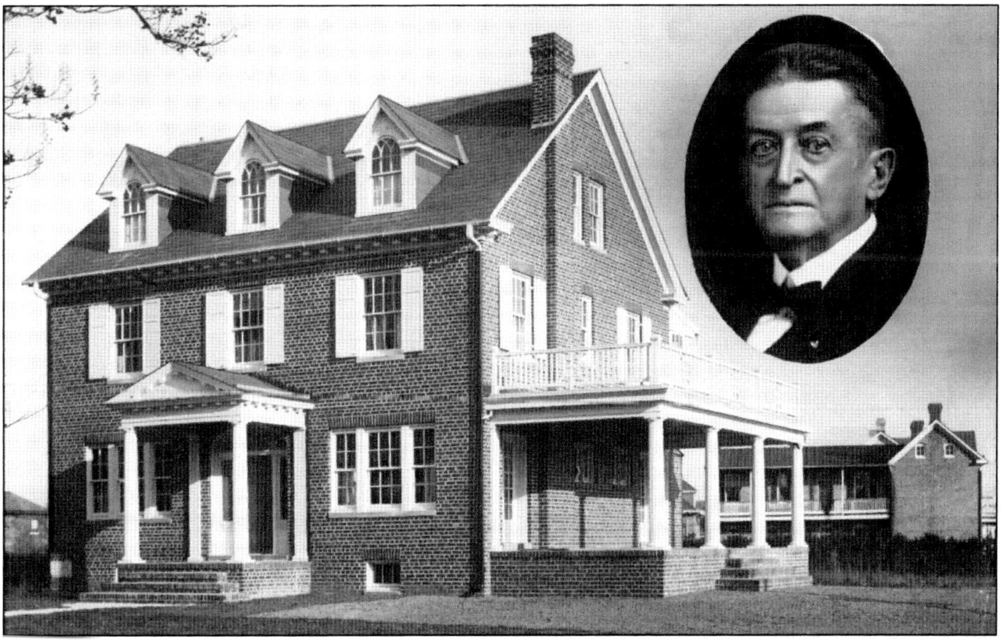

Strawn Cottage, built in 1918 as a home economics laboratory house, was named for David Gates Strawn (inset) of Illinois, whose niece, a home economics major, attended Hood. Apparently, Strawn was so impressed with Hood and his niece's experiences there that he donated the funds to construct the building. Following a fire in 1978, the building was renovated, and it now houses the admissions office.

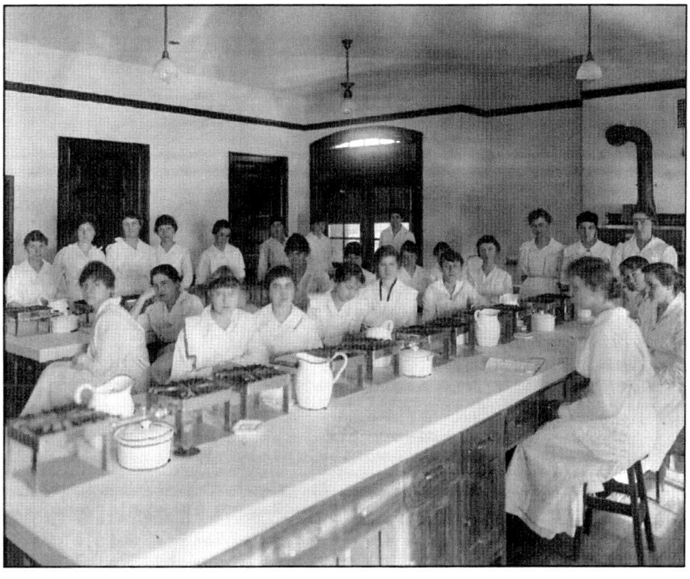

Though home economics had not been a part of the original curriculum of the Woman's College, the additional space afforded by Alumnae Hall allowed the development and expansion of programs. The curriculum covered textiles, clothing, nutrition, household mechanics, and child development. Here, students participate in a nutrition laboratory exercise in a room known as "the White Kitchen" in 1919.

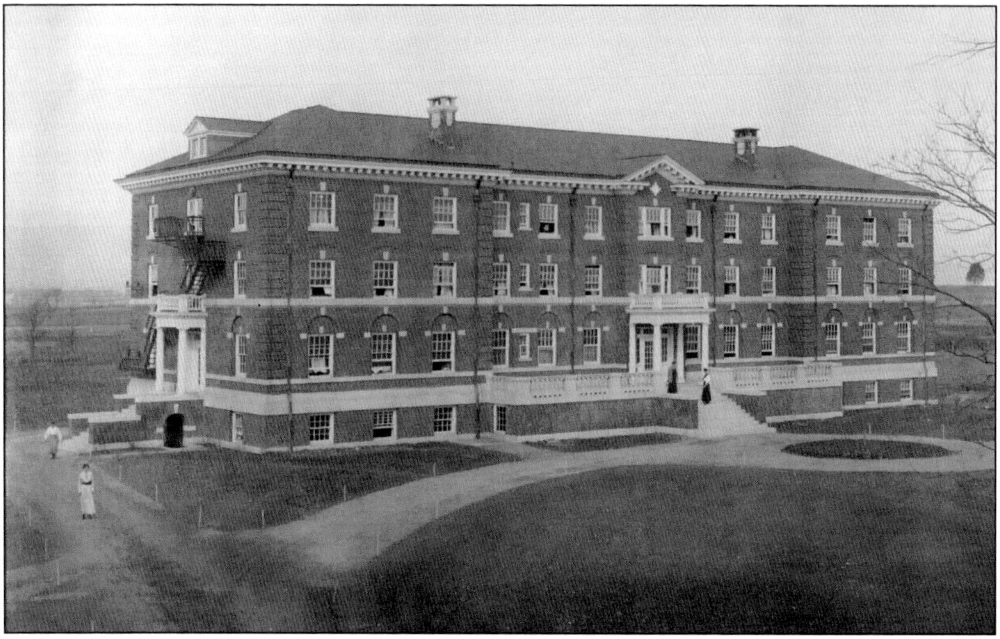

Shriner Hall, originally known as Residence Hall A, was occupied in the fall of 1915 and became the first dormitory on campus. The college later named it in honor of the parents of Edward Derr Shriner Sr., who, like his cousin Margaret Scholl Hood, was a generous supporter of the college. The building was completely renovated in 2001 and 2002.

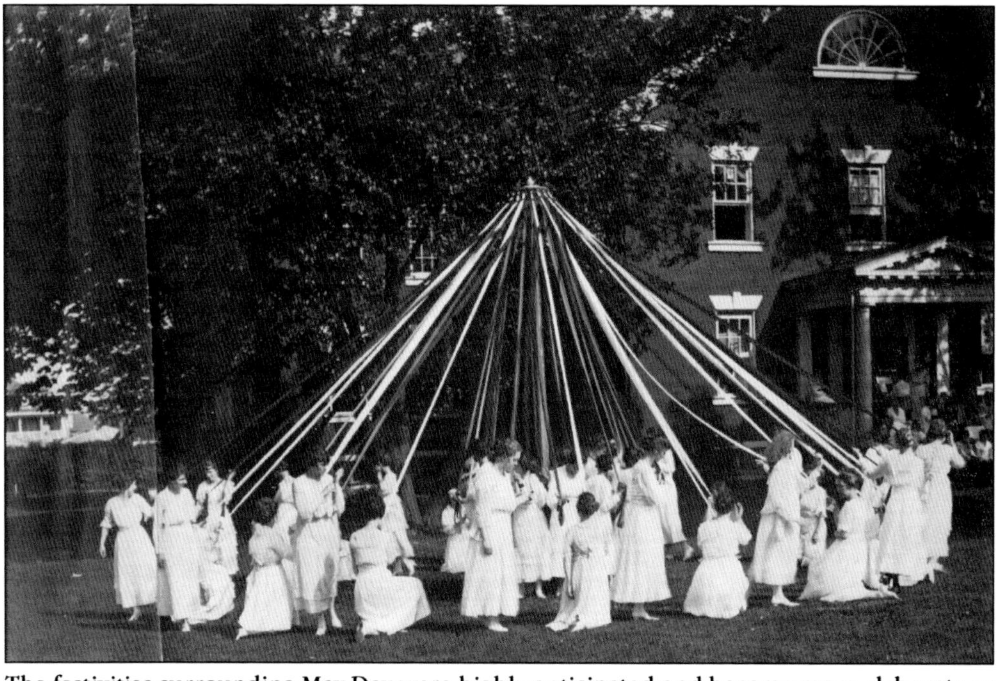

The festivities surrounding May Day were highly anticipated and became more elaborate as years went by. The maypole dance was just one of many activities that students participated in for May Day. Here, students wearing their white "special occasion dresses" weave the maypole ribbons in and out near Brodbeck Music Hall in 1919.

The 1920 *Touchstone* yearbook paid tribute to members of the college community who served their country during World War I. Librarian Miriam Apple (1914, above) served in the Quartermaster's Corps in France; Vice Pres. Charles Wehler (left) and Dr. Thomas Dixon (right), professor of economics, did stateside war work for the YMCA; Lois Johnson Rankin (below), instructor of violin and physical education, worked with the YMCA Canteen Service in France.

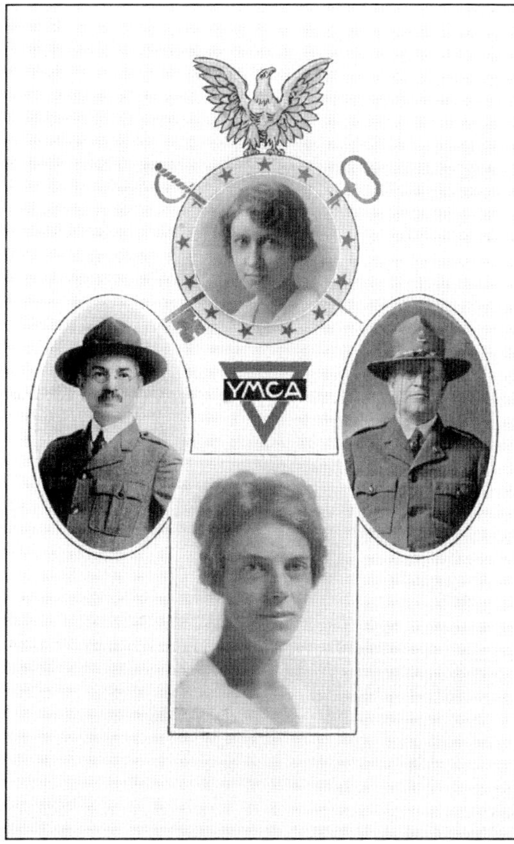

Students have assembled at Alumnae Hall for their 1921 Campus Day photograph. Campus Day was another of the venerable Hood traditions. Each class chose a theme and dressed up in appropriate costumes made in individual class colors. The classes competed against each other in sports, singing, and skits, as well as for having the best costume; the winning class was awarded a trophy by the Athletic Association.

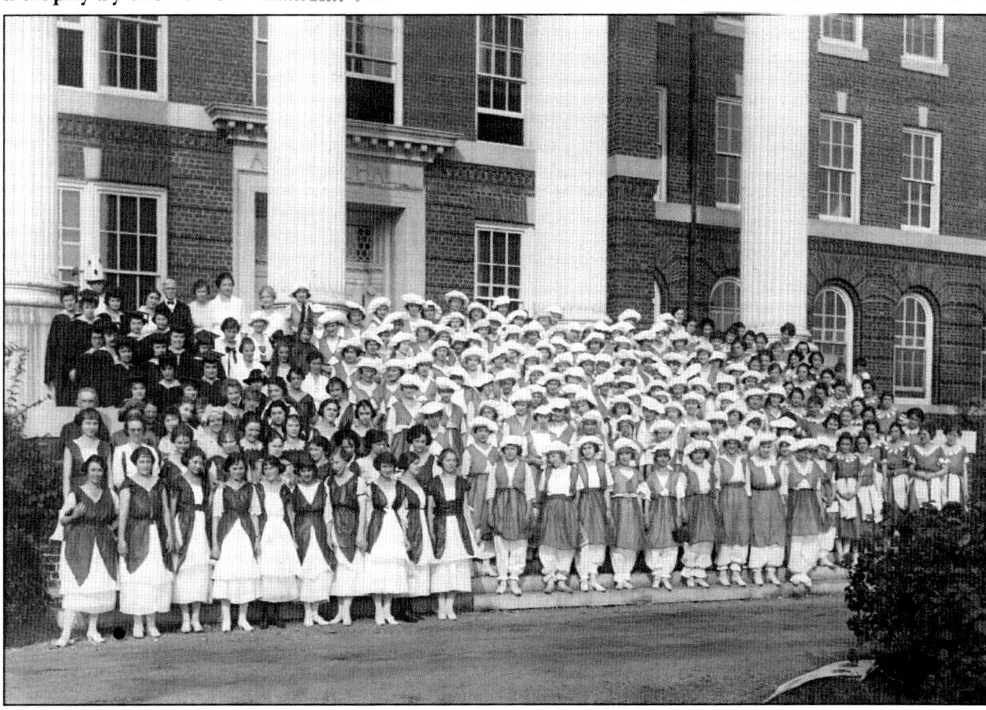

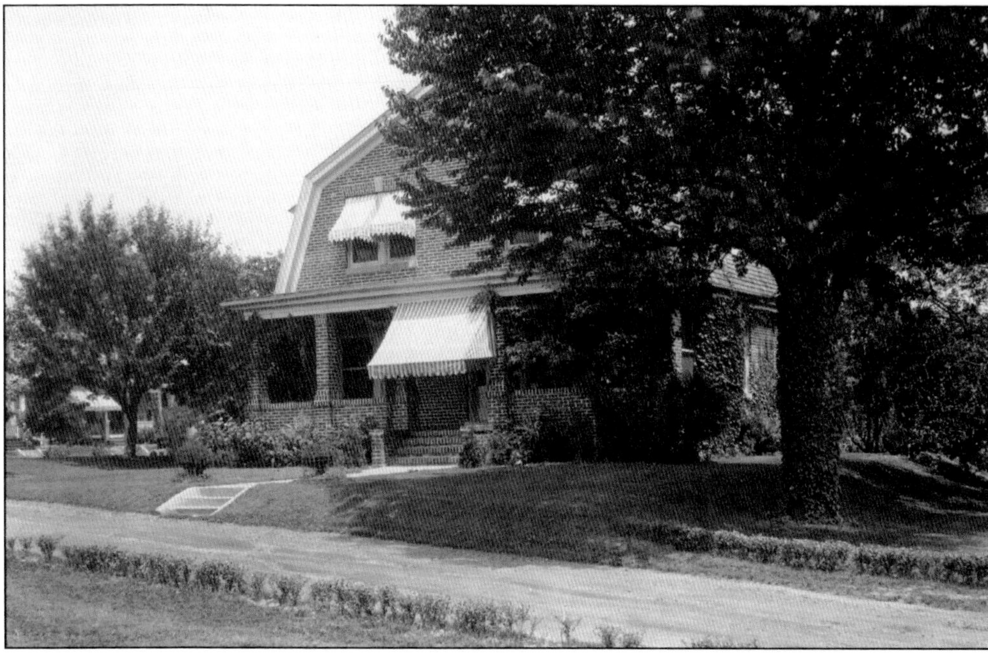

Westview Terrace was built as the vice president's residence in 1921. In 1937, it was renovated to accommodate the nursery school, now the child development laboratory school. The building was renamed in 1971 to honor Onica Prall, who served as the first director of the facility and taught in the education department from 1929 to 1969.

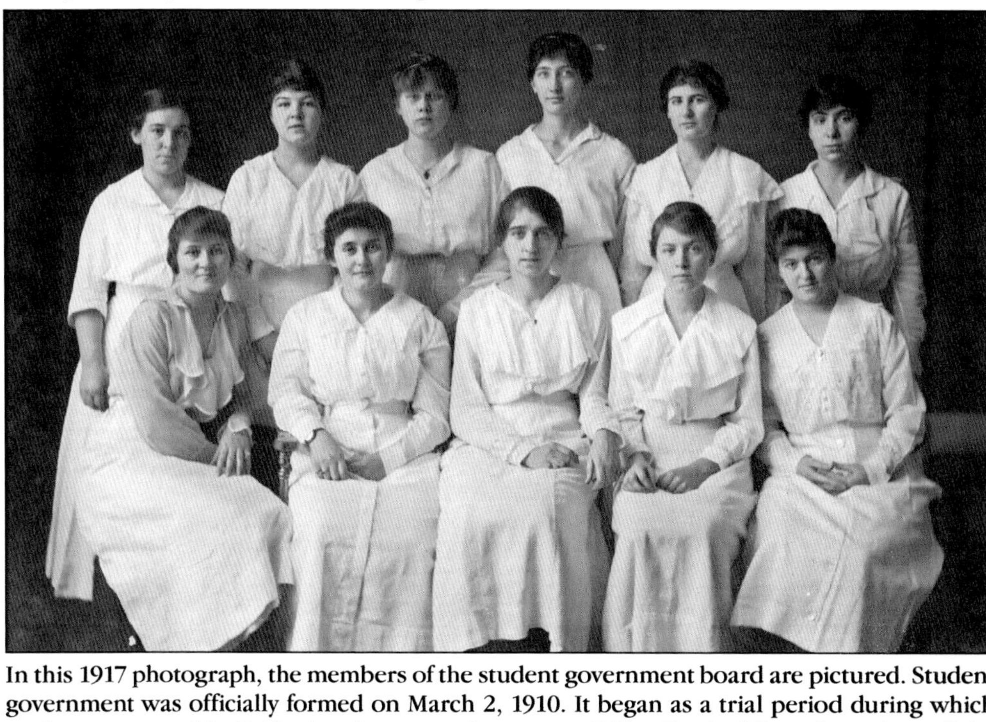

In this 1917 photograph, the members of the student government board are pictured. Student government was officially formed on March 2, 1910. It began as a trial period during which students assumed individual and community responsibility "in the life and conduct of the College, and thus to develop self-control, and to promote loyalty to the College, at all times."

The *Blue and Grey*, the student-run weekly newspaper, began publication in September 1921. In February 1988, the paper became *Hood Today* and was published under that name, though less frequently, until September 2004. At that time, it merged the two older titles and became the *Blue and Grey Today*. In 2011, it resumed its original name: the *Blue and Grey*.

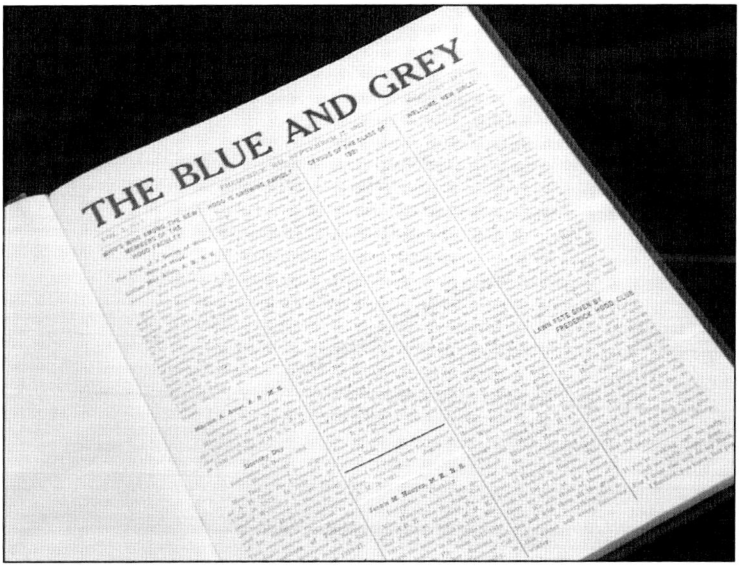

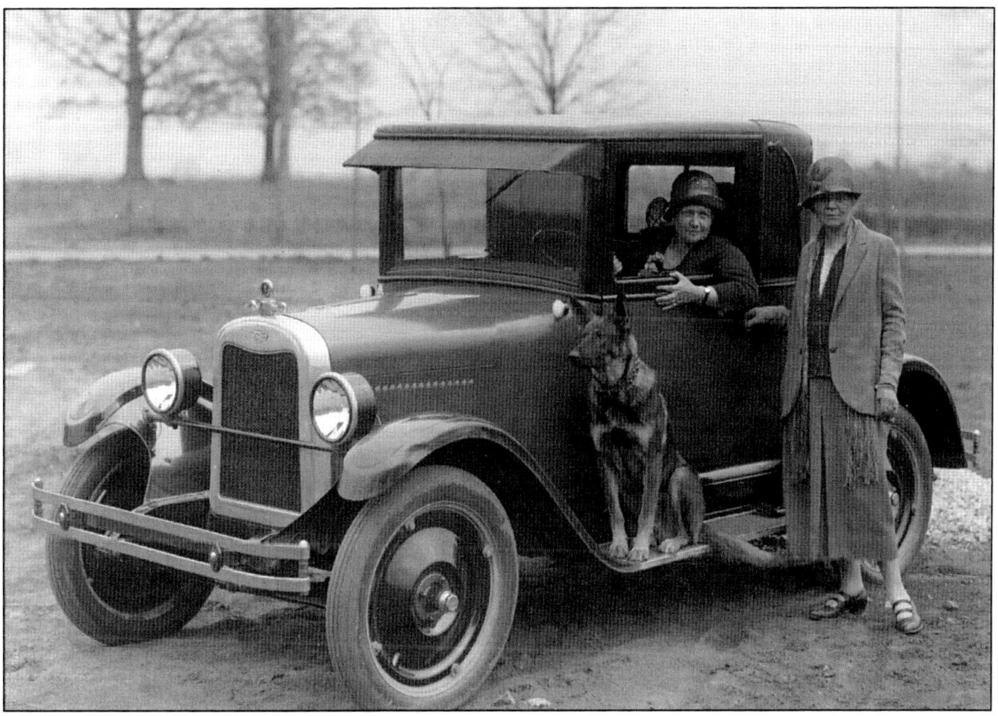

Shown in the 1920s, chemistry teacher Willie Augusta Lantz (sitting in the driver's seat) is going on an outing with her German shepherd, named Wolf of Catawba, and her friend Maria Derendinger, wife of Dr. Ernst Derendinger, a professor of German, Bible studies, and art history. Wolf looks as if he is accustomed to riding on the running board.

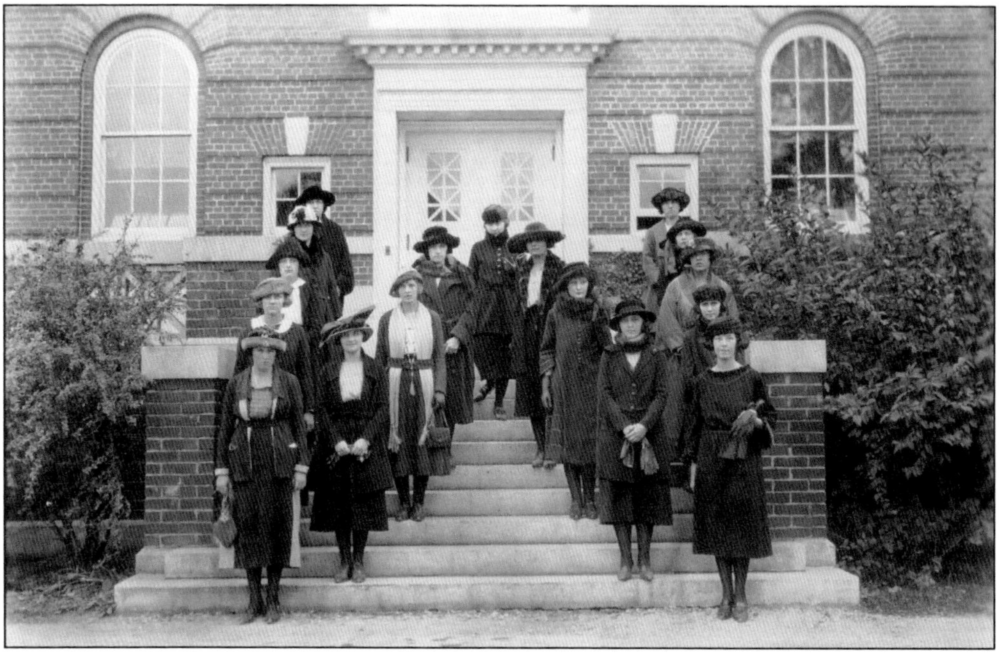

The Wanderers Club forms a "W" on the steps of one of the campus buildings. It is assumed by the name that it was a hiking club, but little about the group is known. Other clubs students could join included the Biology Club, the Mathematics Club, the Home Economics Club, the Glee Club and the Choir, the Cheer Leaders, and Sodalitas Romana for students taking Latin.

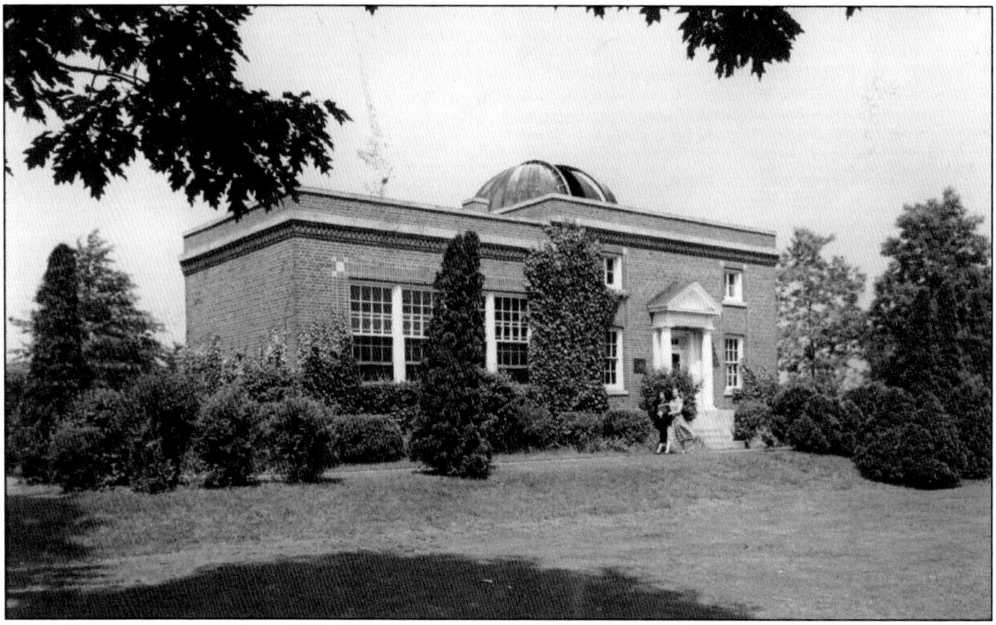

Williams Observatory, which opened in January 1925, was a gift from M. Janet Williams in memory of her late father, John H. Williams, a prominent Frederick lawyer and banker. The telescope, built by Alvan Clark and Sons, has an eight-inch lens made originally for the Harvard College Observatory. The building is now in the National Register of Historic Places.

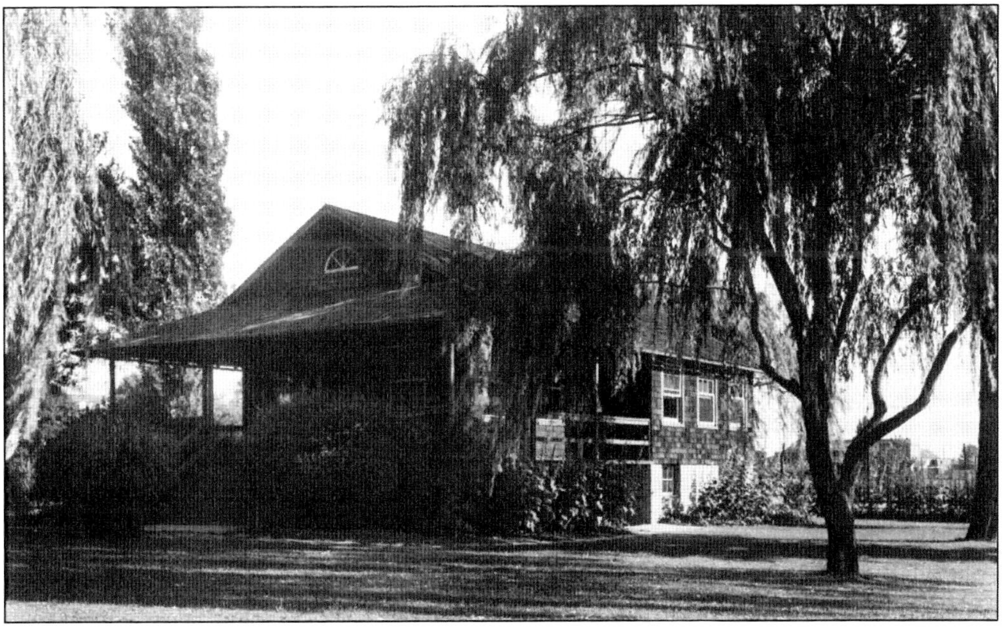

The Y-Hut was built in 1923 as a home for the campus YWCA and also as a base for nonresident students. This is the way it appeared in 1934. In 1954, it was named for Martha Carson, a college matron, dietitian, and instructor in the home economics program, in recognition of her generosity and dedication to the college. She worked at Hood for 34 years, from 1914 to 1948.

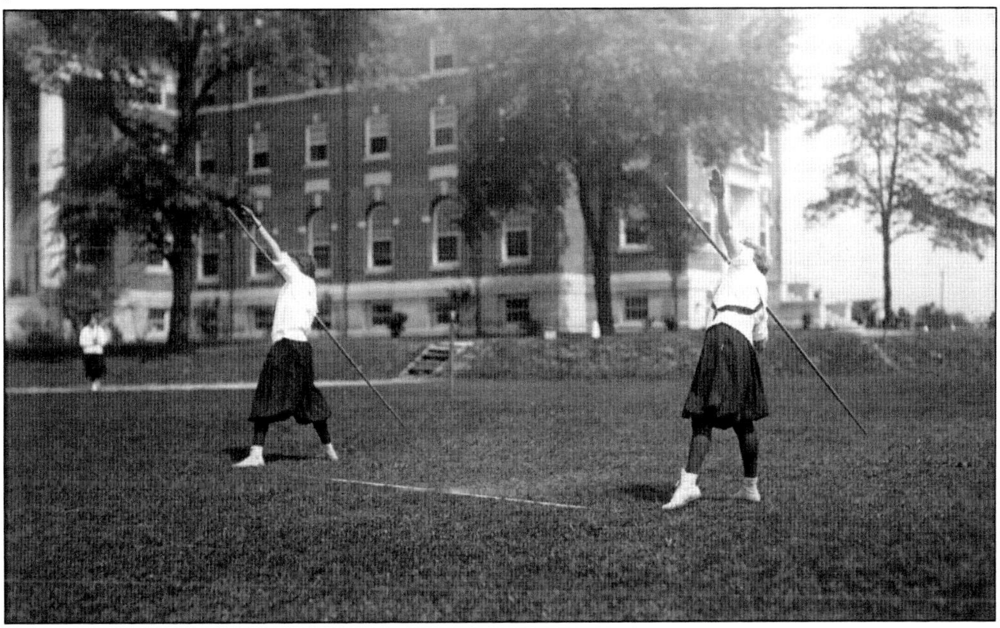

The annual track—or field—day was held in May. Students vied in javelin, discus, shot put, broad jump, hurdles, and sprints. The contests were capped off by a special lunch in the dining hall, the announcement of the winning contestants, and the awarding of the white blazer to the "all-around Hood girl." Pictured are students throwing javelins on Campus Day 1926.

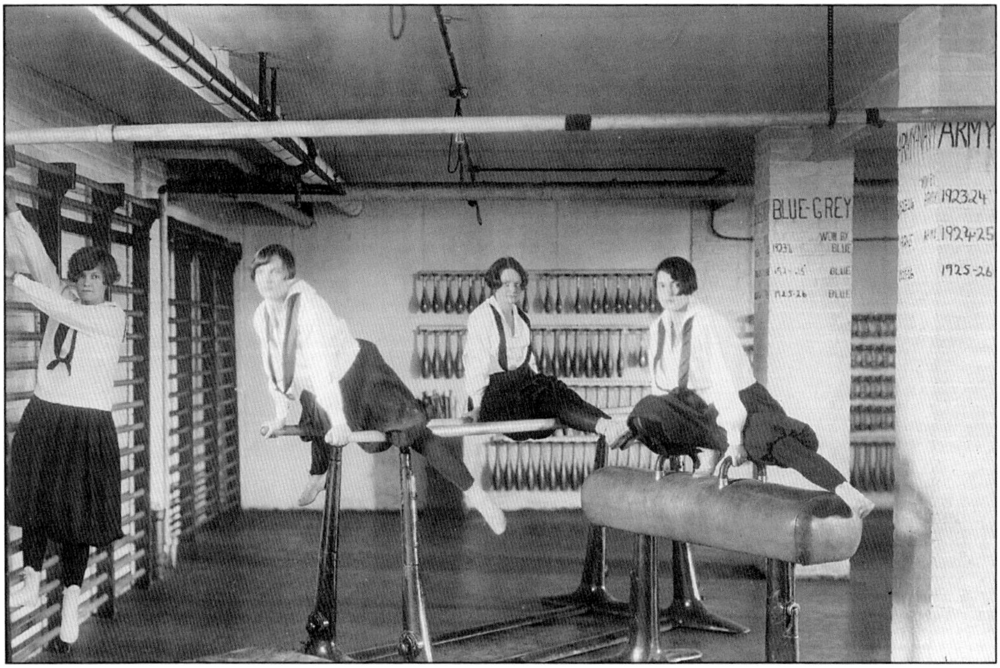

Students demonstrate that they can negotiate the parallel bars and the pommel horse—in spite of bloomers—in this 1926 photograph. Two hours weekly of gymnasium work were required of all but seniors. According to the 1926 catalogue, this included "marching tactics, Swedish floor work, hand apparatus . . . aesthetic and folk dancing, and games. These tend to develop good posture, quickness, accuracy, a sense of rhythm and a spirit of play."

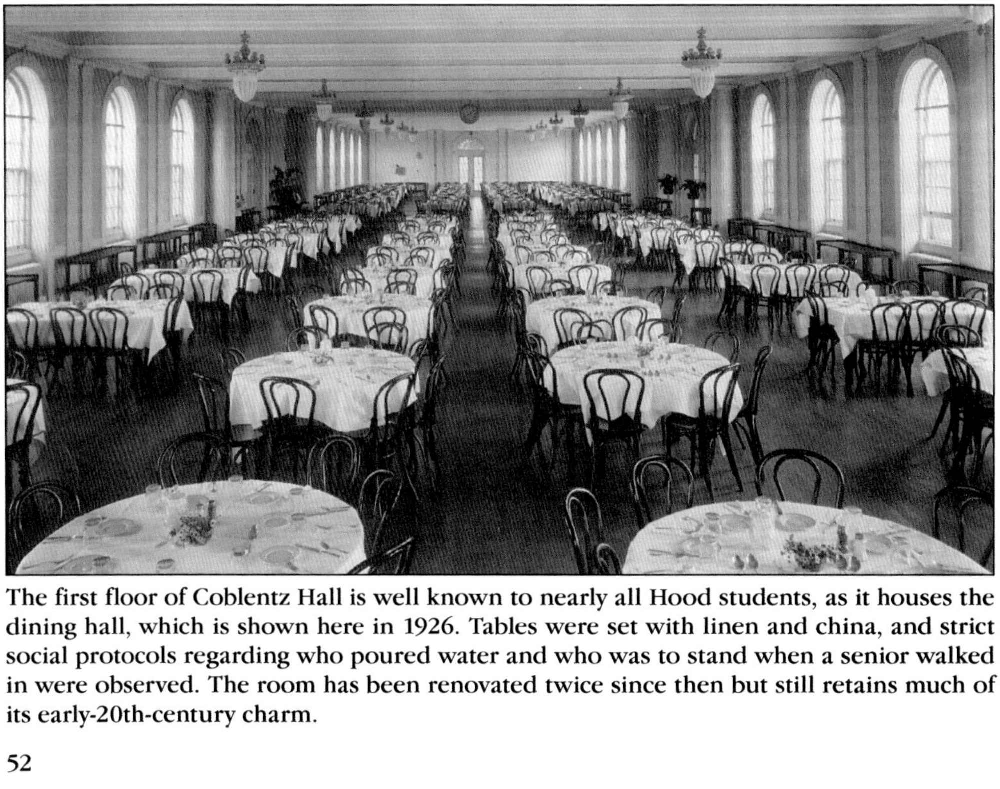

The first floor of Coblentz Hall is well known to nearly all Hood students, as it houses the dining hall, which is shown here in 1926. Tables were set with linen and china, and strict social protocols regarding who poured water and who was to stand when a senior walked in were observed. The room has been renovated twice since then but still retains much of its early-20th-century charm.

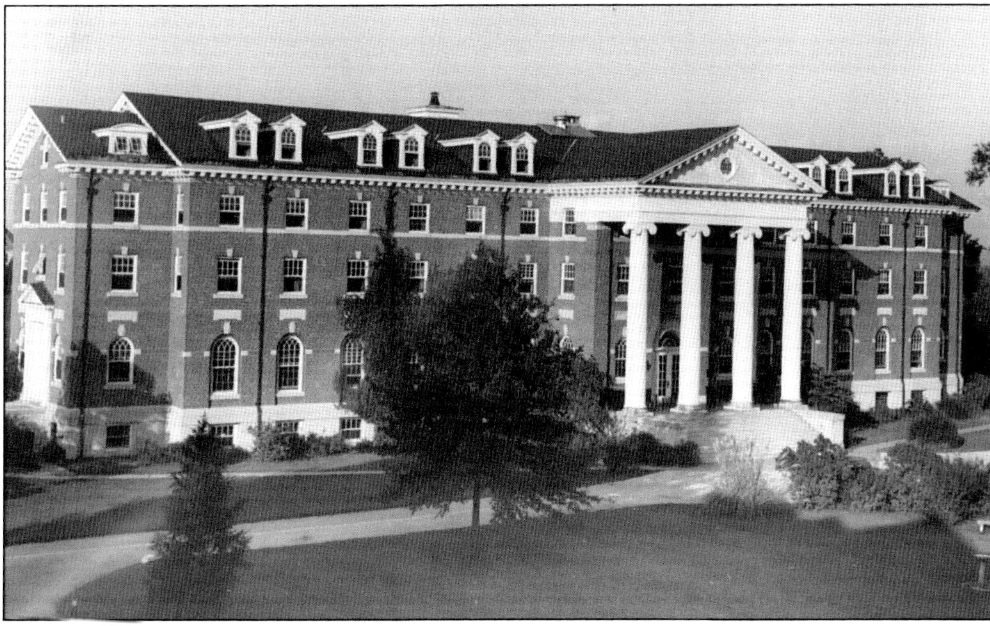

Coblentz Hall, named for Emory Coblentz, Hood director and father of six Hood graduates, became the second dormitory on the "suburban" campus in 1922. Coblentz was a tireless fundraiser, helping in efforts to raise financial support for a dozen campus buildings. He wrote, "Undoubtedly, the greatest service I rendered was in connection with the growth and development of Hood College."

The candidates for May Queen of 1929, all members of the class of 1929, are pictured here. They are, from left to right, Anna Wagner, Cynthia Jones, Anne Davis, Virginia Dunn, and Ruth Moser. Dunn and Frances Norton (not pictured) were proclaimed May Queen and Prince Hood, respectively, by the serenading sophomores. A May pageant depicting a medieval English village drew some 2,000 onlookers as the royalty arrived for their coronation.

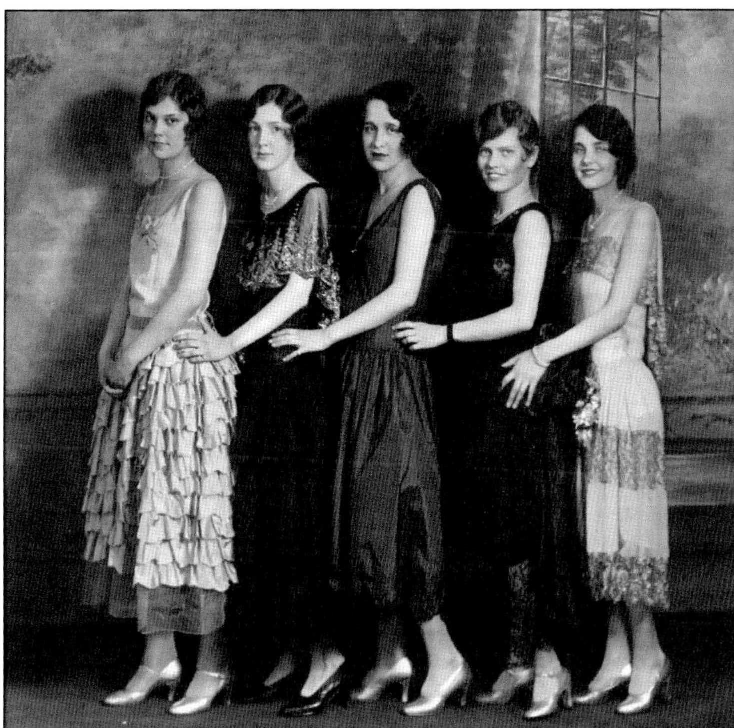

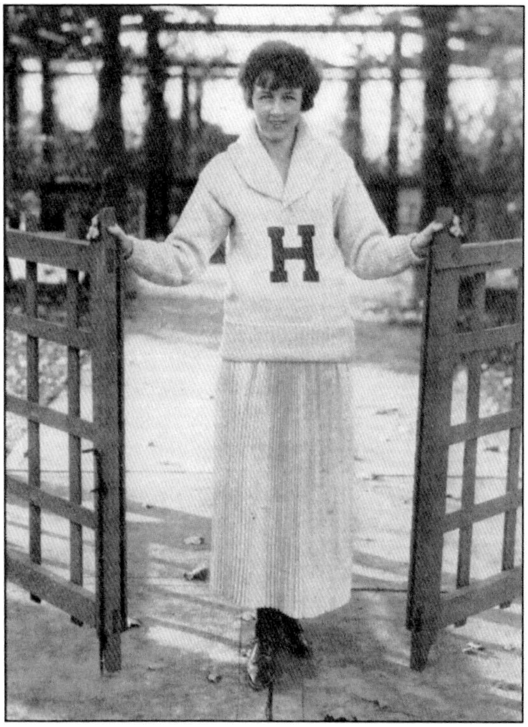

Anna Tisinger (1924) appears in the 1925 *Touchstone* as the White Sweater Girl. The *Touchstone* stated, "A white Spalding slip-on shall be awarded [by the Athletic Association] to the girl of the incoming Senior class having the most all-'round college spirit, showing the best sportsmanship and athletic ability and whose academic standing is not below 'C.' " Later, the white sweater became a white blazer and another college tradition.

Camp Raudy, located a few miles west of Frederick in the Catoctin Mountains, was the scene of many enjoyable outings by the Department of Physical Education and the Recreation Association. Six wooded acres and funds to construct a cabin were given to Hood by a Frederick physician and businessman Rudolph Rau and his wife, Sallie Tetrick Rau, in 1928. Hood sold the property in 2003.

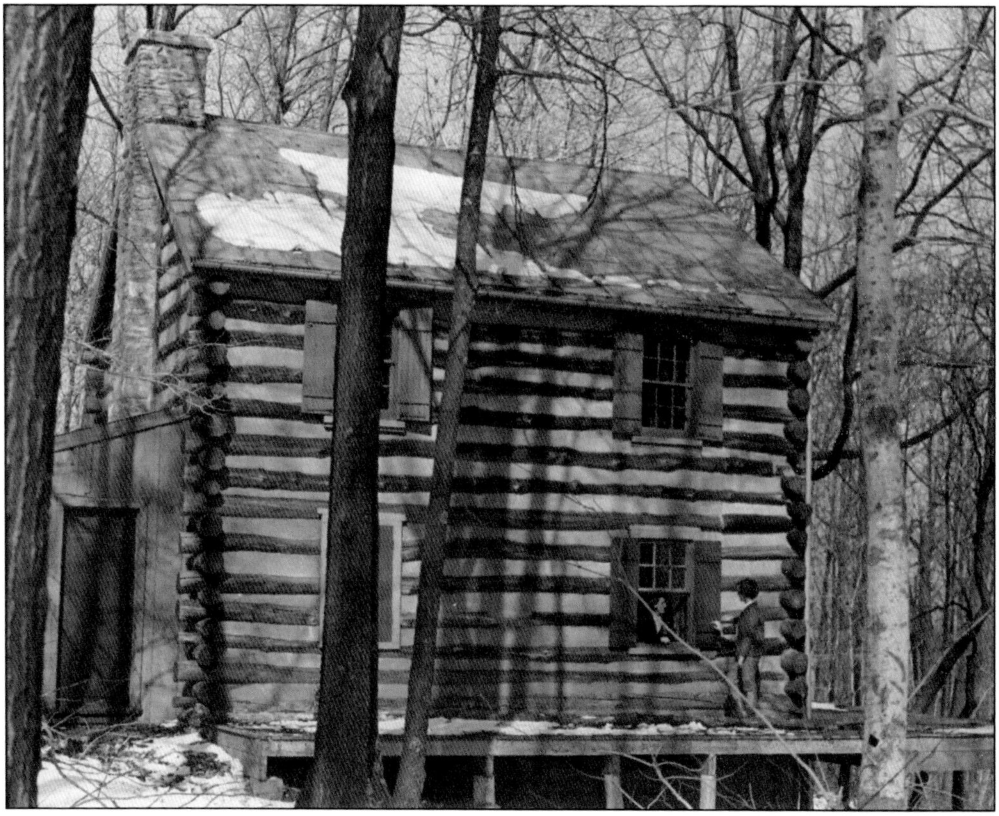

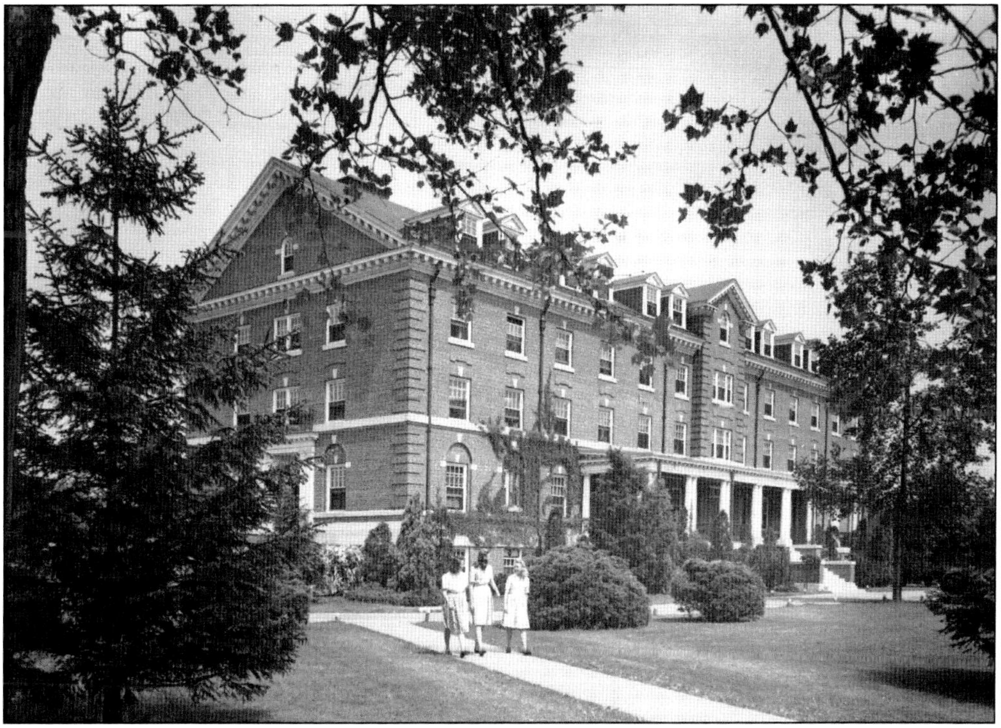

Meyran Hall, shown here in the mid-1940s, was the campus's third dormitory, erected in 1930, largely through the generosity of Louis and Marie Meyran of Pittsburgh, Pennsylvania. The completion of Meyran Hall enabled the college to finally consolidate all operations on the current campus. At that point, the Winchester Hall property was sold to Frederick County, and Hood became a one-campus suburban institution.

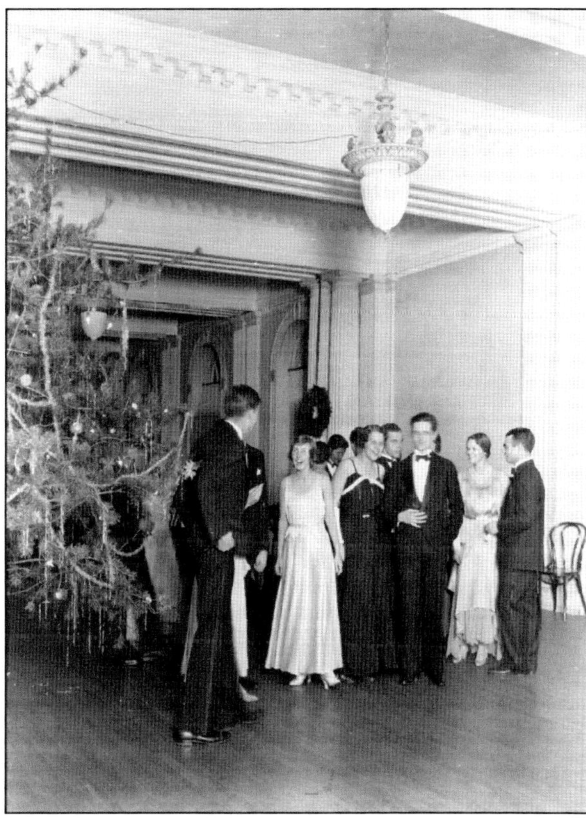

Some of the Christmas traditions of the 1930s included Christmas Vespers, a Christmas play given by the Marionettes (the dramatics club), caroling through Frederick, a tea given by the YWCA, and a dance prior to the students' departure for the holiday break. Pictured here, students gather in December 1932 in Coblentz Dining Hall, dressed in their long gowns, to socialize and relax after a long semester.

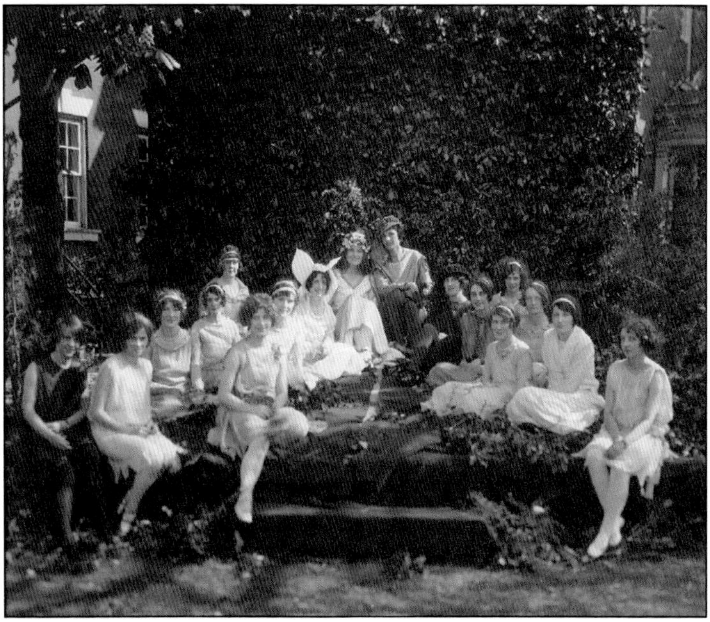

The 1925 May Queen, Helen Bassler, and her court are presented here. The queen and her attendants were seniors, chosen for their beauty by the student body. Prince Hood, Isabelle Bates (next to the queen), was chosen for being the ideal Hood girl. Early on May Day morning, members of the court were serenaded by the sophomore class as a way to reveal their identity to the campus.

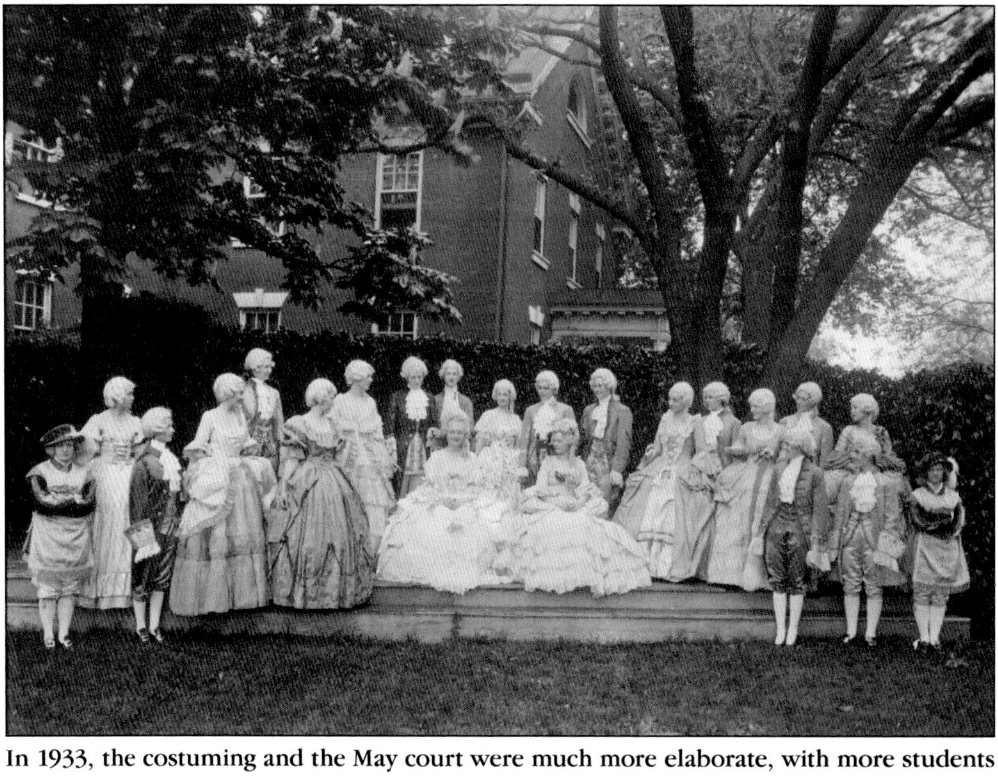

In 1933, the costuming and the May court were much more elaborate, with more students playing male roles in the court. The full-blown May Day tradition gradually faded out: the court shrank in size, Prince Hood became Princess Hood, and finally, by 1967, no queen was selected, and Princess Hood was the sole honoree. In 1964, the May Queen was Cathy Kuralt (1964), sister of the late newsman Charles Kuralt.

Mary Esther Tull (1924) was named the poet laureate of Hood College. One example of her work, though not a poetical one, is a short story published in the *Hood Herald*, the college's literary magazine, in November 1923. The *Herald* was founded by Gertrude Harner in 1896 as a publication of one of the two literary societies of the Woman's College. It ceased publication in 1990.

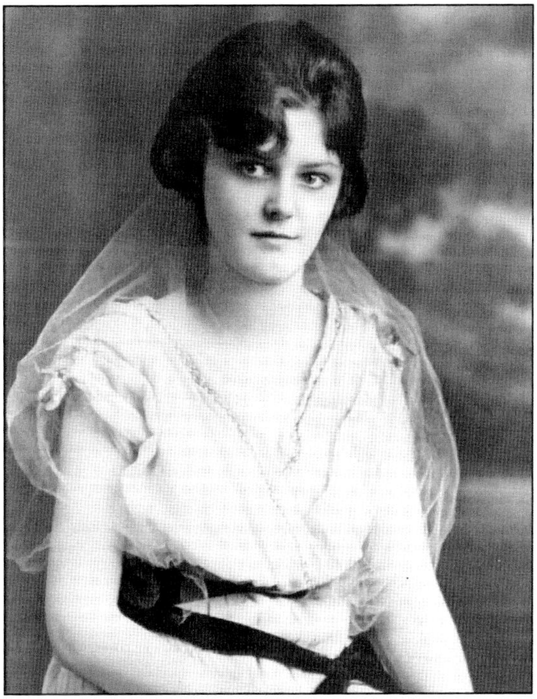

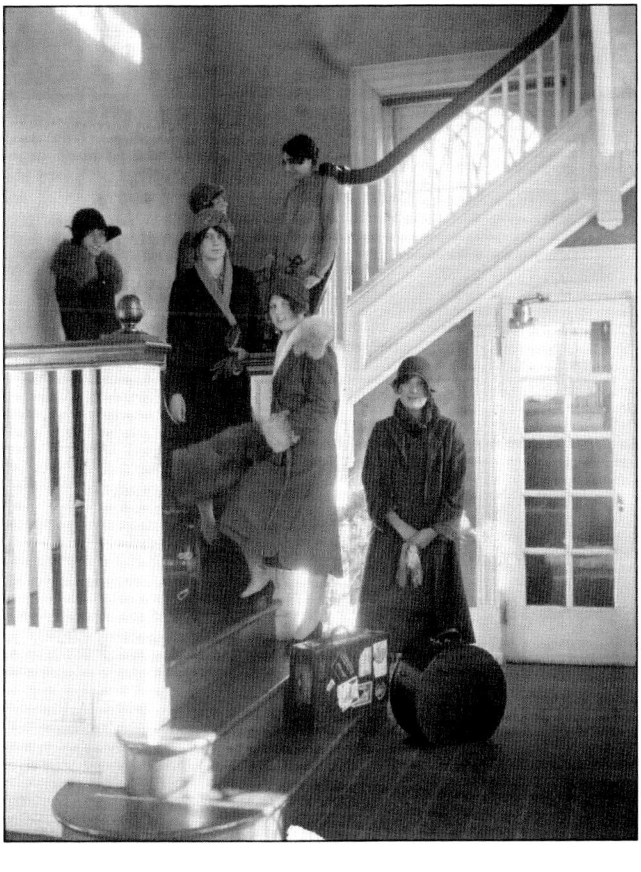

Coblentz Hall was the scene of this classic photograph, taken about 1930, as students depart campus for a holiday break. Of the 1930 student body of 437, nearly two-thirds, or 272 students, came from Pennsylvania; the next largest contingent was Maryland with 82 students, and then New Jersey with 34 students. A total of 15 states were represented at Hood.

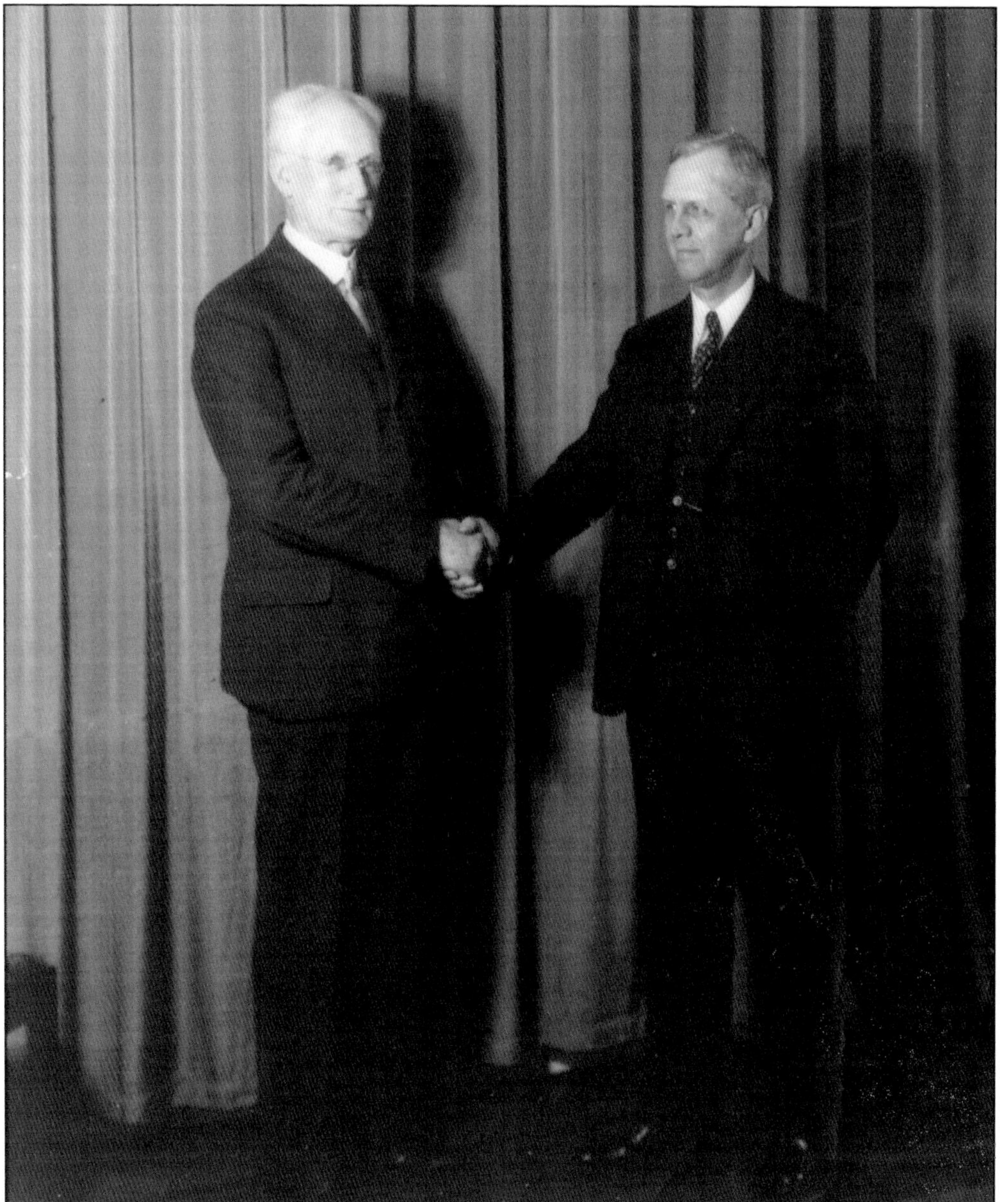

Henry Irvin Stahr (right), the college's second president, shakes hands with President Apple in this 1934 photograph. The college's first president had enjoyed a remarkable career: the institution had grown from a small woman's college to a campus of 125 acres with 14 buildings, and the faculty and staff now numbered over 80 with 500 students. The year before this picture was taken, Dr. Apple's 40th year as president was celebrated with much pomp and circumstance. He was, at that point, the longest continuously serving president at a single college in the United States. His retirement was marked by another outpouring of praise and tributes, but President Stahr was a worthy successor. Emory Coblentz, of Hood's board of directors, told the *Blue and Grey* that, with Stahr, they had named "a person who knew educational principles and had a general knowledge of many more things at the same time." The board had found someone to lead Hood with distinction through the Great Depression and World War II.

Five

Our Changing Face
A New President, a World War, 1934–1948

By the time Dr. Apple retired, Hood had developed a solid reputation on the East Coast and in the Midwest, and that reputation no doubt helped the college through the depths of the Great Depression. Though enrollment was down somewhat, there were still 500 students on campus. Faculty and staff were asked to take pay cuts, but instruction continued.

Henry Irving Stahr, a longtime trustee of the college, assumed the presidency in September 1934. Educated at Franklin and Marshall College, he was an ordained minister in the Reformed Church. Early on in his tenure, the college received the first of many generous gifts from the Hodson Trust. A milestone was reached in 1939 when the Frederick Female Seminary's charter was voided by the State of Maryland, and Hood College, released from its obligations to the seminary trustees, stood as its own entity for the first time. In 1940, the college was accredited by the Association of American Universities.

The Great Depression gave way to talk of war in Europe, and by 1939 the war was a reality. The campus was recovering from the troubled times: the faculty had even gotten raises, and the new Joseph Henry Apple Library was taking shape. By then, it was clear that college business would go on, but not as usual. The college recognized the difficulties of the war by inviting a refugee student to attend Hood. In 1942, a faculty committee on the war emergency was established, and the college adjusted its curriculum to recognize the need for nurses and stenographers. War bonds were being sold, and blood drives were organized on campus.

Still, Hood was looking to the future, and in 1944 the college marked its 50th anniversary. Fundraising had begun for a new gymnasium. The French and Spanish language houses were established in 1945 and 1946 respectively, and courses in early childhood education were added to the curriculum. In 1948, Dr. Apple died, Dr. Stahr retired, and Dr. Andrew G. Truxal, a widely respected educator, was named president.

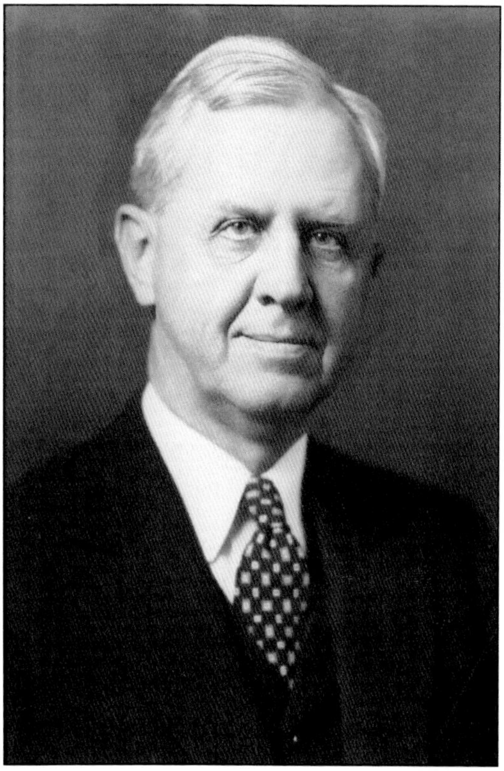

The next era literally began with a change of face: Dr. Joseph Henry Apple's 41-year presidency—the entire history of Hood College—was giving way to the presidency of Dr. Henry Irvin Stahr and movement into some of the darkest times of the 20th century. The country was in the middle of the Great Depression and would only really emerge as World War II began.

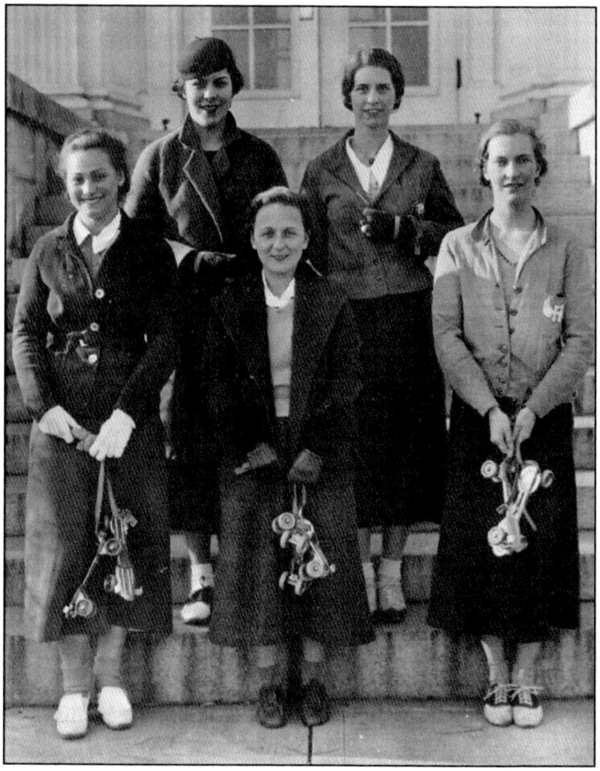

Members of the Roller Skating Club pose for a photograph around 1935. Apparently, these ladies loved wheels, as they also constituted the members of the Bicycle Club. During this period, a number of athletic groups came into being under the aegis of the Athletic Association, including the baseball team, the Wanderers Club, the Aesthetic Dancing Club, the Hiking Club, the Horseback Riding Club, and the Outing Club.

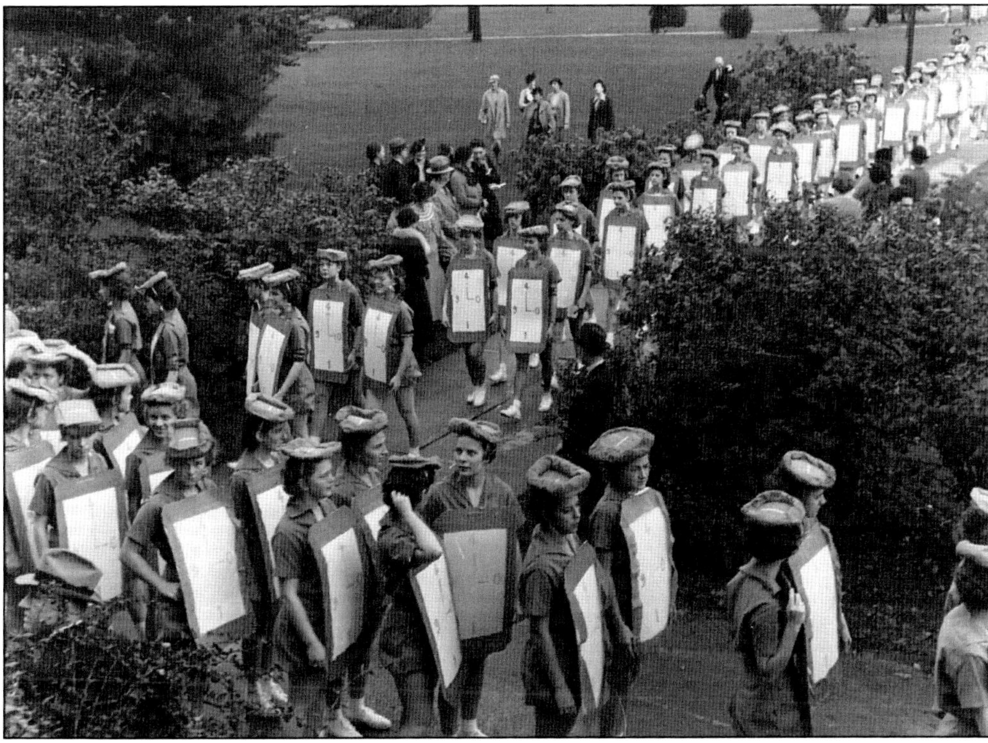

Members of the class of 1940, in their freshman year, march while wearing their Campus Day costumes in the fall of 1936. Their theme was *The March of Time*, and the costumes were intended to resemble clocks. The numbers on the clock face were 1-9-4-0, for their class; the headgear was intended to represent a watch stem. Their creativity won them second place in the Campus Day competition.

The college was old enough that the daughters of its alumnae were now attending and graduating from Hood. These women from the class of 1937 are all daughters of former students. They are, from left to right, (front row) Jean Hoffmeier, Betty Markey, and Ella Greisemer; (back row) Patty Kurtz, Betty Genger, Sarah Leiter, and Betty McPherson.

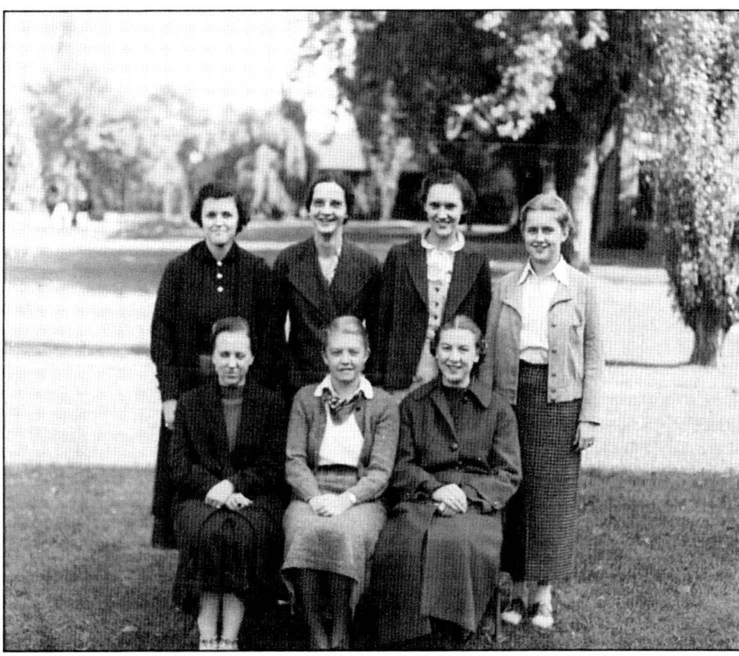

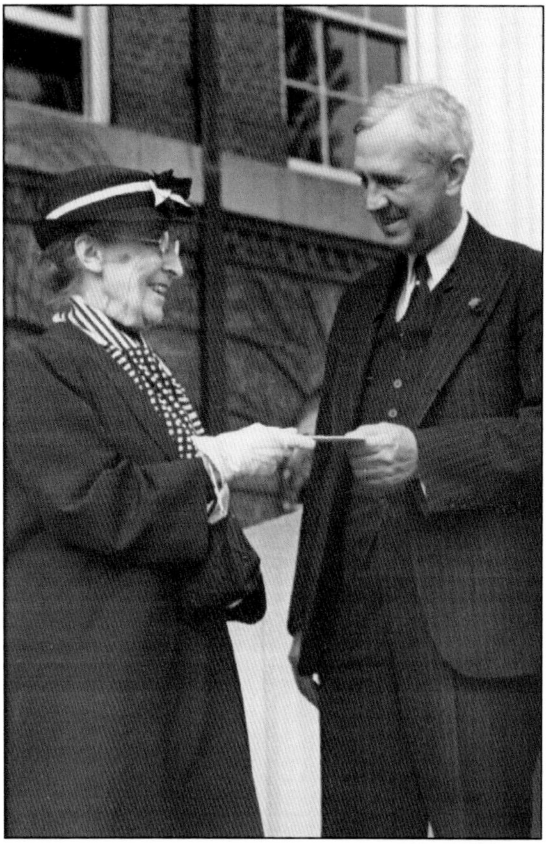

The Frederick Female Seminary alumnae club, called the Pioneers, was very active in the life of Hood College. The group was one of the first chartered women's clubs in the United States. In this photograph, Bertha Trail, an 1880 Frederick Female Seminary alumna, presents a check to President Stahr for the library building fund in May 1938.

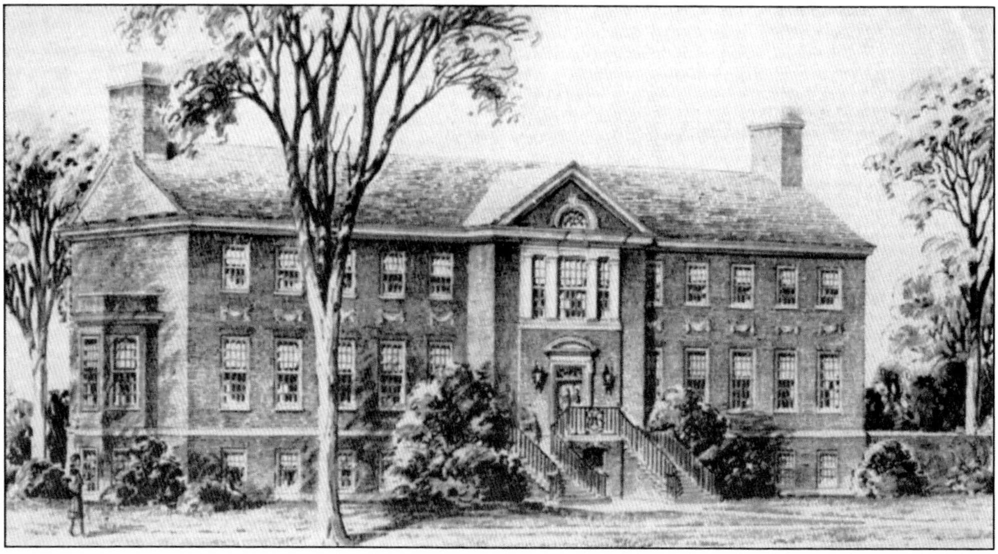

Among the needs of the college was a larger library space. By the late 1930s, rooms on the third floor of Alumnae Hall no longer met the requirements for the growing library collection of a serious institution of higher education. Fundraising had been actively under way for several years by the time this architectural rendering of the proposed building was presented about 1939.

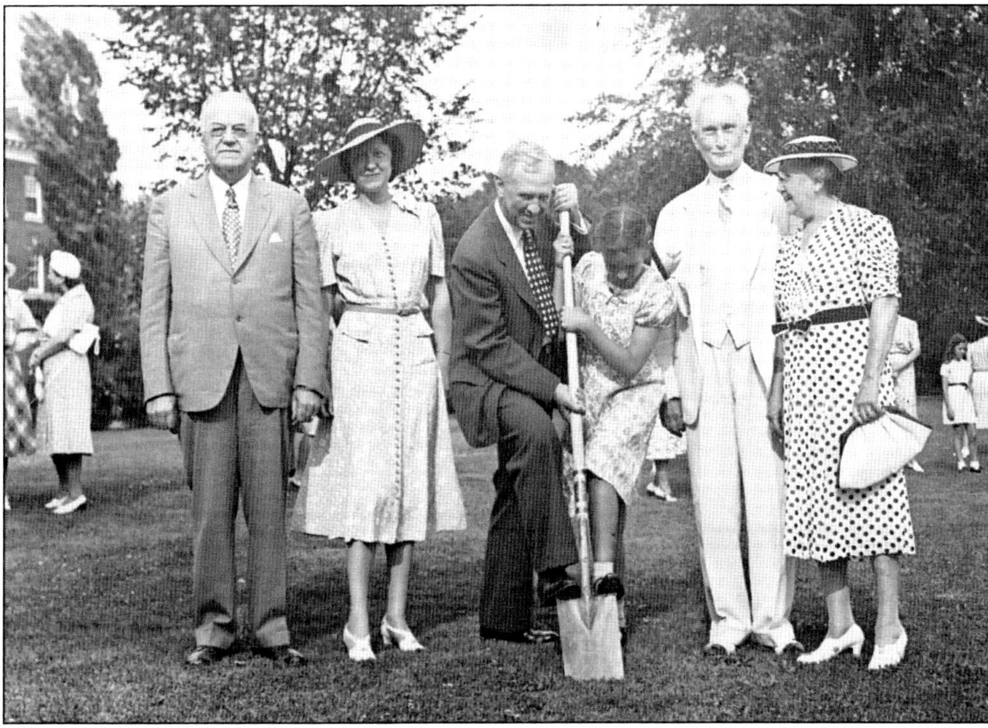

In July 1940, ground was broken for the new Joseph Henry Apple Library. Seen here wielding the shovel are President Stahr and Betsy McCain (1951), Dr. Apple's granddaughter; on the right are Dr. and Mrs. Gertrude Apple, and on the left are Charles P. Rice, president of the board of trustees, and Miriam Rankin Apple (1914), college librarian and daughter of Dr. Apple. The new library opened in 1941.

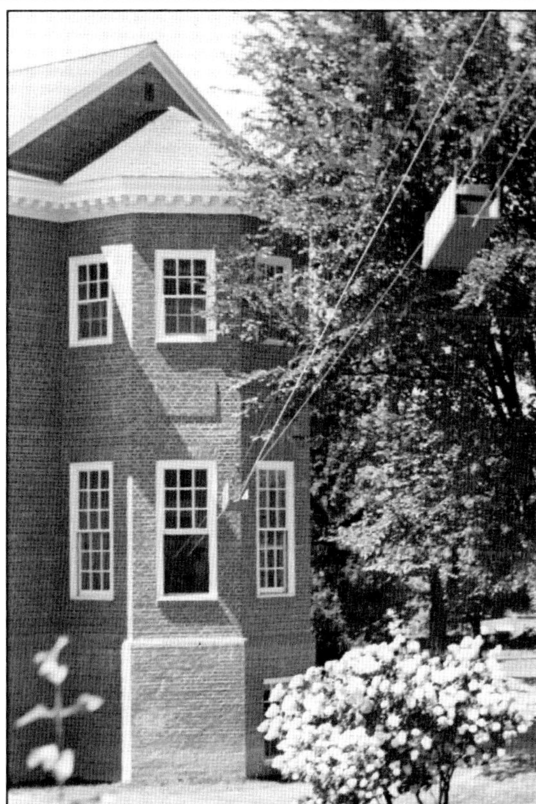

Construction on the new library was complete, and the college moved the current library book stock from Alumnae Hall to the Joseph Henry Apple Library. An ingenious pulley system was rigged from a window on the third floor of the administration building, where the old library had been located, to a window in the new building. Here, a load of books makes its way across the street.

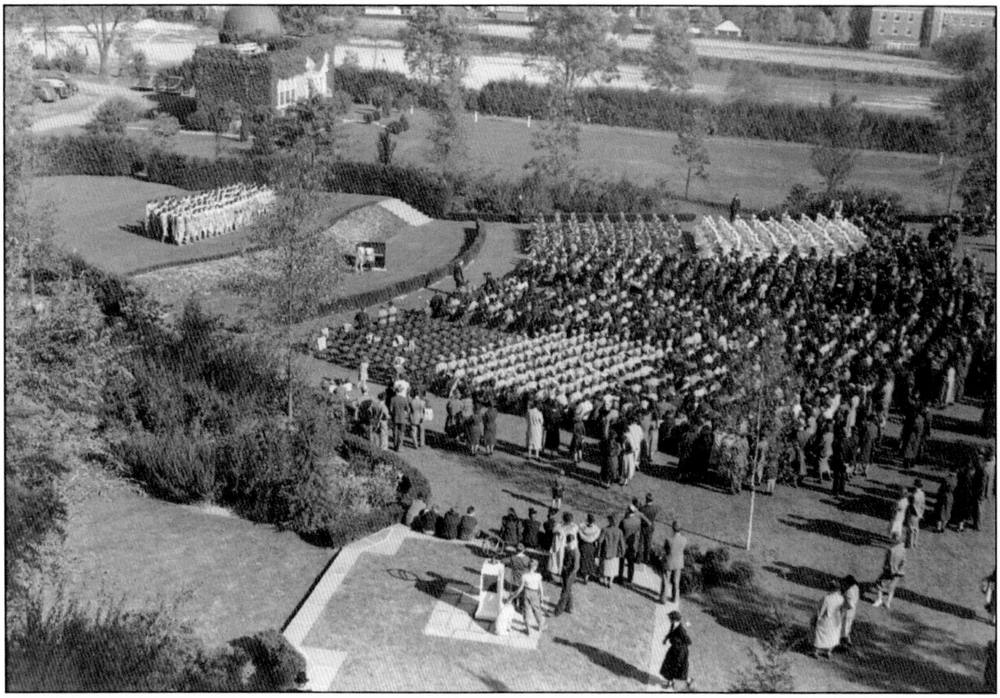

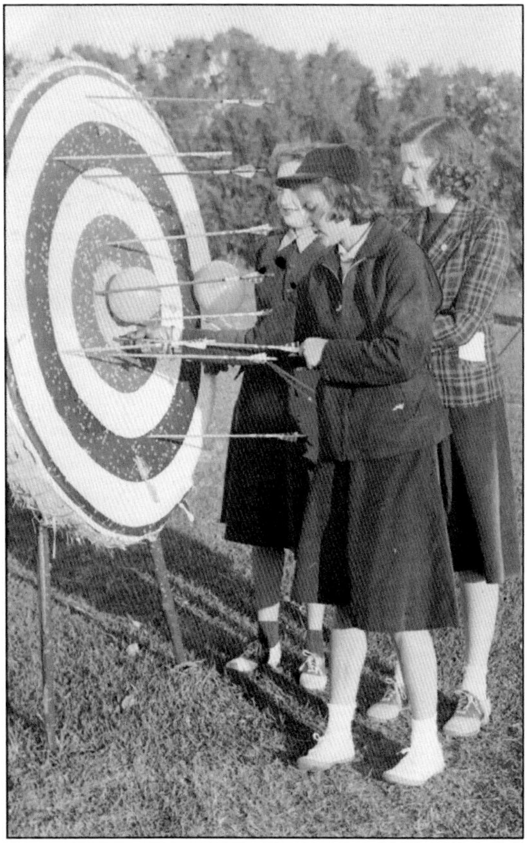

Campus Day 1938 was one of the first events held in the Hodson Outdoor Theater. The theater has been the scene of many pageants, plays, convocations, commencements, and concerts. The Hodson Trust has given more than $72 million to Hood since 1936, with the following facilities also bearing the Hodson name: Hodson Science and Technology Center, Beneficial-Hodson Library, Hodson Swimming Pool, Hodson Gallery, and Hodson Theater in Rosenstock Hall.

Amateur archers check their arrows during Spring Sports Day in 1940. Organized by the Athletic Association, this event was attended by students and faculty who could compete in volleyball, ping-pong, tennis, and a variety of races, including potato, sack, three-legged, and wheelbarrow. In addition, the Athletic Association arranged play days with women's teams from other colleges, providing for informal intercollegiate sports since there was essentially no league play then.

A greater variety of sports was being played at Hood by 1940. Here, students wearing more practical gym clothes play volleyball. Soccer, archery, tennis, field hockey, basketball, and lacrosse were also being played. Hood did not have a gymnasium at this time, so basketball, the "winter sport," was played in the gym of the Frederick National Guard Armory on West Second Street.

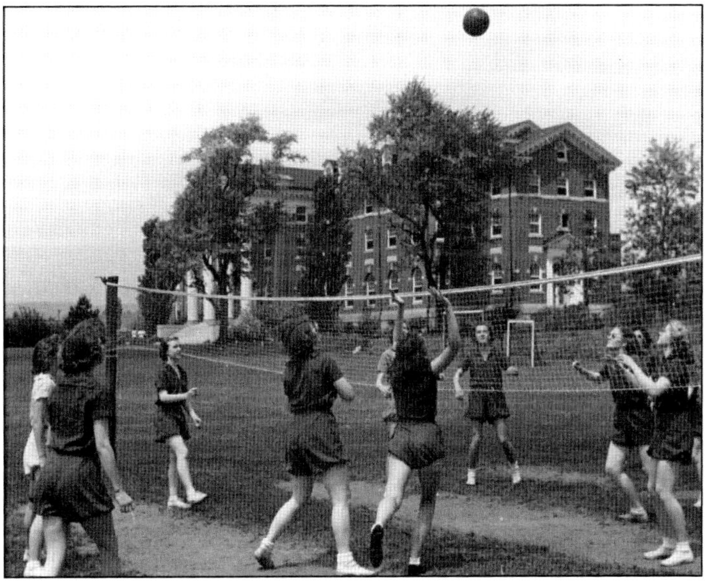

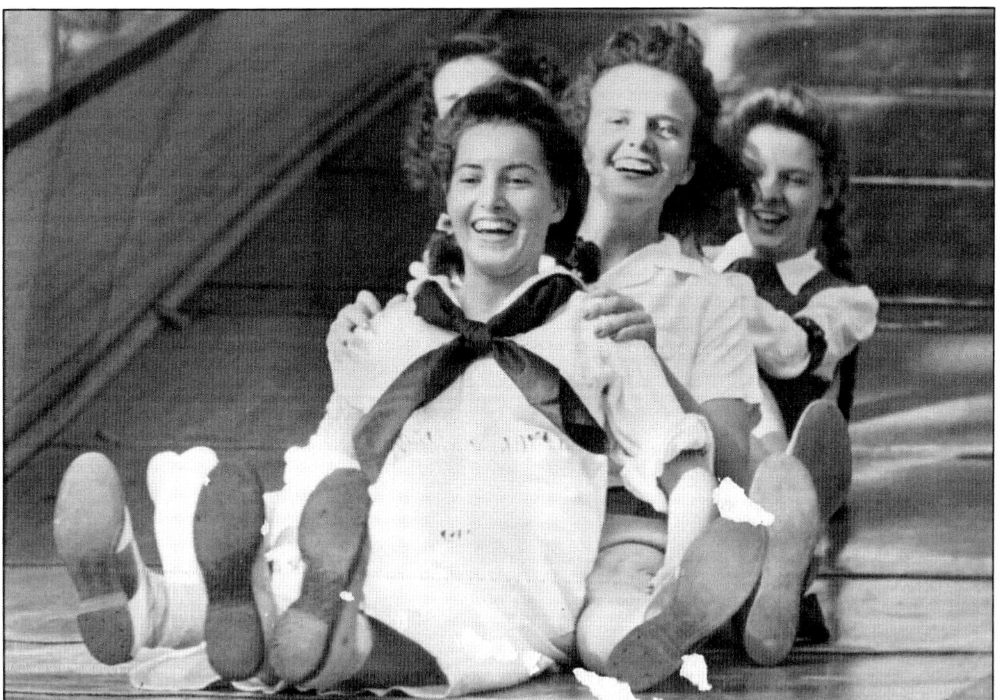

The Braddock picnic continued to be one of the favorite fall events. These students reach the end of the giant sliding board in Braddock Heights, Maryland. The summer resort area was in its infancy when Hood's Braddock tradition began, but by 1941, when this photograph was taken, a number of amenities, including a merry-go-round, an indoor skating rink, a swimming pool, and the slide, had been added.

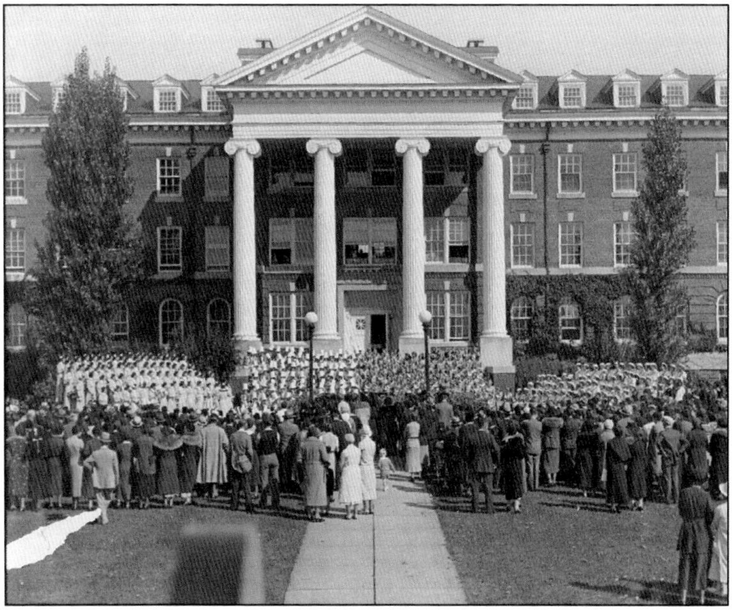

Donning their costumes, the student body stands on the steps of Alumnae Hall for Campus Day 1942. Not only was this day a time for friendly class competitions, it also provided an opportunity for alumnae to gather for homecoming activities. The individuals in civilian clothes watching the proceedings are family members of the students and returning alumnae.

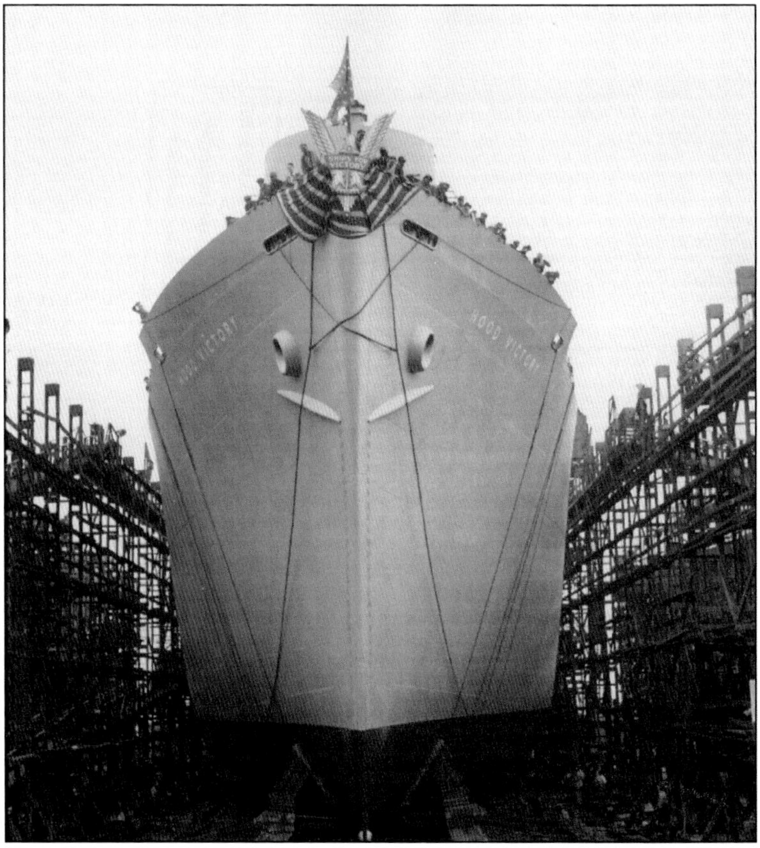

In 1945, the SS *Hood Victory* became one of 414 victory ships built for wartime use. A number of these fast cargo ships were named for American colleges and universities. The *Hood Victory's* keel was laid on April 25, 1945; she was launched on June 9, just 45 days after construction began. Hood equipped the ship with a library of 175 books, including one entitled *How to Abandon Ship*.

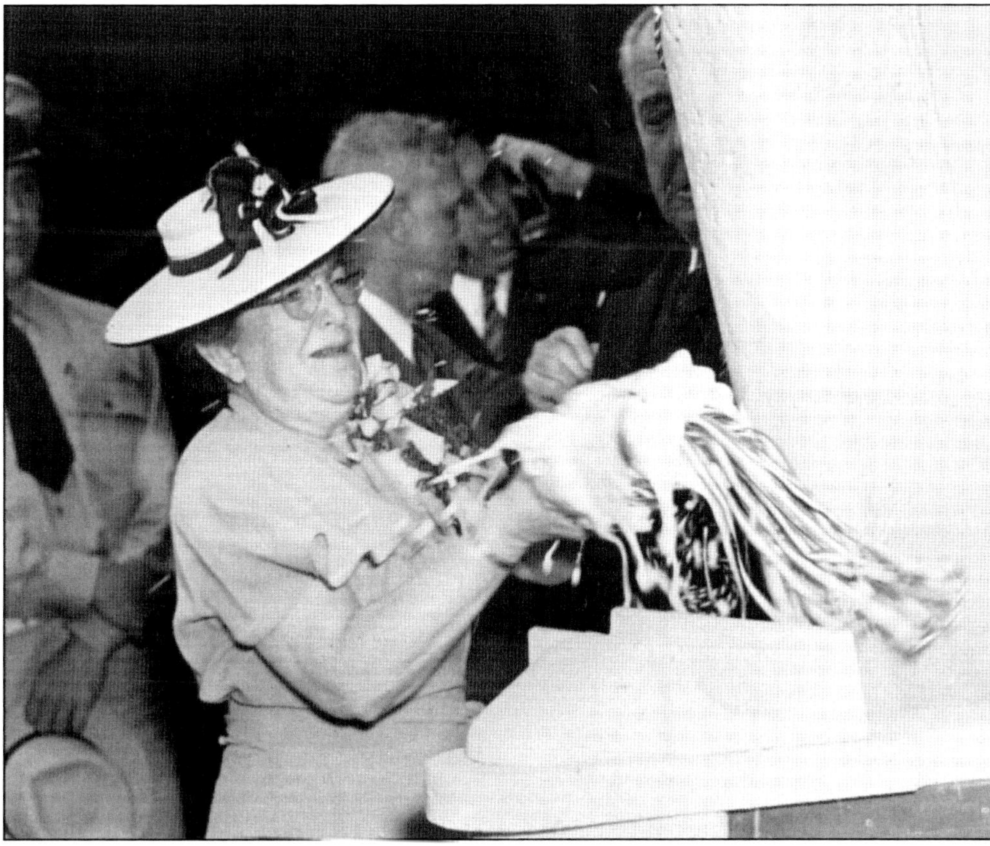

On June 9, 1945, Alice Stahr broke a heavily beribboned bottle of champagne across the bow to christen the SS *Hood Victory*. The ship was built by the Bethlehem-Fairfield Shipbuilding Company in Baltimore, the world's largest shipbuilder. She departed immediately to take supplies to Europe and bring troops home. In 1947, no longer needed by the military, the vessel was sold to a Greek shipping company.

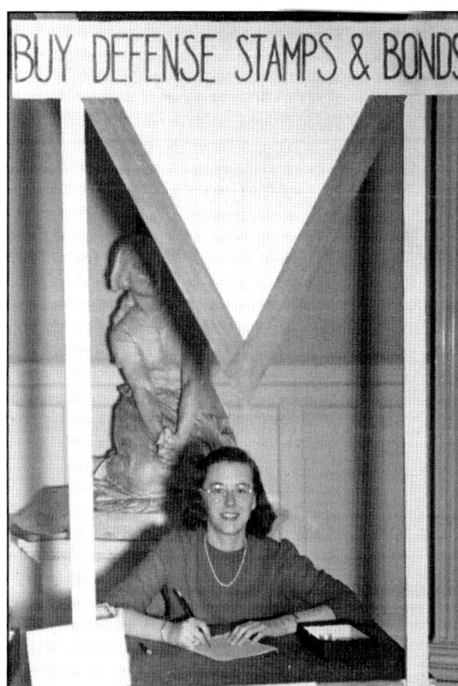

Marcia Ludlum (1943) sells defense stamps and bonds to raise money for the war effort. One way that Hood students responded to the conflict was by forming the Women Organized to Relieve the Manpower Shortage (WORMS). At Hood, "flatworms" did the ironing, "cutworms" prepared food in the kitchen, and "earthworms" maintained the campus grounds. Other activities included blood drives and the preparation of surgical dressings to be sent to field hospitals.

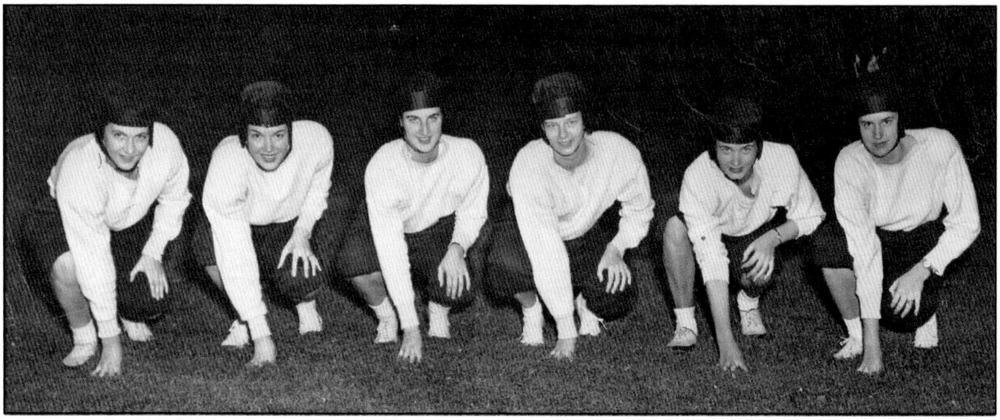

On Campus Day 1946, the junior class fielded Hood's first varsity football team as their theme for the day. Decades later, one of Hood's most popular T-shirts read, "Hood Football—Undefeated Since 1893." The linemen pictured here are, from left to right, Isabel Gill, Jean Herman, Katherine Maguire, Margaret Thacher, Ellen Bindon, and Bette Blome. After two consecutive years taking first place, these juniors rated a disappointing third.

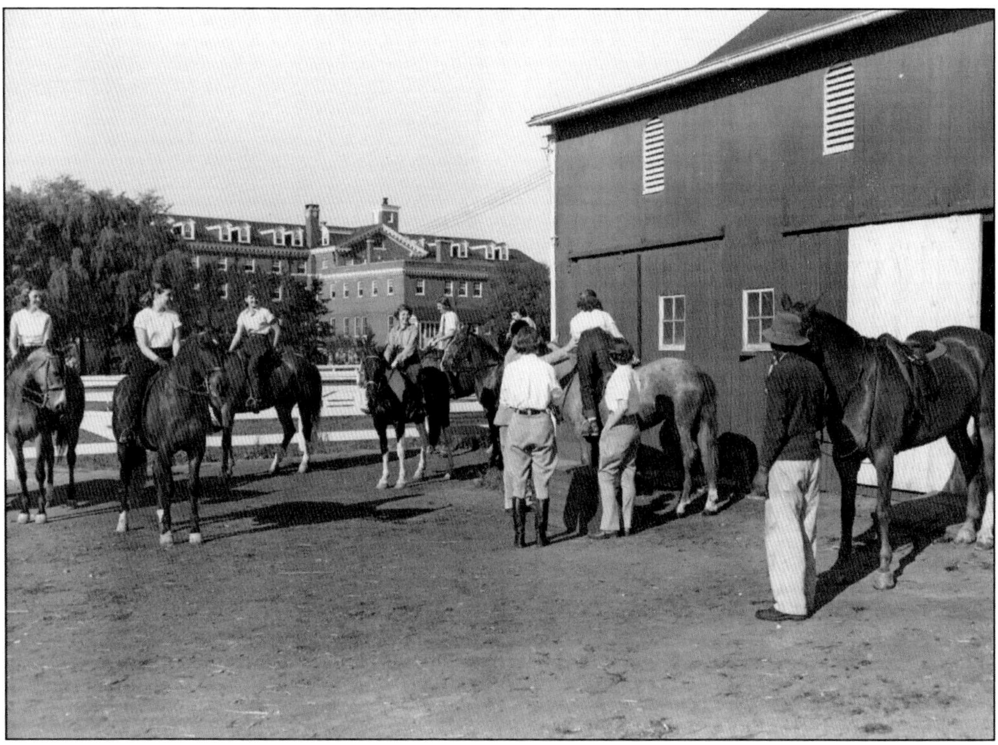

This 1947 picture of a group of equestriennes saddling up for a ride shows the stables behind Coblentz Hall. By 1984, the stables were no longer in use and were intentionally burned to the ground in a spectacular form of building removal. Pictured in the right foreground is Krebs Benchoff, the beloved college riding master, who worked with students and their horses for over two decades.

In this 1940s photograph, Prof. Leah Allen (standing to the left of the student using the telescope) works with an astronomy class in the Williams Observatory. The observatory was frequently opened to the public for viewing and lectures. On dance nights, students got special permission to bring their dates to the observatory between musical sets.

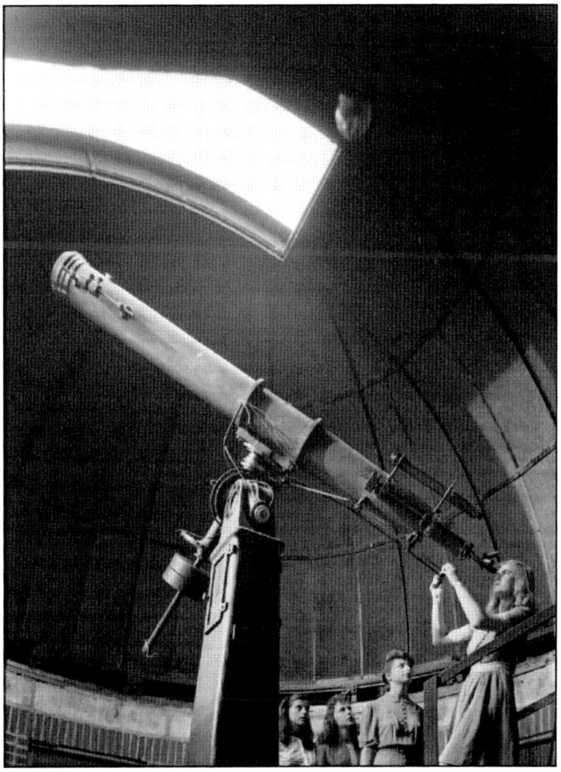

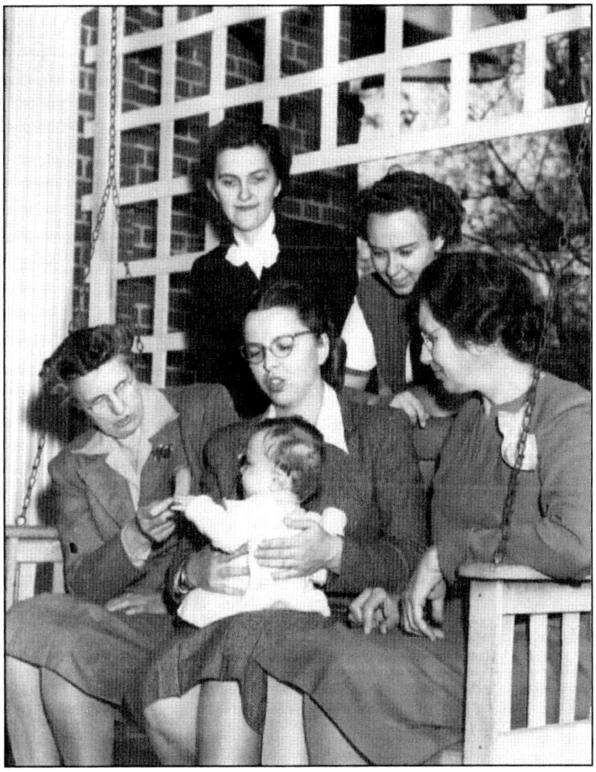

Students in the home economics program developed their child-care skills by working with orphaned infants who were brought to campus. They worked with a different child each year. The children were known as "Strawn babies" after Strawn Cottage, home to the child development and home management program of the home economics department. In this 1946 photograph, students and faculty get to know one of the babies.

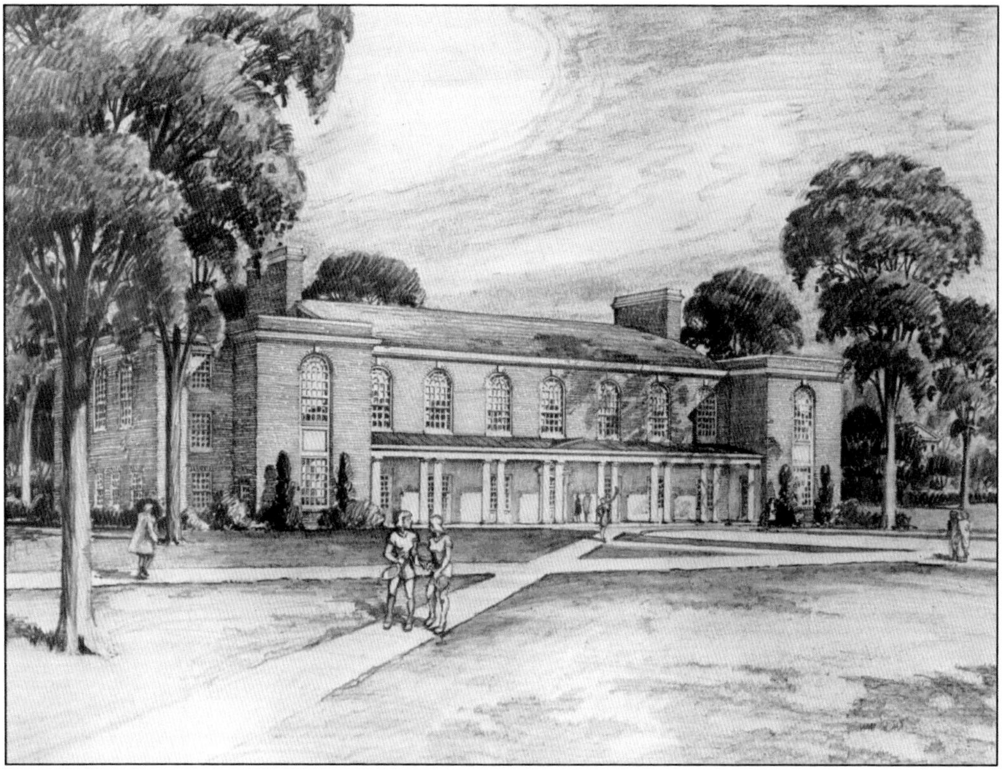

Besides building a new library, Dr. Stahr was tasked by Hood's accrediting body with improving the athletic facilities. A fundraising campaign had been under way for several years before this architect's rendering of the proposed gymnasium was introduced in 1947. The building was named for James H. Gambrill Jr., a Frederick businessman who served on Hood's board of trustees from 1916 until his death in 1951.

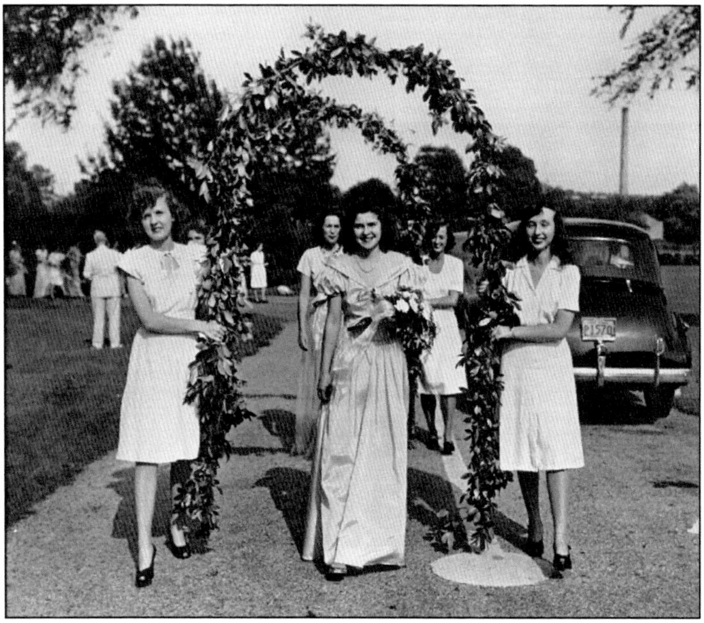

Flanked by white-clad "little sisters" carrying the traditional laurel chain, the class of 1947 parades to Hodson Theater to sing their favorite Hood songs and hear their class history. This is what Class Day was all about: giving the seniors a moment to look back over their four years at Hood on the day before commencement. Senior class president Elizabeth Bishop (center) leads the procession.

Beauty pageants were becoming the rage in the 1940s, and Hood needed to have its own. In 1948, junior Mildred Lou Hittinger was named the first Miss Touchstone, after the yearbook, which sponsored the contest. Photographs of the candidates were sent to entertainer Bob Hope, who selected Miss Hittinger. He said in the letter announcing his decision, "May I . . . congratulate Hood on having so many beautiful women from whom to choose."

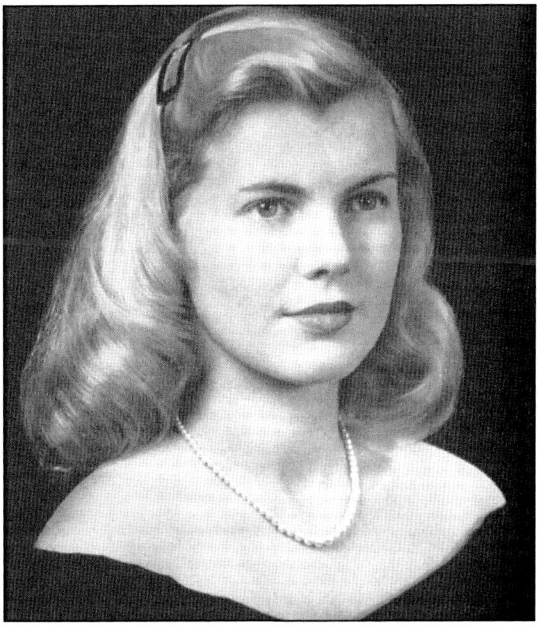

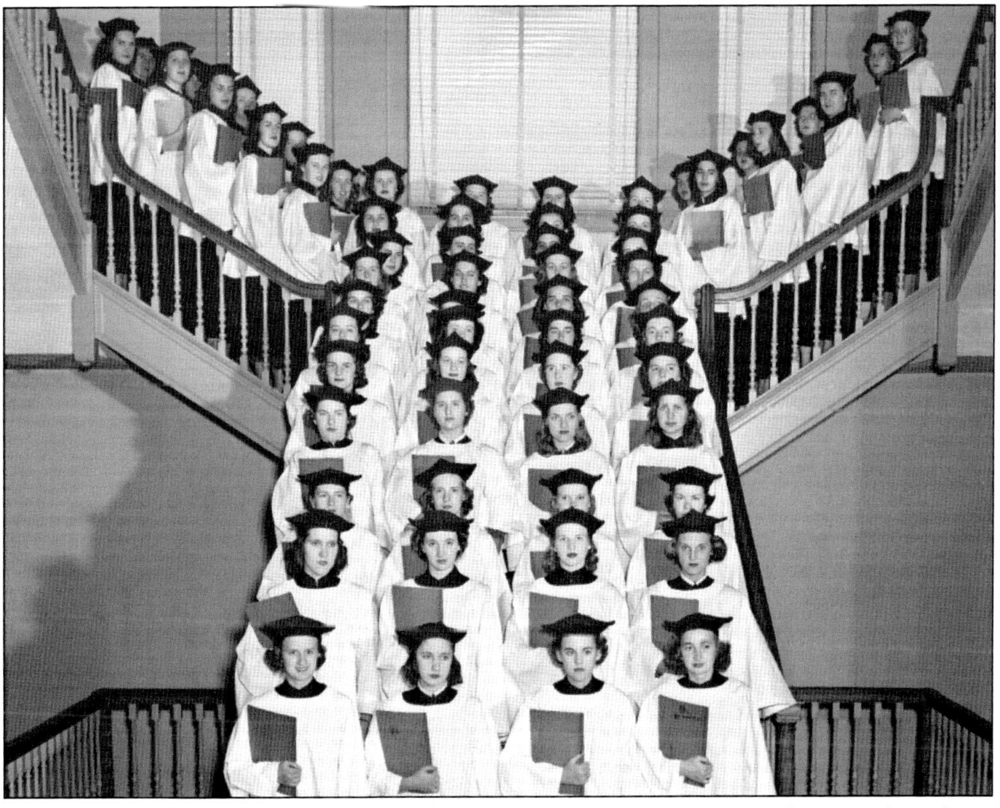

December 1948 marked the first year of the acclaimed Hood College and US Naval Academy combined choir performances of Handel's *Messiah*. For more than 60 years, the performances and formal dances held afterward have been a treasured tradition at Hood. More than a few Hood students dated and wed midshipmen whom they met during Messiah Weekend.

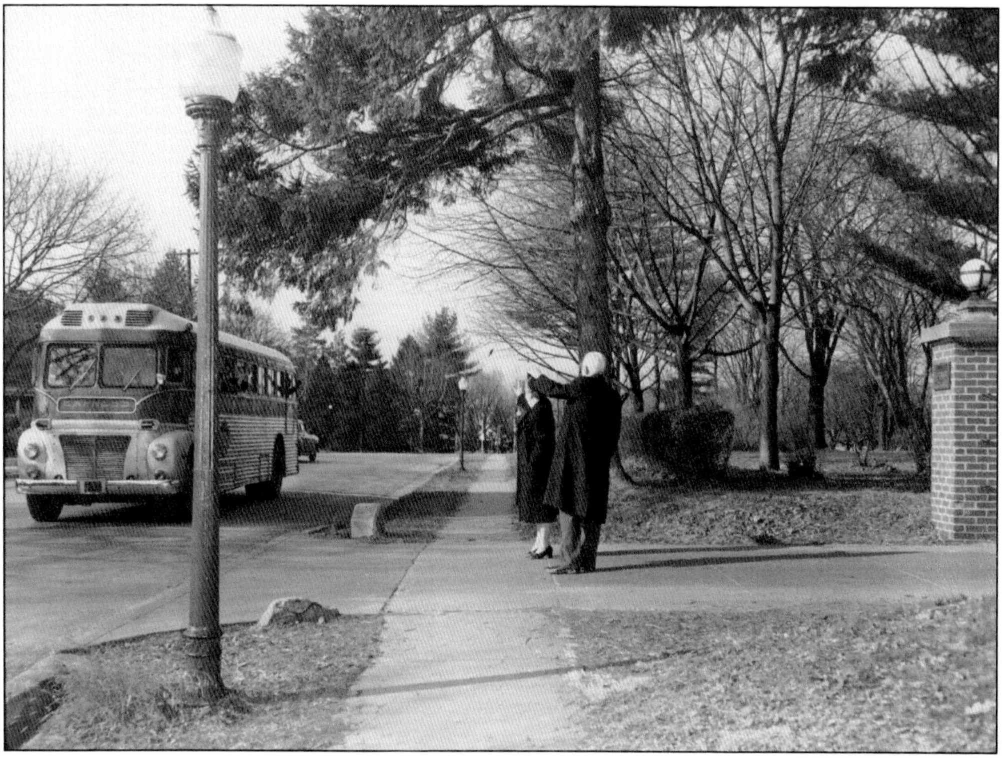

President and Mrs. Stahr welcome students returning to campus. The Stahrs were moving into a new phase of their lives. Dr. Stahr announced plans to retire at the end of the 1948 academic year, saying, "It's better to go before people wonder why you don't go." After leaving Hood, he assumed the pastorate of a small Reformed Church congregation in Scituate, Massachusetts.

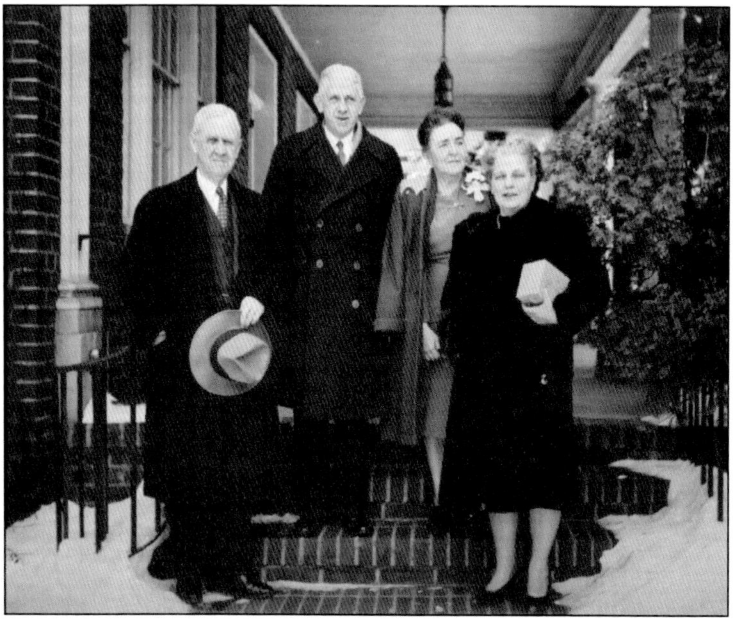

In December 1947, Andrew Gehr Truxal, a minister and former faculty member at Franklin and Marshall College, met with Hood's board of trustees and was offered the presidency of the college. He assumed the new office on July 1, 1948, though his inauguration did not take place until October 21. From left to right are, Dr. Stahr, Dr. Truxal, Mrs. Alice Stahr, and Mrs. Leah Deldee Truxal.

Six

Our Halcyon Days
Dr. Truxal's Presidency, 1948–1961

In the autumn of 1948, the nation was settling into postwar life, and Hood was becoming acquainted with its third president, Andrew Gehr Truxal. Dr. Truxal arrived at Hood as things were changing in higher education. The growth in public institutions to accommodate soldiers on the GI Bill and other factors had increased competition for students. Hood was seeing declining enrollment as students opted for coeducational schools and declining retention as students dropped out to get married. Vigorous recruitment efforts led to an increase in students by the mid-1950s.

Despite the early gloomy enrollment prospects, Dr. Truxal developed an ambitious advancement plan, launching the Hood Forward campaign, raising funds for much-needed additions to the physical plant. Between 1955 and 1961, the college built Coffman Chapel, the Hodson Science Hall, the R. Paul Smith Hall (dormitory), a new president's house, and the Thomas Annex to the Apple Library. Dr. Truxal worked tirelessly to fund scholarships and improve faculty salaries, and he doubled the endowment to $2 million. Concerned about bettering Hood's public image, he hired the college's first public relations staffer. He organized the Hood College Board of Associates to advise on long-range planning and was instrumental in the formation of what became the Maryland Independent Colleges and Universities Association.

The faculty wrestled with issues of curriculum, discussing core courses, considering the necessity of foreign language study, eliminating the nursing and secretarial programs, and adding independent study courses. A disagreement with the Reformed Church arose over the elimination of the religion requirement.

Students were finding that, though unbecoming behavior could still result in dismissal, campus life was less regulated, except for freshmen, who continued to be bound by traditional rules established by students themselves. The college newspaper decried violations of the honor code, as well as the general student demeanor, such as clothing that was too revealing, litter on the campus, or the objection to required chapel attendance. Students were becoming more aware of politics and world affairs. A dialogue about desegregation was taking place. More states, and some foreign countries, were represented in the student body.

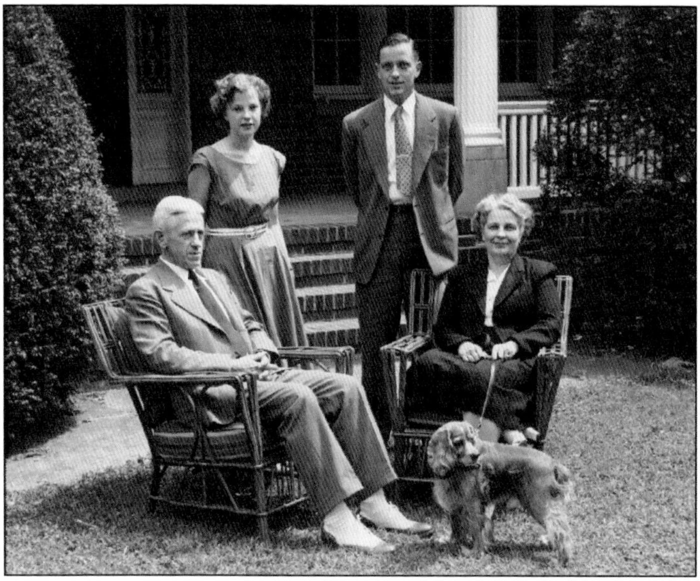

The Truxal family moved into their new home on the Hood campus in July 1948. Pictured from left to right are Dr. Truxal, daughter Noradel (1953), son John, wife Leah Deldee Truxal, and the family dog. Both of the Truxal children became academics, and Noradel served as a member of Hood's board of trustees.

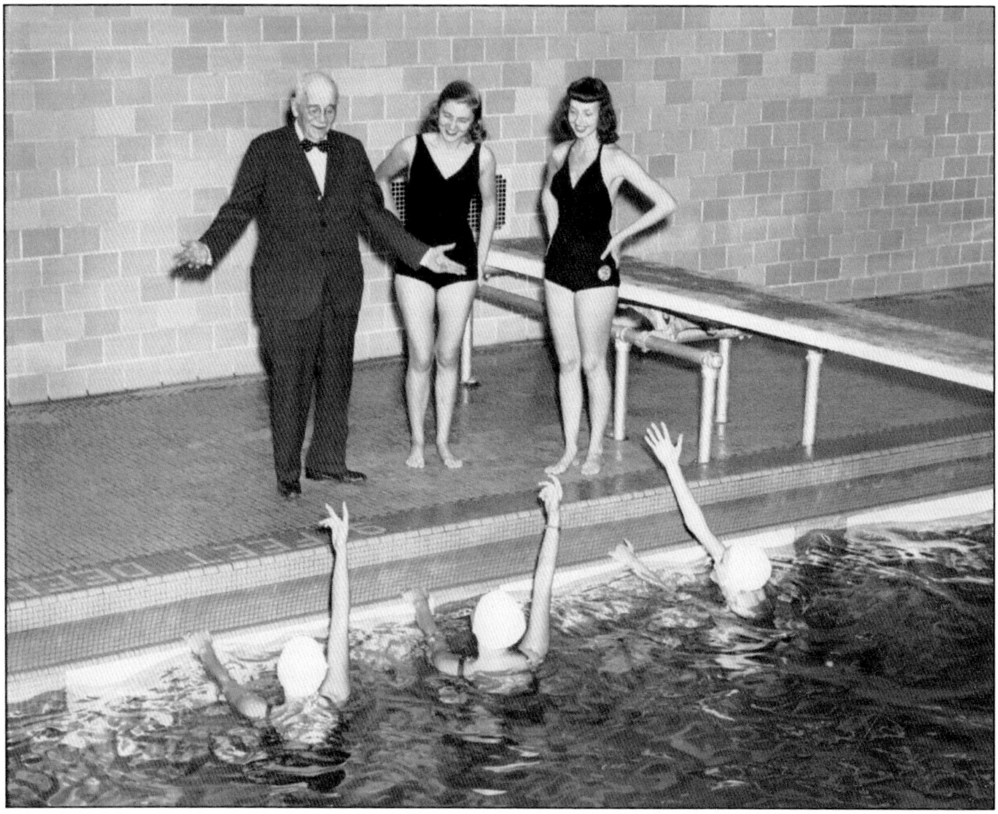

Hood swimmers appear to be urging James H. Gambrill Jr. to join them in the Hodson Pool at the dedication of Gambrill Gymnasium in November 1949. The gymnasium was named for Gambrill, a prominent local businessman who served on Hood's board of trustees from 1916 to 1951. In 1975, Hood built the Huntsinger Aquatic Center, providing an additional swimming venue on campus.

President and Mrs. Leah Deldee Truxal remove their shoes before entering the home economics dining room to attend a dinner being served by the food preparation classes. Korean student Shin Hyung Kim, standing behind Dr. Truxal, inspired the home economics students to cook Korean food. Kathy Strachan (1951) wears a Korean costume for the event. Ruth Perry, director of student personnel, sits on the floor, awaiting the family-style dinner.

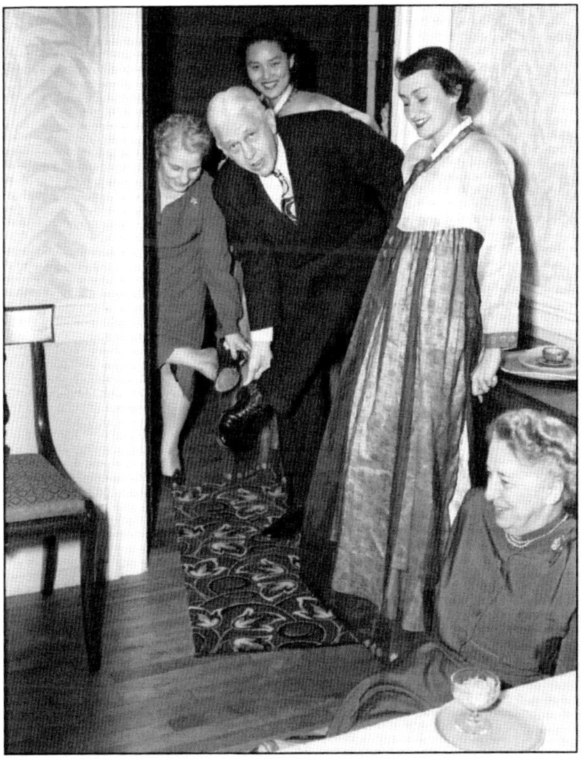

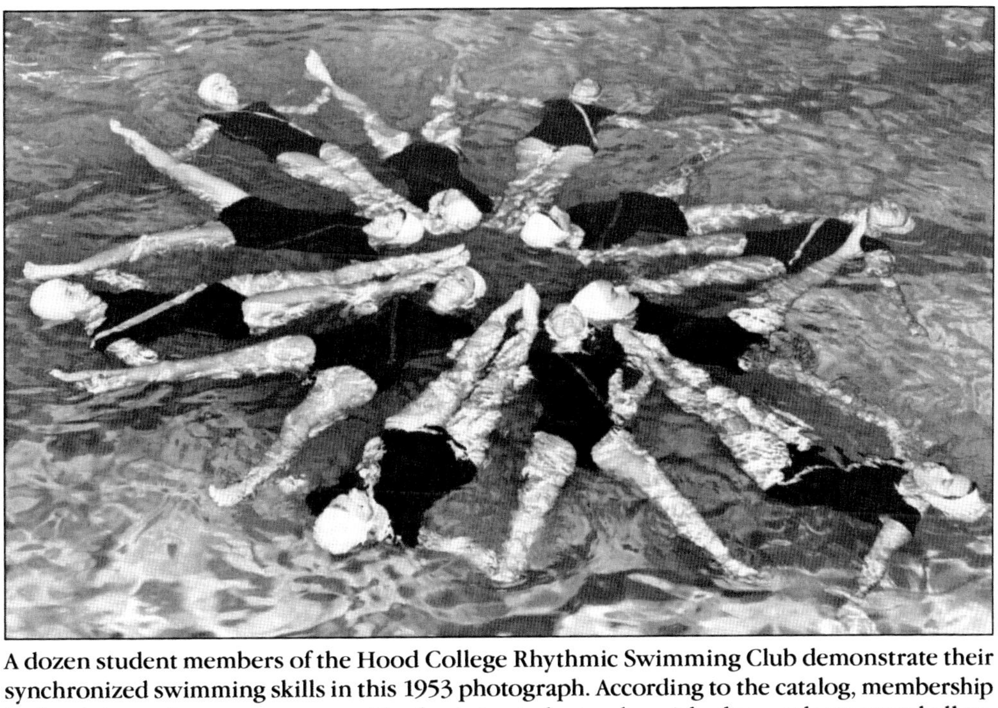

A dozen student members of the Hood College Rhythmic Swimming Club demonstrate their synchronized swimming skills in this 1953 photograph. According to the catalog, membership in the club was "open on a competitive basis to students who wished to work on water ballets, festivals, and rhythmic swimming patterns." The student-run Athletic Association administered a number of sports clubs, including dance, hiking, riding, and swimming.

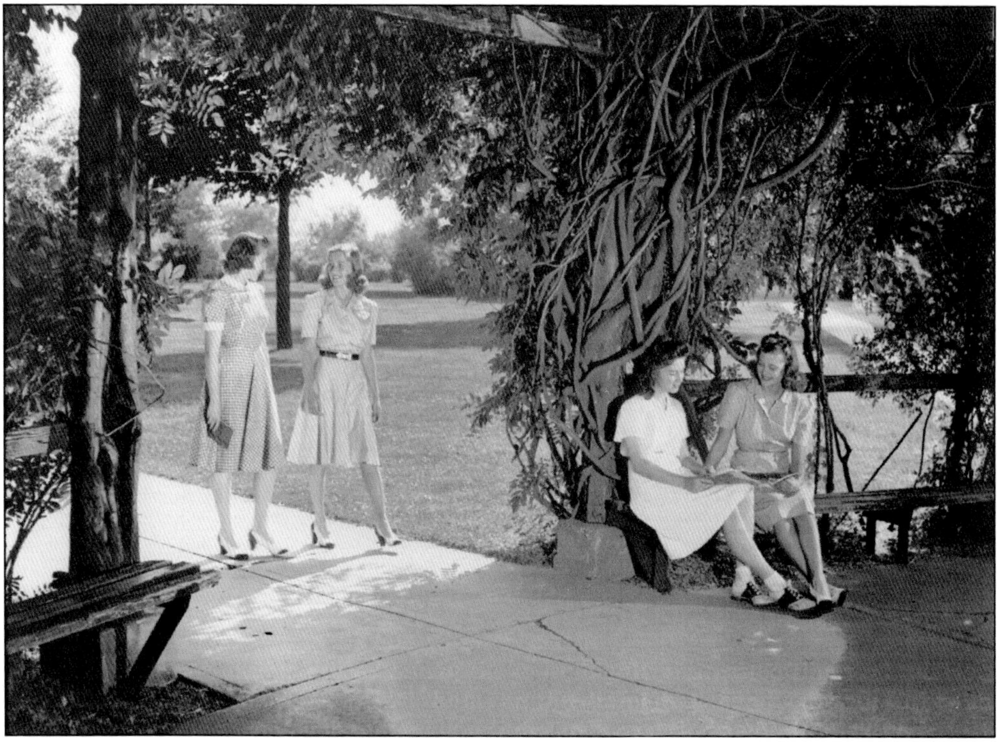

The wisteria-covered pergola, originally built in 1915, was dedicated and named in honor of President Truxal in 1999. Hood customs regarding the pergola are traditional: friends don't "split the poles" as they walk side by side, but both pass a support on the same side to keep the friendship intact; and only kind words are to be spoken about others when one is in the pergola's confines.

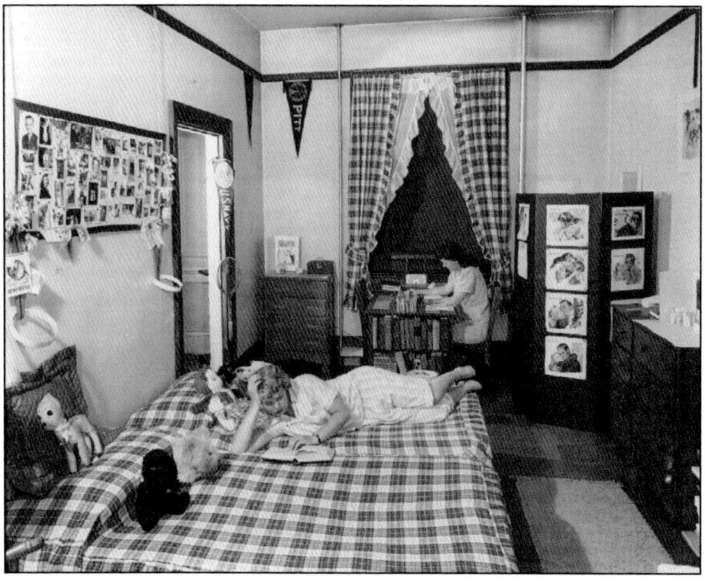

Each dormitory was supervised by the head of house. Residents worked closely with her to decide how best to serve the welfare of individuals and the group. These students, seen in a typical room, set an example for others to follow. At this time, there were the three major dormitories—Shriner, Meyran, and Coblentz—as well as the smaller French House, Terrace House, and Rayford Lodge.

Begum Liaquat Ra'ana Ali Khan, the first lady of Pakistan, is welcomed to the Hood campus in 1950 by students Anne Tetlow (1951), Louise Mistlebower (1951), and Barbara Henderson (1951) and Dr. Olive Reddick, professor of economics and sociology. It was a point of pride for Hood's news service that newsreels of Begum Ra'ana's visit to Hood were being shown in Iran and India.

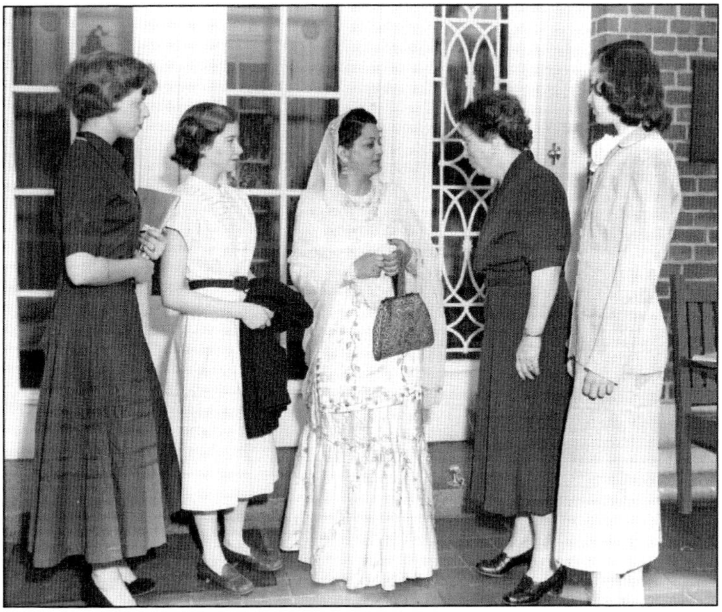

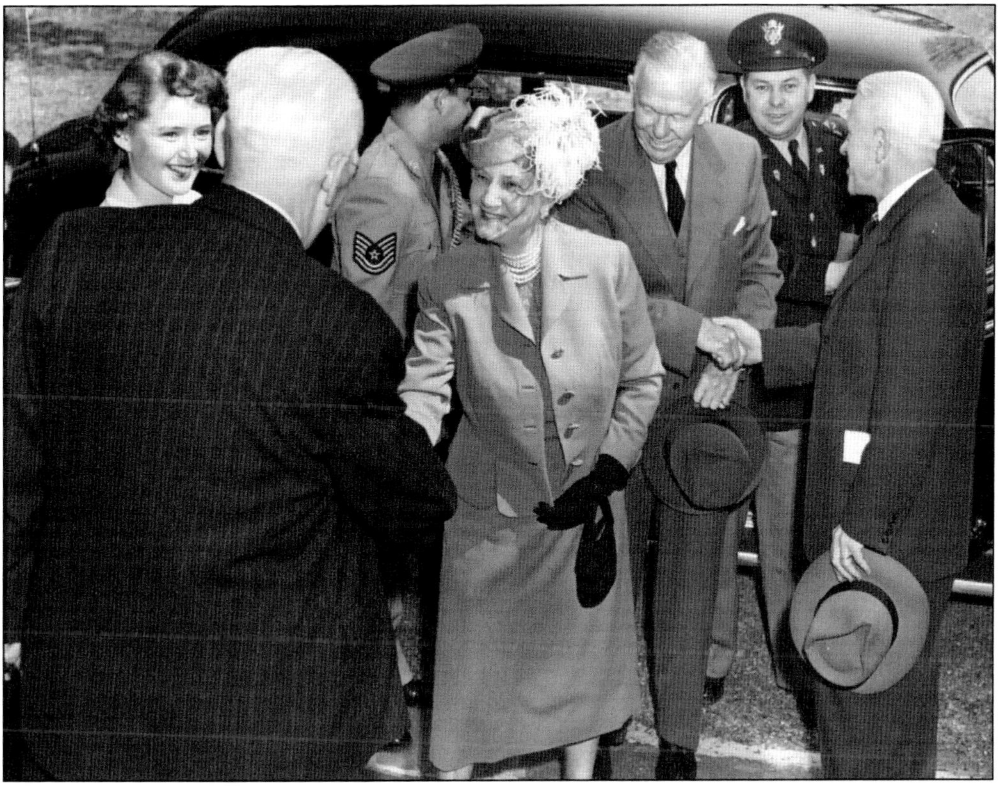

In April 1951, President Truxal launched his Hood Forward fundraising campaign with a three-day convocation called "The Role of Women and the Family in the Defense of Democracy." The featured speakers were US Secretary of Defense Gen. George C. Marshall and Maine senator Margaret Chase Smith. Smith and General Marshall's wife, Katherine Tupper Marshall, were awarded honorary doctorates at the convocation.

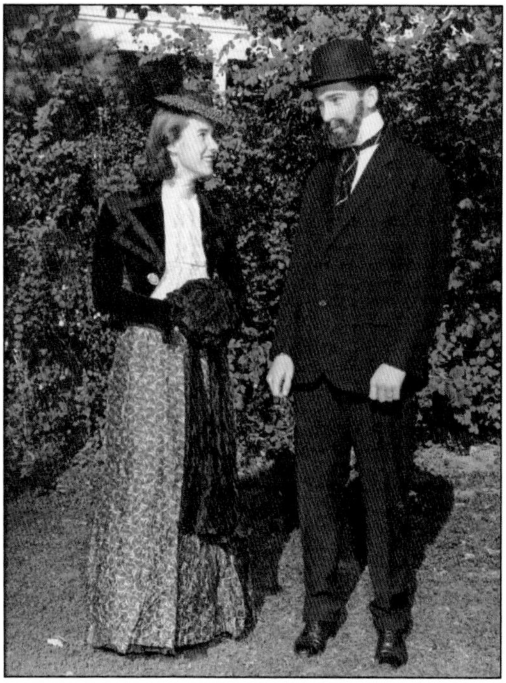

Campus Day 1951 must have been especially meaningful for Betsy McCain McAlpine (1951), shown here with Frederick lawyer and Maryland state senator Edward Storm. The two portrayed Joseph Henry Apple and Gertrude Apple in a Campus Day skit. Betsy McCain is the Apples' granddaughter, and since her graduation she has served Hood in numerous ways, including as a member of the board of trustees.

Among the many fun events on campus was the Athletic Association circus. In 1952, students dressed up in comical costumes, staged a parade with the dormitories competing for best float, ran an arcade with games like ring toss, and presented circus acts such as the equestrian drill team depicting gypsy riders and the dance club portraying snake charmers; clown acts and a clown car were also part of the circus.

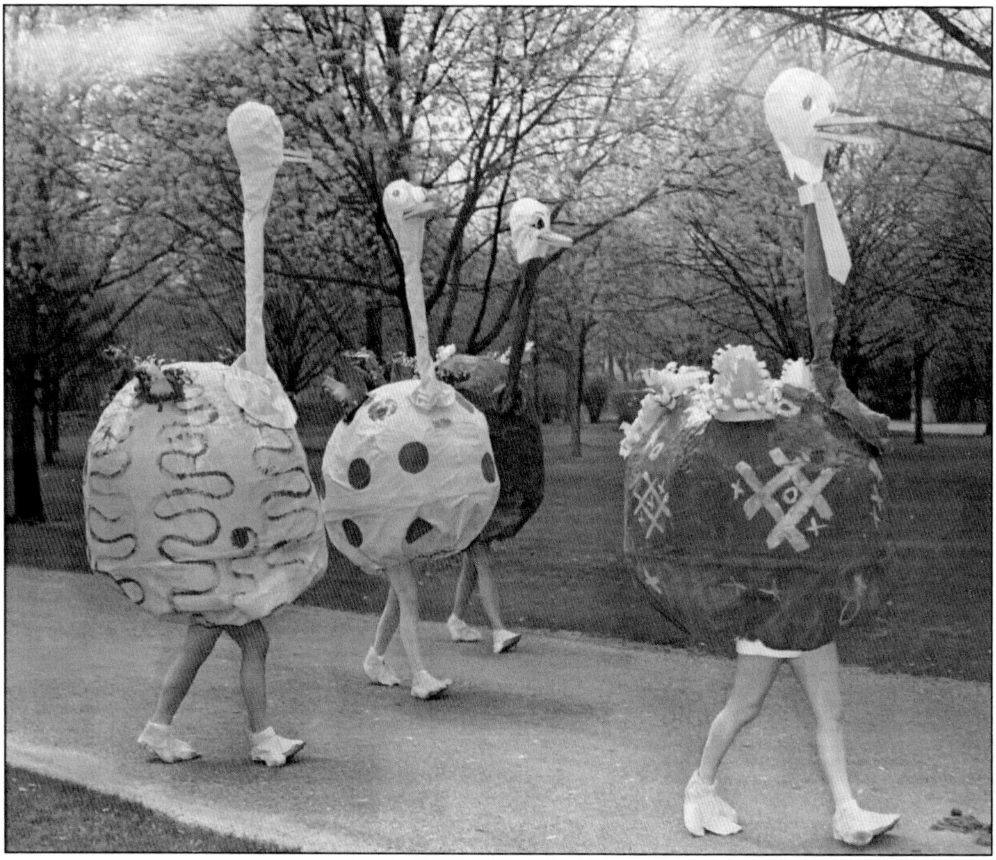

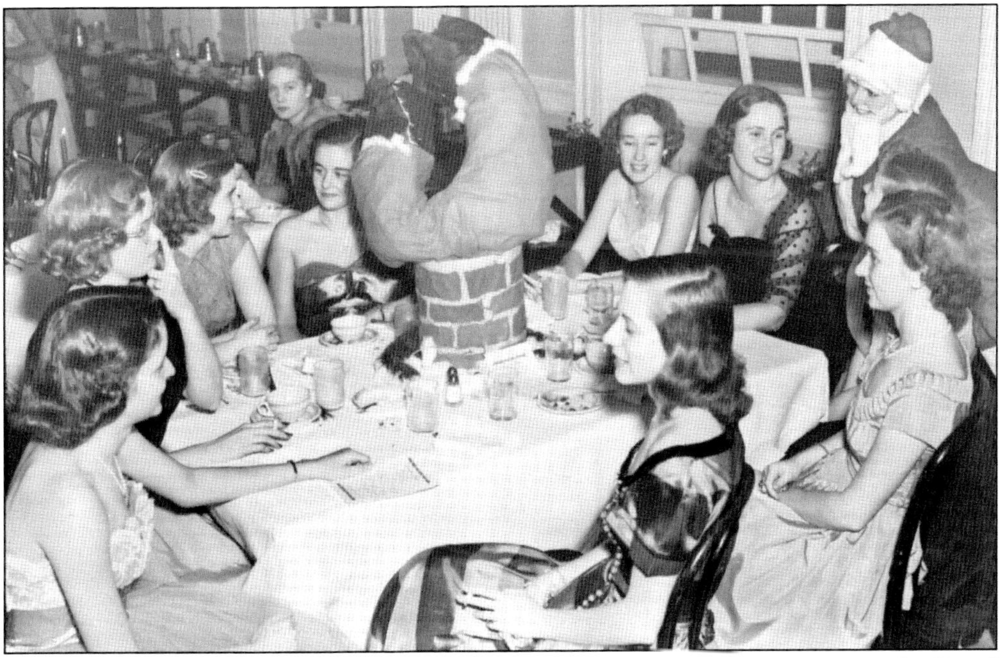

Little Christmas continued to be one of the more highly anticipated times on the Hood calendar. Students enjoyed a formal dinner in the dining hall, complete with turkey and oyster dressing and flaming plum pudding with hard sauce, and a visit from St. Nick.

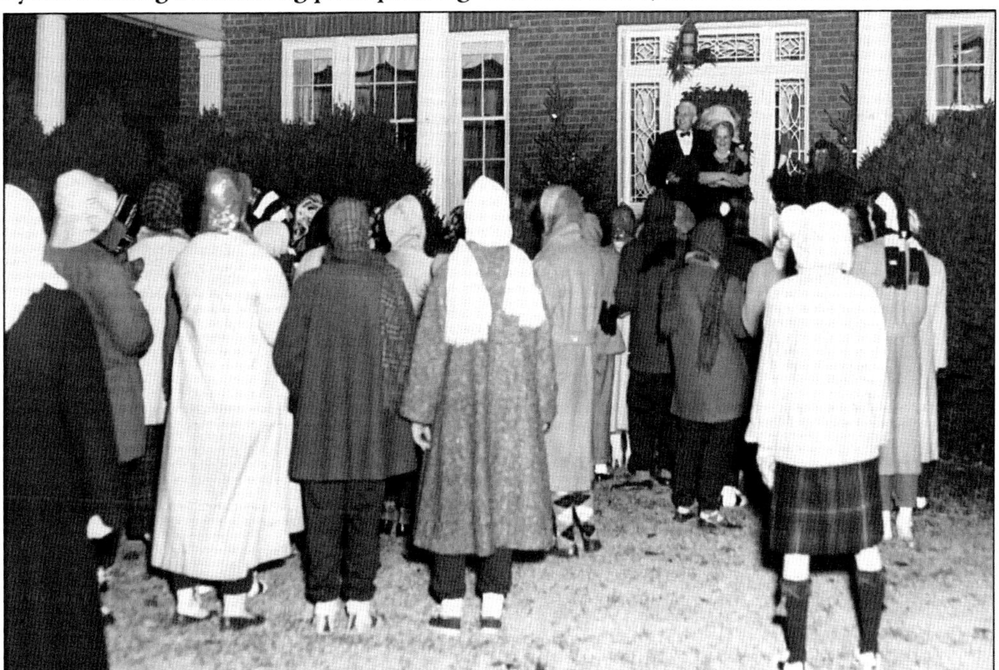

In 1957, Little Christmas traditions included singing carols and sharing the Christmas spirit with President Truxal and his wife in front of the president's house. While it appears that this was an evening outing, in some years the students rose at 5:00 a.m. in order to be out and singing to folks at 6:00 a.m.—on campus and in Frederick—in their pajamas.

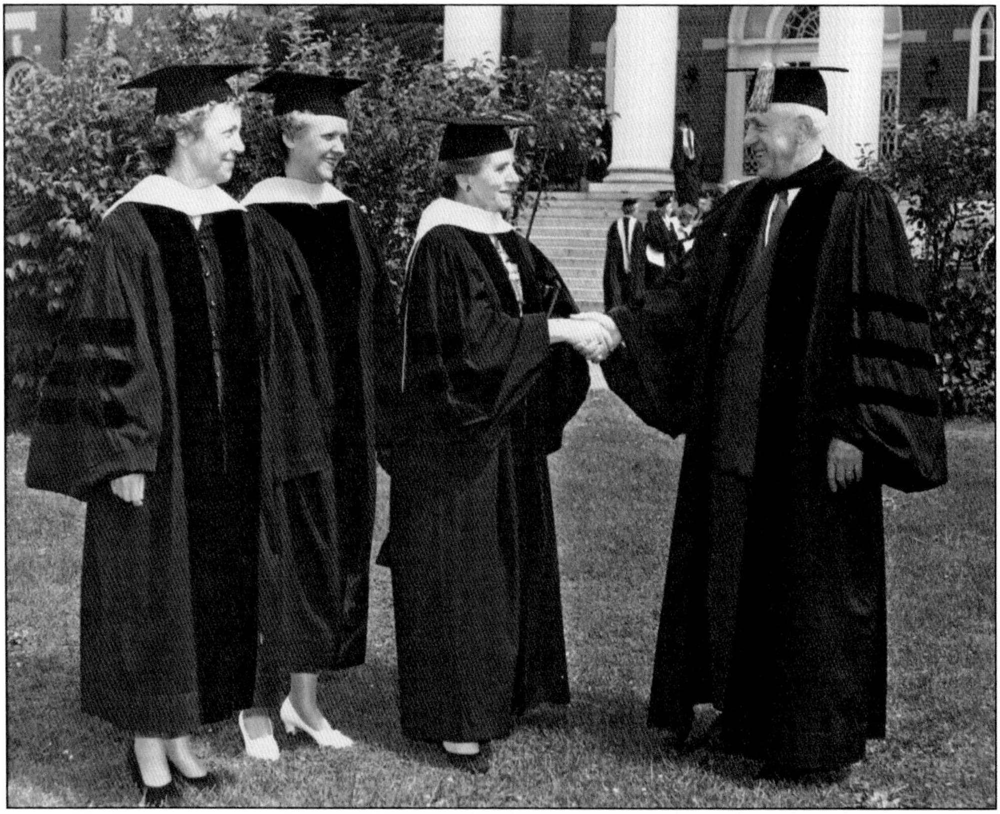

President Truxal confers honorary degrees on, from left to right, Margaret Wehler (1918), Ruth Sleeper, and Ruth Isabel Seabury. Hood has bestowed this honor on over 175 individuals since 1951; among them are educator Ernest Boyer (1984), former first lady Barbara Bush (1983), children's rights activist Marian Wright Edelman (1992), journalist Charlayne Hunter-Gault (1986), thanatologist Elisabeth Kübler Ross (1976), Maryland senator Paul Sarbannes (2006), and actress Jean Stapleton (1978).

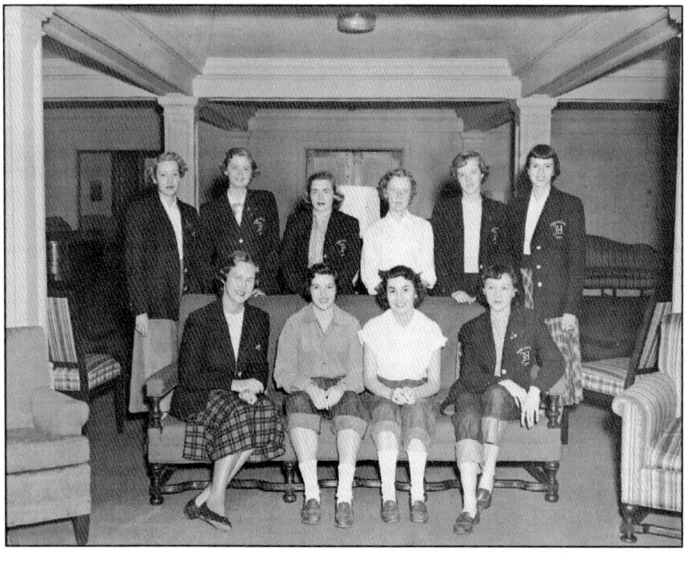

Students in Beta Beta Beta, the biology honorary, gather for a photograph in 1954. Today, Hood has 15 single-discipline honoraries that recognize academic excellence in those disciplines, as well as Phi Kappa Phi and Mortarboard (formerly the Keystone Society), all-discipline honoraries; Alpha Lambda Delta, the first-year honorary; and the Ionic Society, a service honorary.

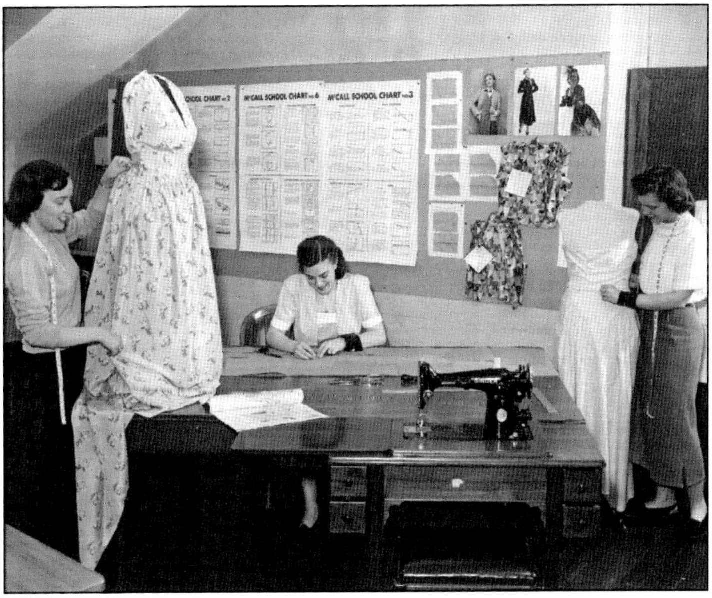

During the mid-1950s, home economics as a major seemed in decline in part due to the nursery school having been moved to the education department; however, the courses continued to be popular with students who were majoring in other subjects. Students demonstrate their skills in dressmaking in one of the home economics laboratories on the fourth floor of Alumnae Hall in this 1954 photograph.

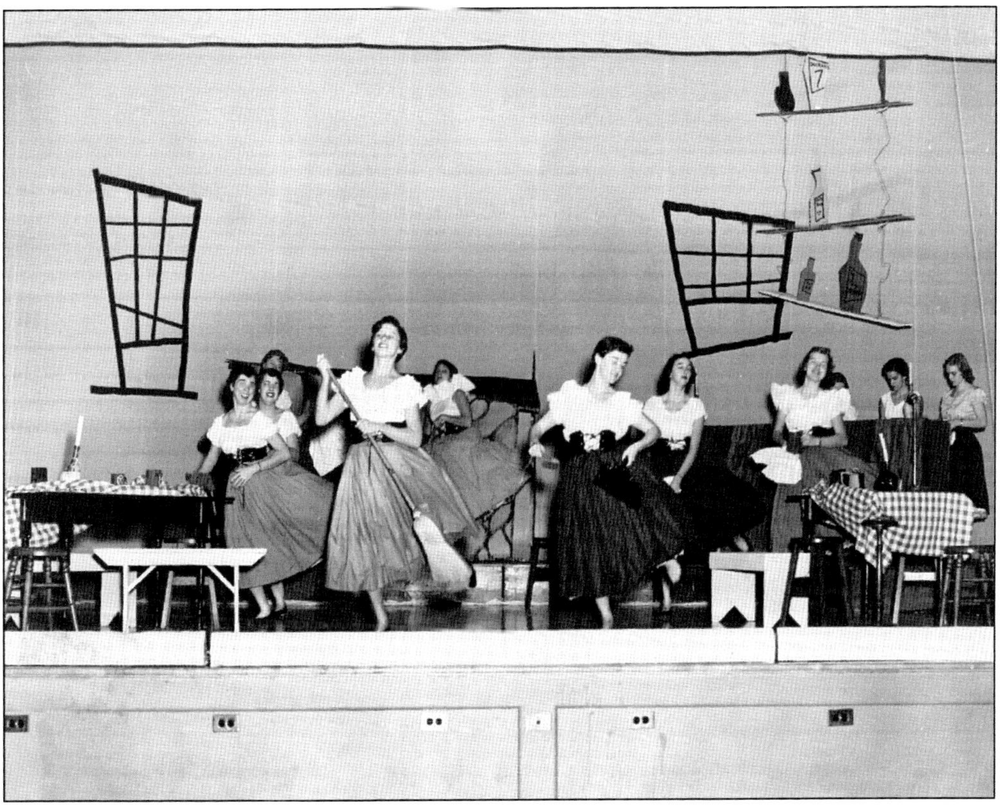

The Soph Revue was produced each year by the sophomore class. Sometimes called "the forgotten class," the sophomores took this opportunity to shine. The revue featured 90 minutes of hilarious skits that parodied faculty, staff, and sometimes even the college president. The 1955 Soph Revue was called *Inn and Out*.

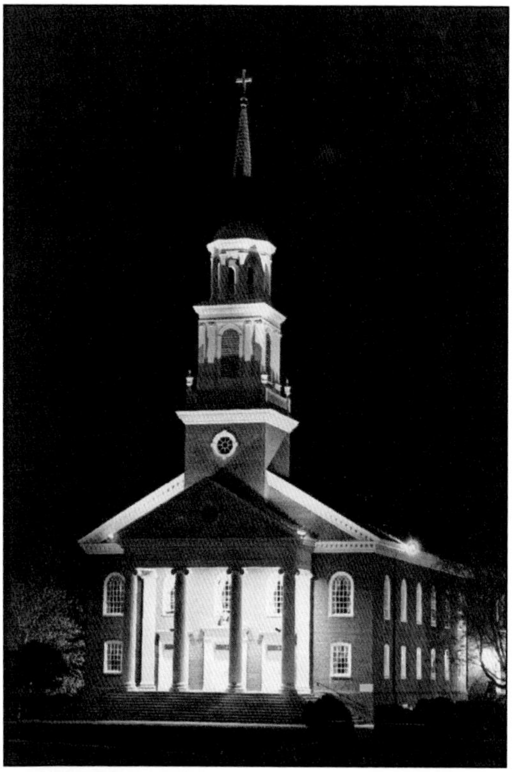

In 1949, an anonymous donor came forward proposing to cover half the expense ($150,000) of erecting a chapel on the campus. Dr. Truxal used the offer as a starting point for the Hood Forward fundraising campaign. Gifts totaling $750,000 were received. Later, the anonymous donors were identified as Hood trustee Andrew Coffman and his wife, Gladys. Construction on Coffman Chapel was completed in 1955.

By the mid-1950s, Hood's enrollment had increased enough that another dormitory was opened in 1957. R. Paul Smith, for whom the new building was named, laid the cornerstone in 1956. Smith, president of the Potomac Edison Company and longtime chair of the board of trustees, was the father of two Hood alums, including Lois Smith Harrison (1945), who also served as chair of the board.

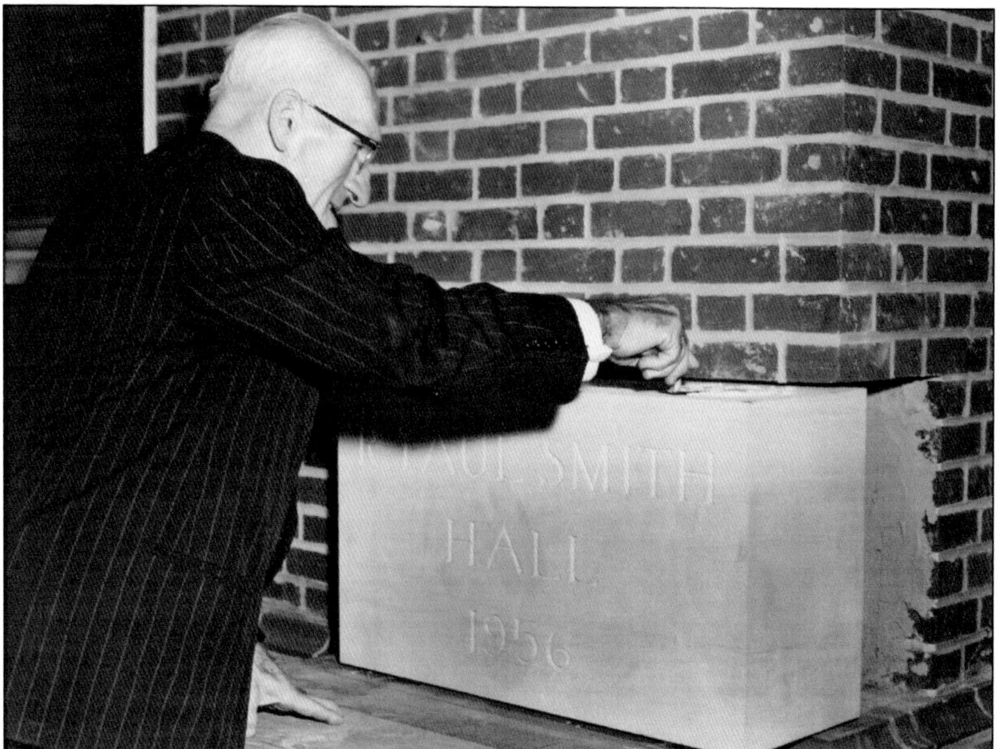

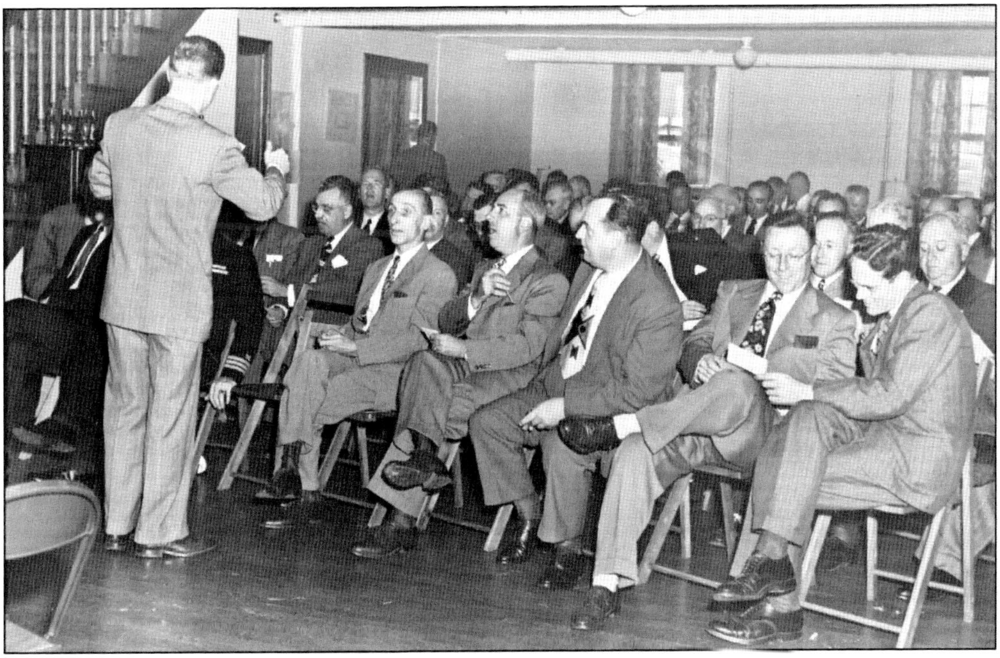

Hood's Fathers' Club was initiated in 1944. By 1956, their meetings had transitioned into the Dad and Daughter Weekend when the fathers joined their daughters on campus for two days of fun and games. The Mothers' Club, established by Lee Deldee Truxal in 1951, met during May Day festivities; the women volunteered time and money for projects such as redecorating the infirmary and installing an intercom system in the dormitories.

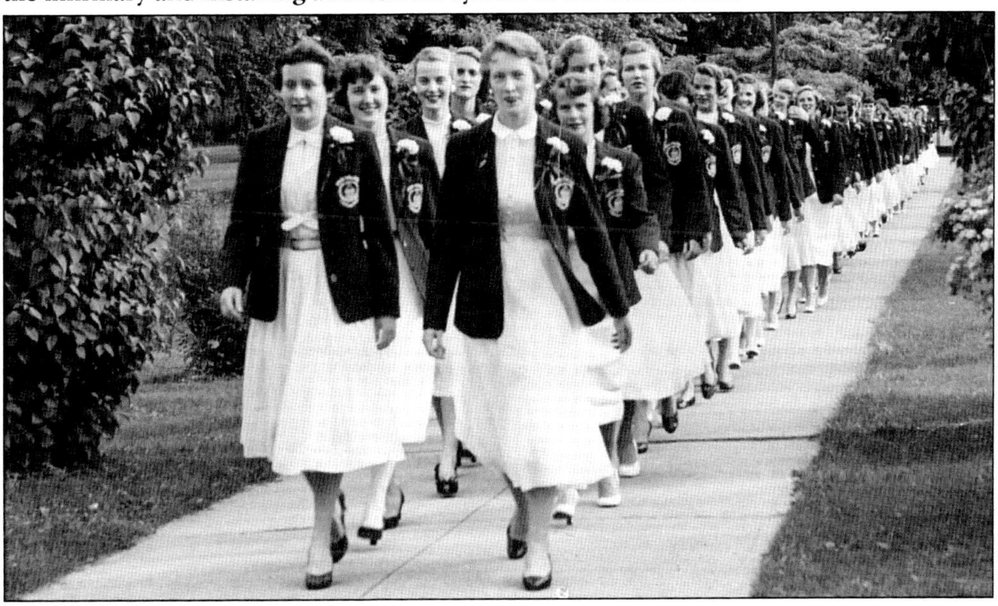

The class of 1957 wears their new blazers on Moving Up Day during their sophomore year. Moving Up Day recognized the advancement of each class to its next level. The classes customized their blazers with embroidered insignias of their own design. The blazers were either blue or gray, alternating every year. Hood sports teams, in a nod to this tradition, are known today as the Blazers.

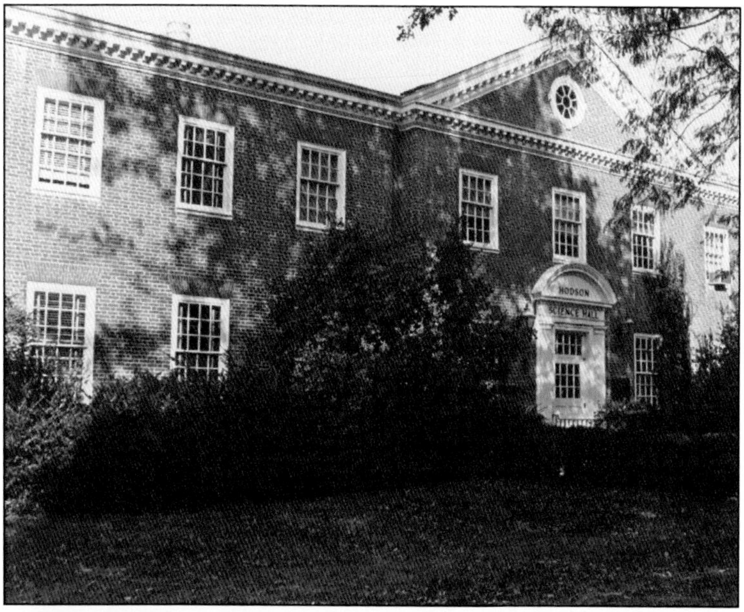

President Truxal was able to mark another goal off his to-do list that Hood's accrediting body had recommended. Along with a new dormitory in 1957, he saw the addition of an up-to-date science facility. The Lillian Brown Hodson Science Hall, named for the wife of Col. Clarence Hodson, became the third location on campus to bear the Hodson name.

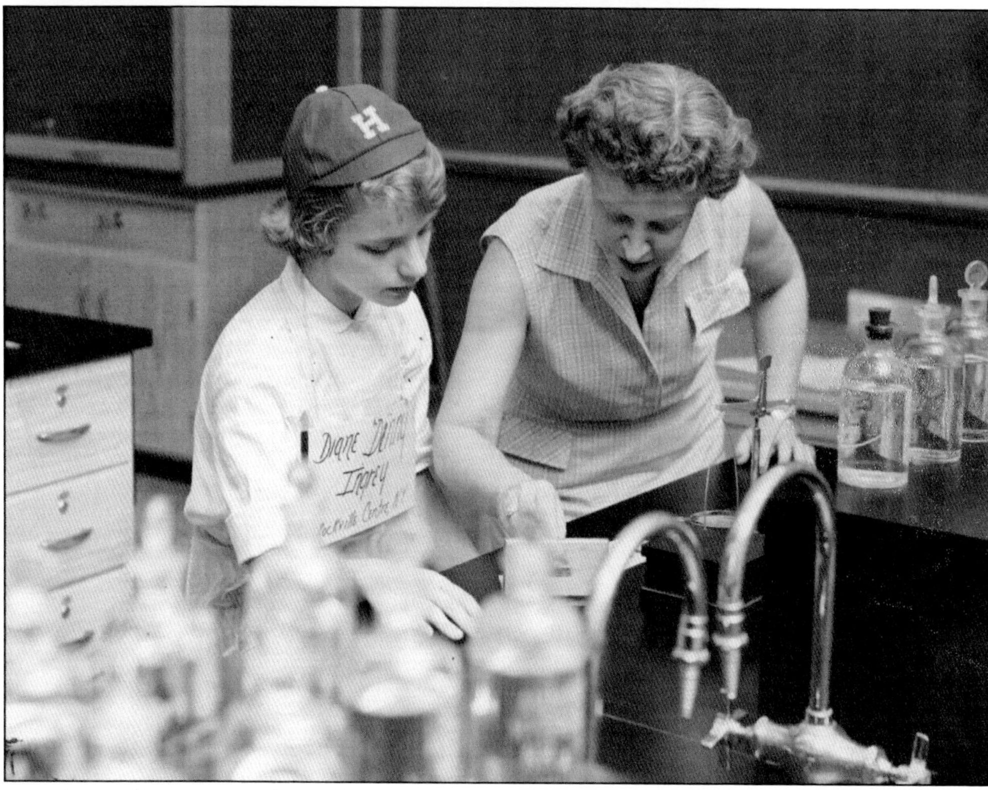

A tradition that apparently surfaced in the early 1950s, "dinks" are caps worn by freshman. Each class gets a color—red, blue, yellow, or green—which they keep throughout their four years at Hood. The dinks provide a way for freshmen to proclaim their class color and for upperclassmen to identify them as freshmen. In this 1959 photograph, professor of chemistry Margaret Neely works with freshman Diane Ingrey (1963), wearing her dink.

One of the most enduring of Hood traditions is the Hood ring. The unique piece of jewelry evolved from a pin (lower left) and went through several iterations before being standardized in 1925, with the letter "H" in gold on a lapis lazuli field. Because of its fragility, the lapis lazuli stone was replaced by blue spinel in 1945. These older rings demonstrate the evolution of the ring.

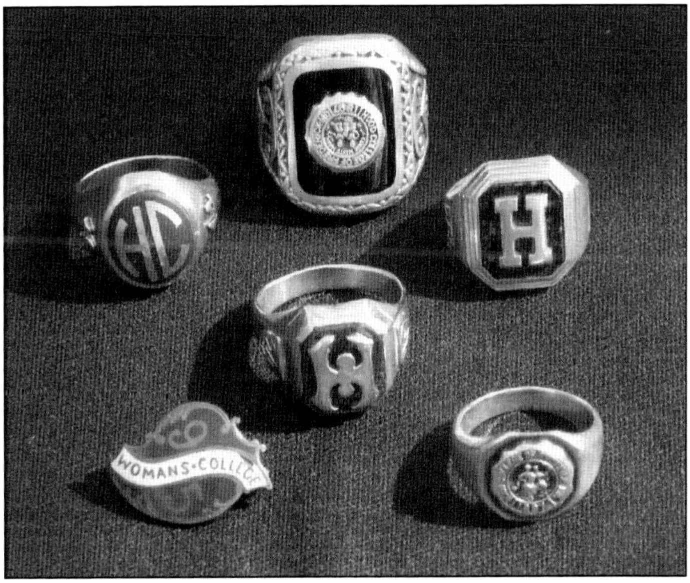

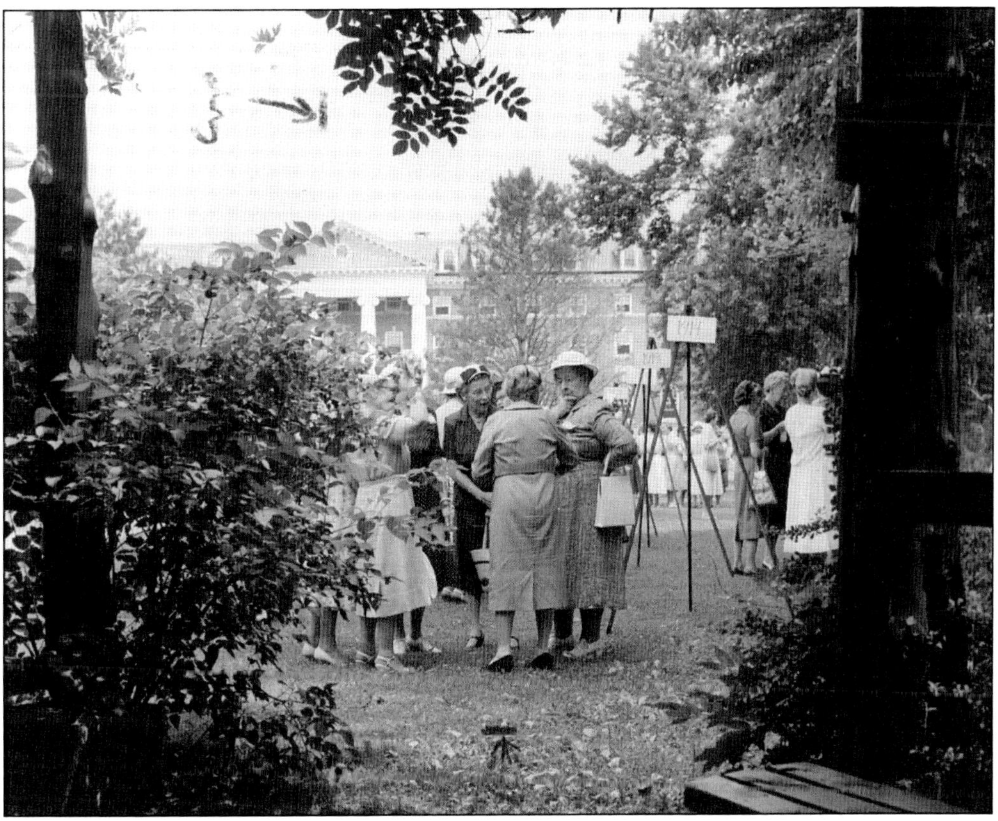

The 1959 Alumnae Weekend featured, among others, the classes of 1919 and 1914. Here, some of the first alumnae of the newly named Hood College gather to share their memories. Alumnae Weekend is now known as Reunion Weekend, traditionally held at the beginning of June. In 2012, nearly 500 alumni and their family members and friends returned to campus to reconnect with their classmates and college.

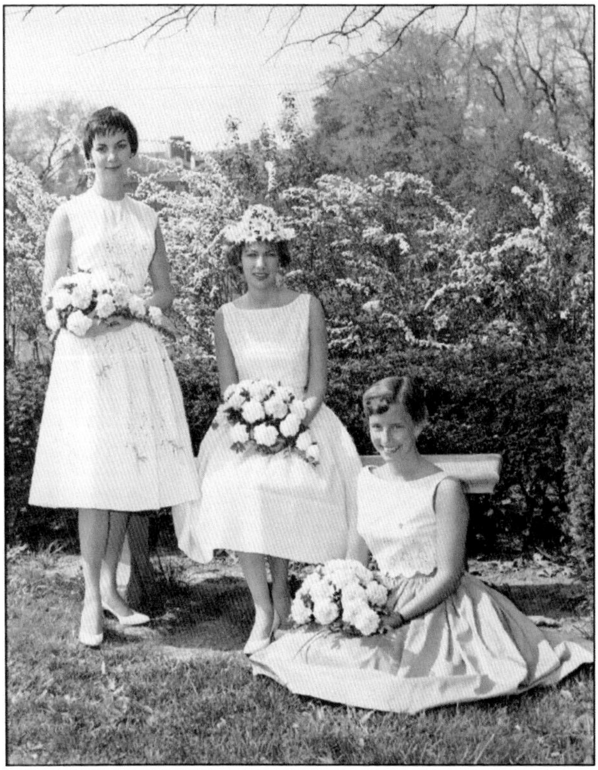

While the May Day concept continued into the 1960s, it had become rather more simplified when compared with the elaborate costumes and courts of the 1930s. By 1959, Prince Hood had become Princess Hood. Carol Lumb (1959), seated on the ground, received the honor that year. The May Queen, Gail Mulliken (1959) is identified by her flowered hat. Janet Knecht (1959), the Maid of Honor, rounds out the modest court.

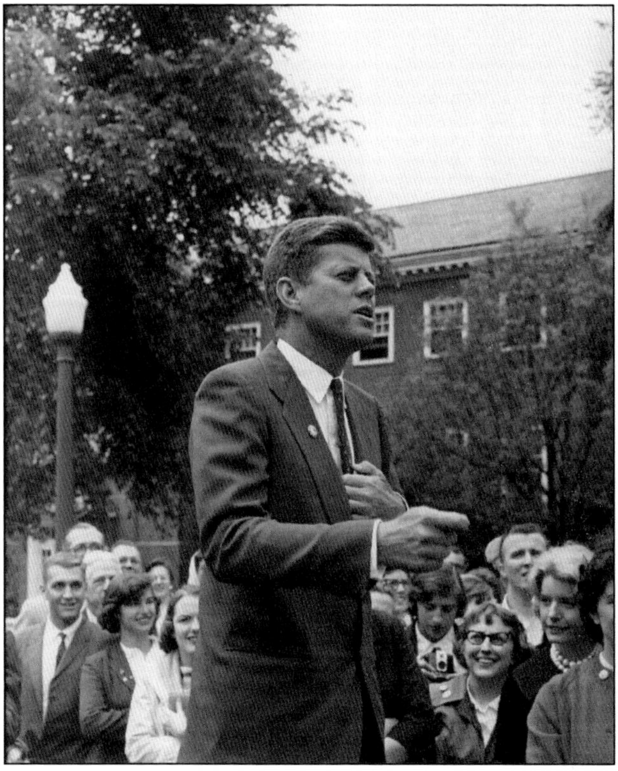

In May 1960, John F. Kennedy visited the Hood campus as he campaigned for the Democratic Party nomination for president. No one could have imagined the tragic end he would meet three years later. Coincidentally, Hood came to house one of the largest private collections of documents on the Kennedy assassination in its archives, amassed by the late researcher Harold Weisberg of Frederick.

Seven

Our Changing Times
Politics and Presidents, 1961–1975

After Dr. Truxal retired from Hood, international affairs specialist Randle Elliot assumed the presidency of the college. During his tenure, Coblentz Memorial Hall, Tatem Arts Center, and Rosenstock Hall were added to the campus buildings. Enrollment was growing, and the extra space was put to good use. Predictably, Dr. Elliott worked hard to strengthen Hood's sense of global connectedness, enrolling the college in the US-India Women's College program in 1966 and creating Hood's well-regarded Junior Year Abroad program in 1967. The campus was becoming more diverse with the arrival of the first African American student in 1964 and the establishment of a student exchange with Morgan State University. The college charter was amended in 1970 to admit men as commuters.

Unfortunately, enrollment was dropping, and faculty vacancies were left unfilled. To attract students, Hood adjusted requirements, increased financial aid, and liberalized some social restrictions. The Cooperative Government Constitution was completely revamped, and discipline was placed in the hands of students. Students were taking an interest in the national political scene, but rather than protests they were engaged in more constructive activities such as running blood drives. A teach-in involving 200 students and faculty was one campus response to the Vietnam War. Disagreements between the administration and the rest of the Hood community led to the resignation of Dr. Elliott in 1971.

Dr. Theodore Erck, a classicist, was hired to serve as interim president from 1971 to 1972. Continuing attempts to improve recruitment, he threw out all graduation requirements except English composition and physical education. He oversaw the establishment of the Hood College Graduate School in 1971.

Dr. Ross Pritchard, an international economist, became president in 1972 and made the addition of professional programs, such as graphic arts courses, a radiological technology program, and the addition of journalism classes, the hallmark of his administration. Hood's successful continuing education program for adult students began in 1973. Pritchard was also instrumental in reaffirming Hood's role as a women's college, though men were being admitted.

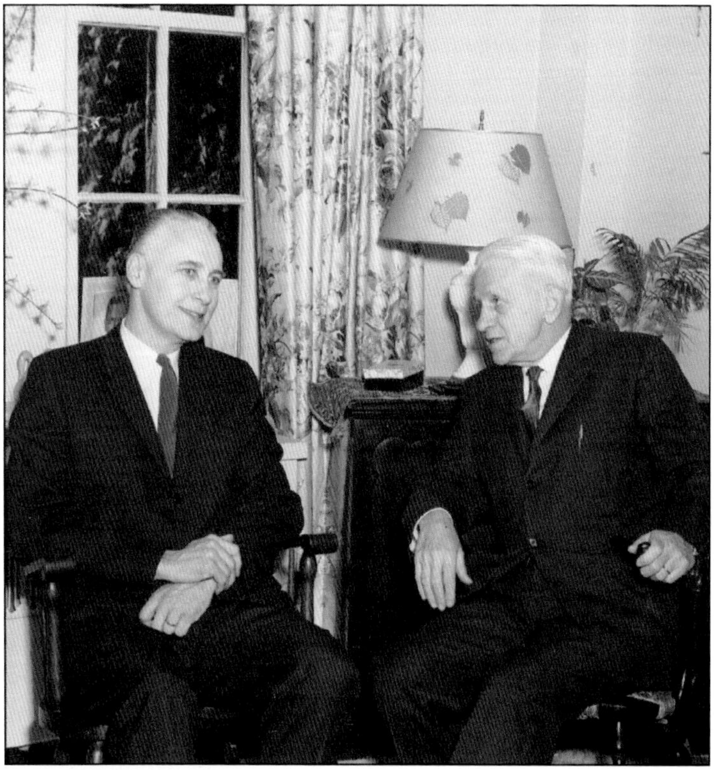

Randle Elliott (left) officially became Hood's fourth president on October 14, 1961. In this photograph, he is shown with outgoing president Andrew Truxal, whose tenure was one of great accomplishment, marked by new buildings, an enlarged endowment, enhancements to Hood's academic standing, and a growing student body. Dr. Truxal announced his resignation in 1960 and left the college in 1961.

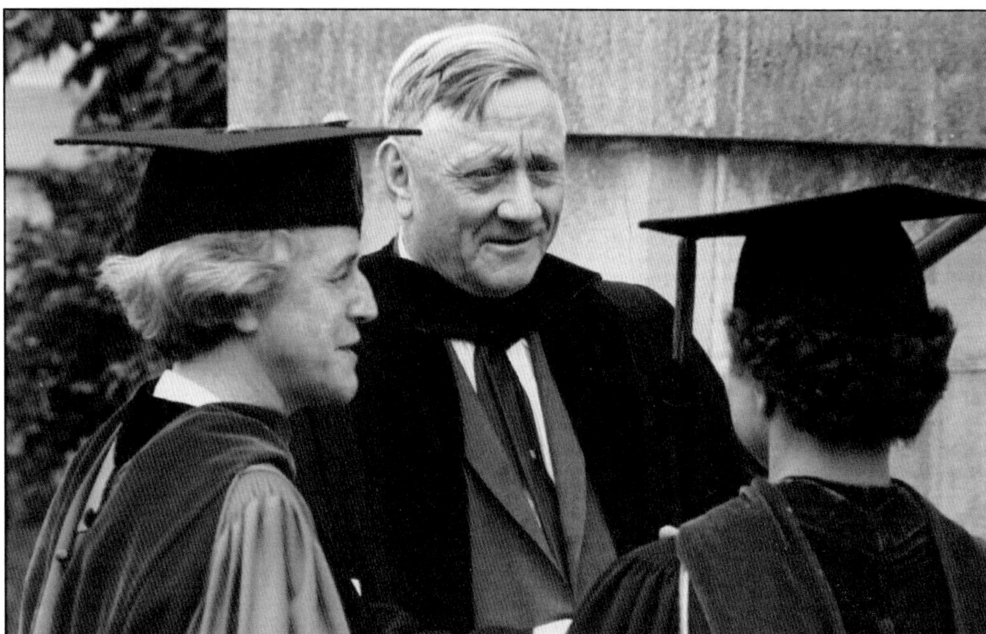

Supreme Court Justice William O. Douglas addressed the class of 1962 at their June 3 commencement. Here, he and dean of faculty Mary Frear Keeler speak with a faculty participant in the ceremony. At that time, Justice Douglas urged the graduates to "show the path of freedom" to the many new nations that were emerging, especially in Africa.

For a number of years, Hood students selected the best dressed from among their ranks to vie with other college women from across the country in *Glamour Magazine's* annual 10 Best Dressed competition, which considered not only the clothes but the characteristics of the woman wearing them. In 1962, Betsy Anne "Sunny" Griffin (1962) was one of the winners. She went on to a highly successful modeling career.

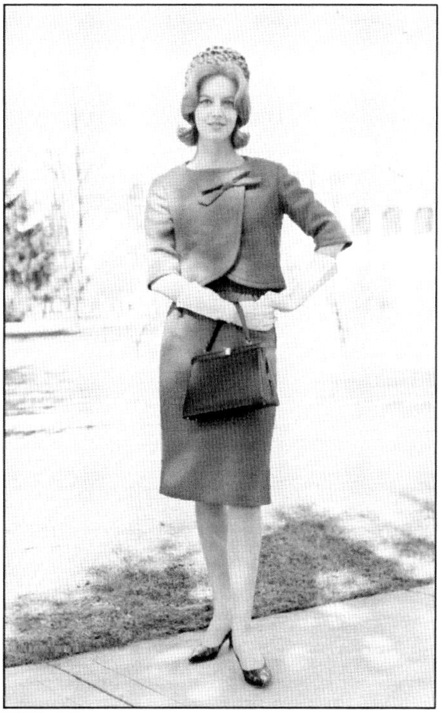

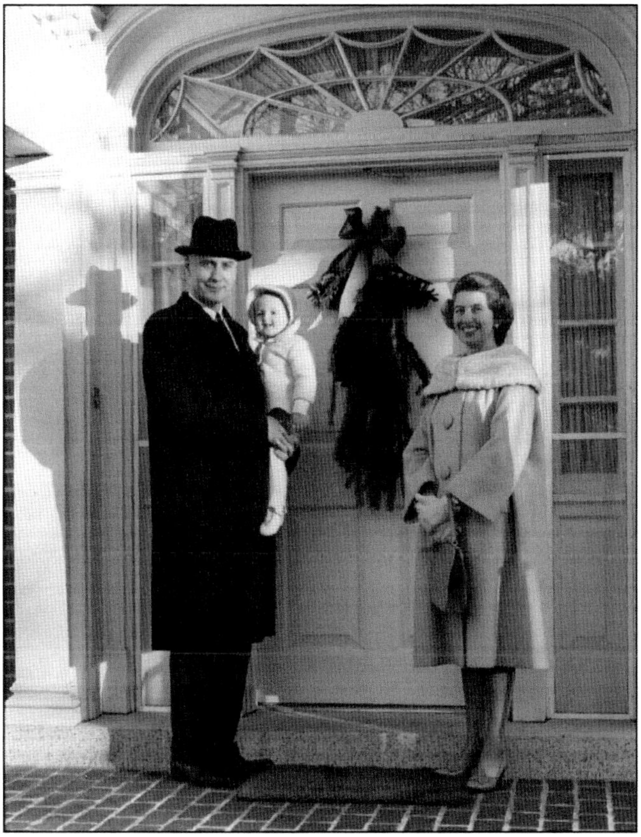

President Elliott, wife Dr. Gwendolyn Crawford Elliott, and their daughter Dawn were photographed at the door to the president's house in December 1962. At the time of her husband's appointment to the presidency of Hood, Dr. Elliott was the dean of women at the University of Delaware, a position that she resigned to become Hood's full-time first lady.

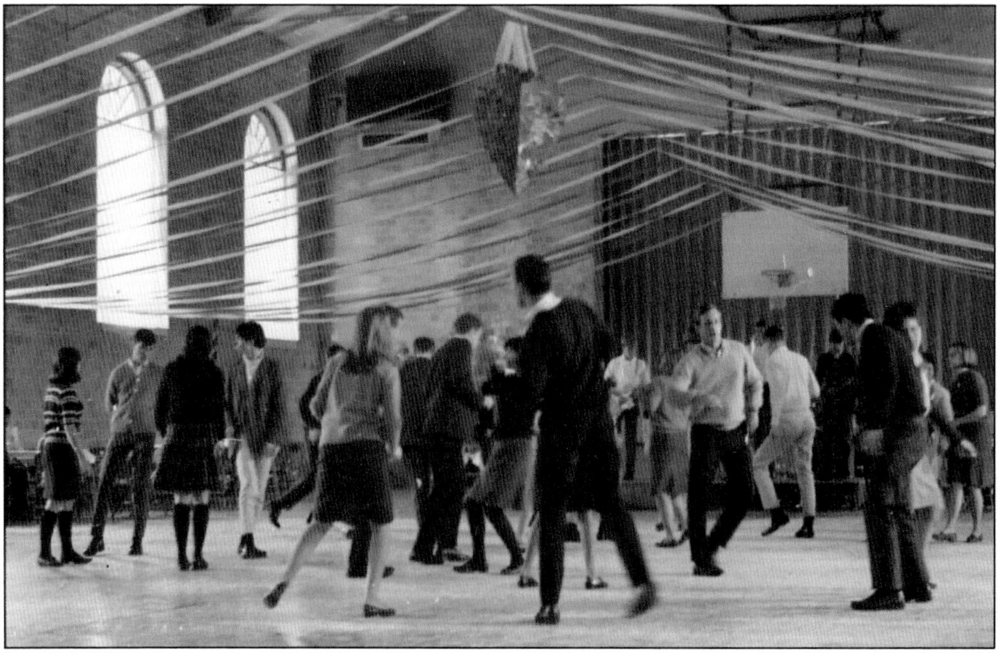

Students dance in Gambrill Gymnasium, which is seen festooned with crepe paper streamers, in 1966. Hood held a variety of regular formal and informal dances, sometimes busing dates in from other colleges. For a time, there was even a student-run service—one might call it a matchmaking service—that worked to pair such men up with compatible Hood students.

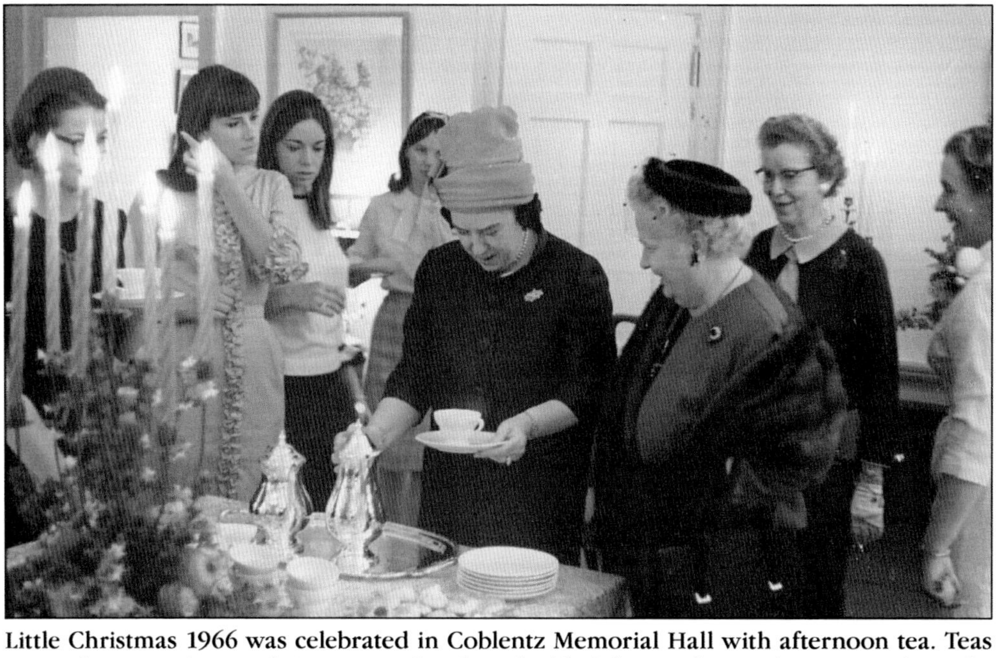

Little Christmas 1966 was celebrated in Coblentz Memorial Hall with afternoon tea. Teas were a long-standing tradition at Hood and marked holidays and special occasions from the Woman's College days. The heads of houses eased the tension at exam time by hosting teas in the dormitories. It was also common practice for the presidents, or their wives, to host teas for special occasions or holidays.

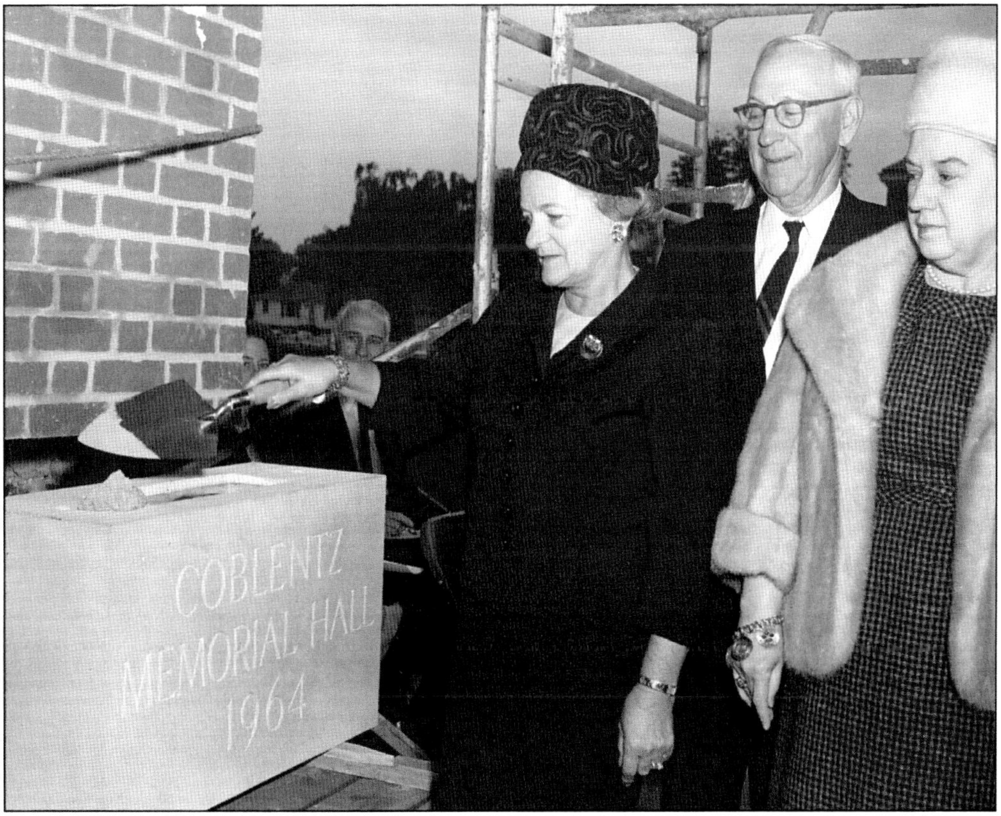

In 1964, Clyde Thomas, chair of Hood's board of trustees, and Angela Coblentz watch as Katharine Coblentz Crook (1929) places the cornerstone of Coblentz Memorial Hall, Hood's fifth dormitory. It is named in memory of Margaret Pontius Coblentz (1901) and her son Edward P. Coblentz, a member of Hood's board of trustees. Katharine, daughter and sister to the memorialized Coblentzes, was the mother of two Hood alumnae.

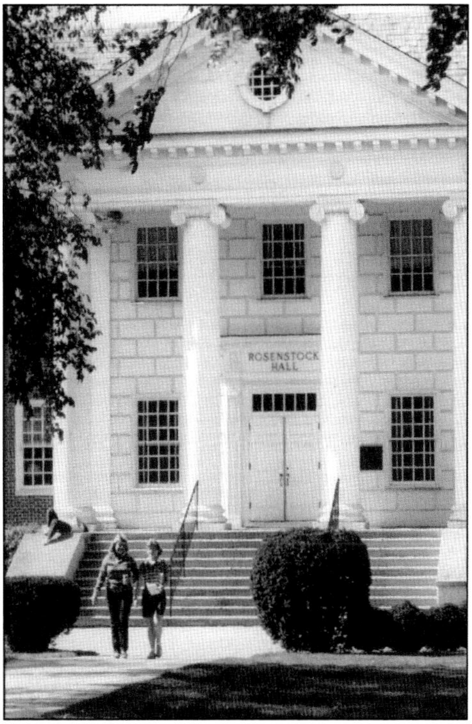

Rosenstock Hall was built in 1970 to meet the need for additional classroom space. It was named for Henrietta and Samuel H. Rosenstock. Samuel was a founding member of the board of associates. The building houses the economics and management, English, and history departments, as well as the 400-seat Hodson Auditorium.

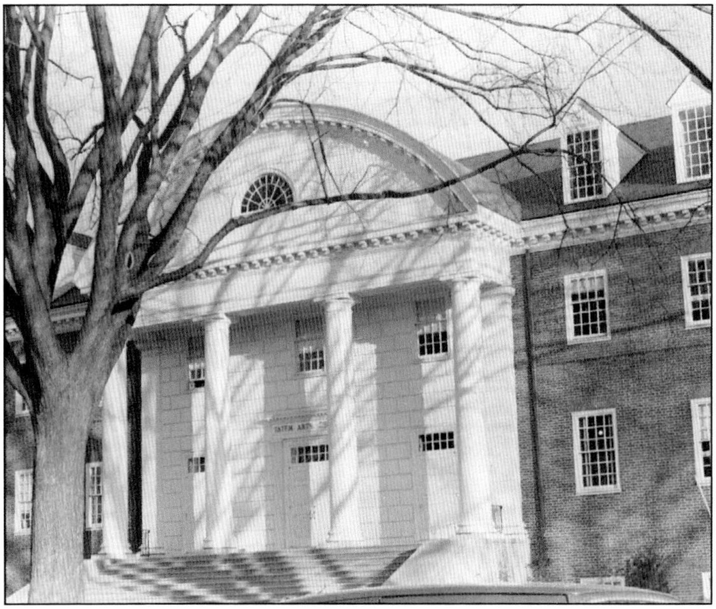

A new classroom building, Tatem Arts Center, was dedicated in 1966. It was named for Minnie Antoinette Moore Tatem of Haddonfield, New Jersey, who was the mother of Antoinette Tatem Driscoll (1929), a member of the Hood College's board of trustees. Today, it houses the Departments of Art and Archaeology, Education, and Foreign Languages and Literatures, as well as the Hodson Gallery.

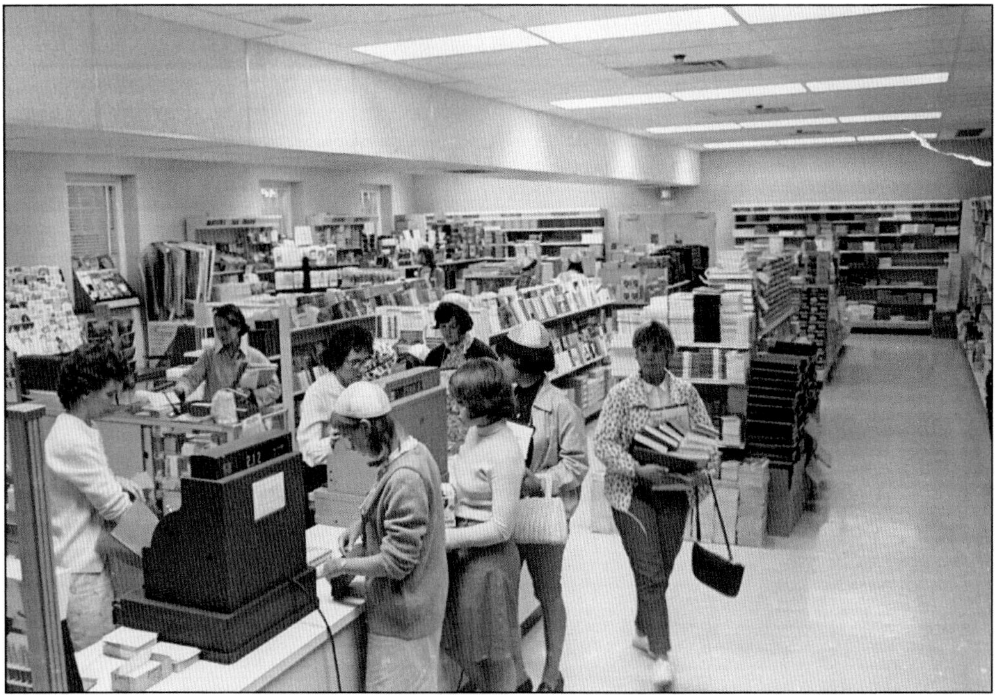

Tatem Arts Center was also home to another very important campus agency. Until the construction of the Whitaker Campus Center in 1997, the bookstore was located in the basement of Tatem. This photograph, taken early in the fall semester of 1966, shows freshmen in their dinks lined up at the checkout counter as they purchase textbooks.

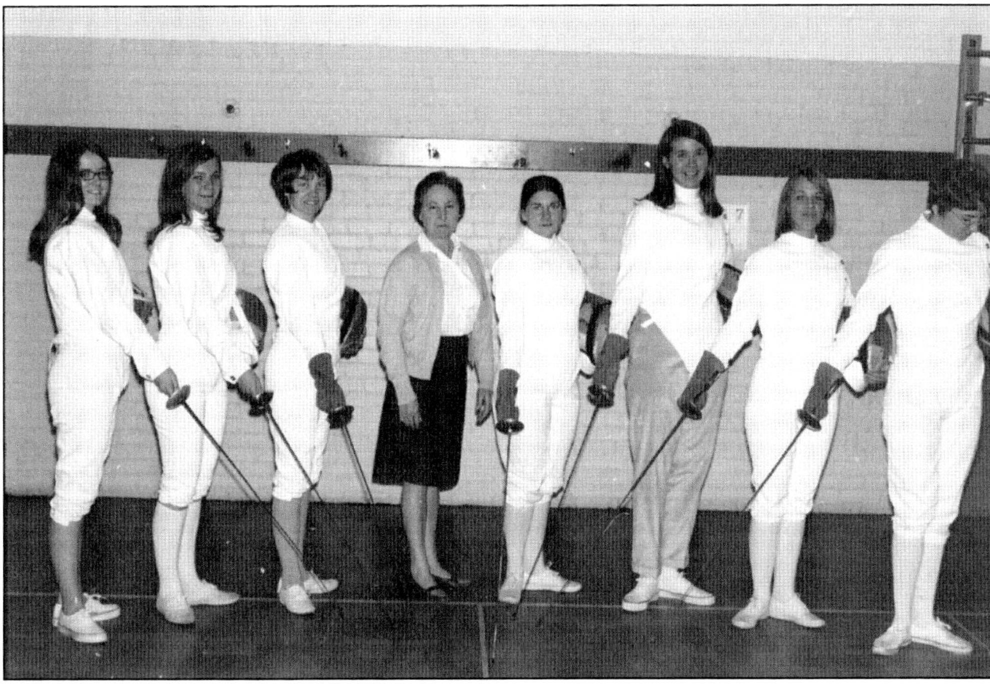

The varsity fencing team finished its 1969–1970 season with a 5-1 record. By this time, intercollegiate play was well established at Hood. The fencing team met Penn State and the University of Maryland once during the season and Wilson College and Goucher College twice each; the team was bested only once—by Wilson College.

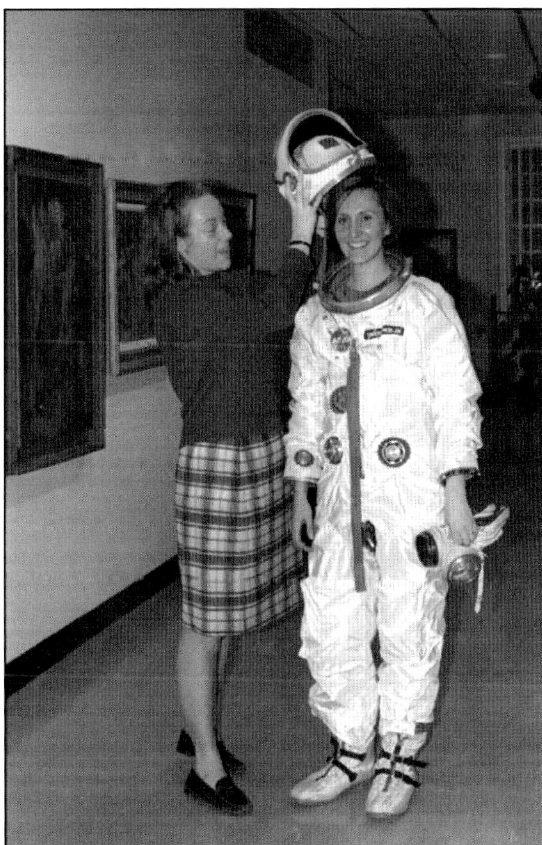

Student Jane Cross (1967) is getting suited up in an authentic Gemini space program astronaut suit in April 1967. The suit was demonstrated by a NASA official who also presented a lecture on the "Space Application of Textiles." The lecture was sponsored by the home economics department and Beta Beta Beta, the biology honorary. Interestingly, Cross went on to fly, not as an astronaut but as an airline stewardess.

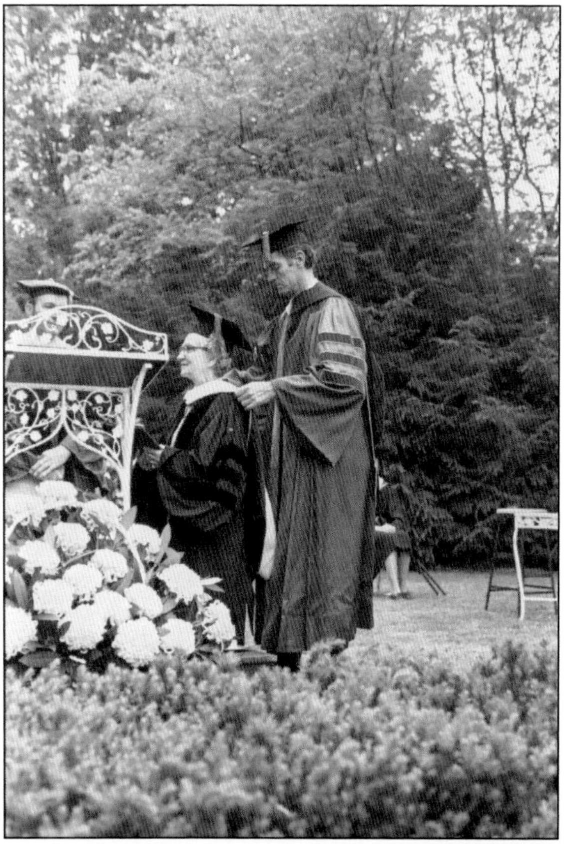

Eleanor Johnson, cofounder and editor of *My Weekly Reader*, was awarded an honorary doctor of letters during the 1971 commencement in Hodson Outdoor Theater. Following tradition, a member of the faculty adjusts her new academic hood. Several generations fondly recall the weekly publication of kid-friendly news and information that Dr. Johnson helped launch in 1929, published today as *Weekly Reader*.

In the spring of 1971, a crisis of confidence in some of the college's administrators led to several resignations, including that of President Elliott. A search was initiated for an interim president, and Theodore Erck, a classicist from Vassar College, was selected for the 1971–1972 academic year. Here, Dr. Erck and his wife, Dr. Myrtle Soles Erck, also a Vassar classicist, greet students at the president's house.

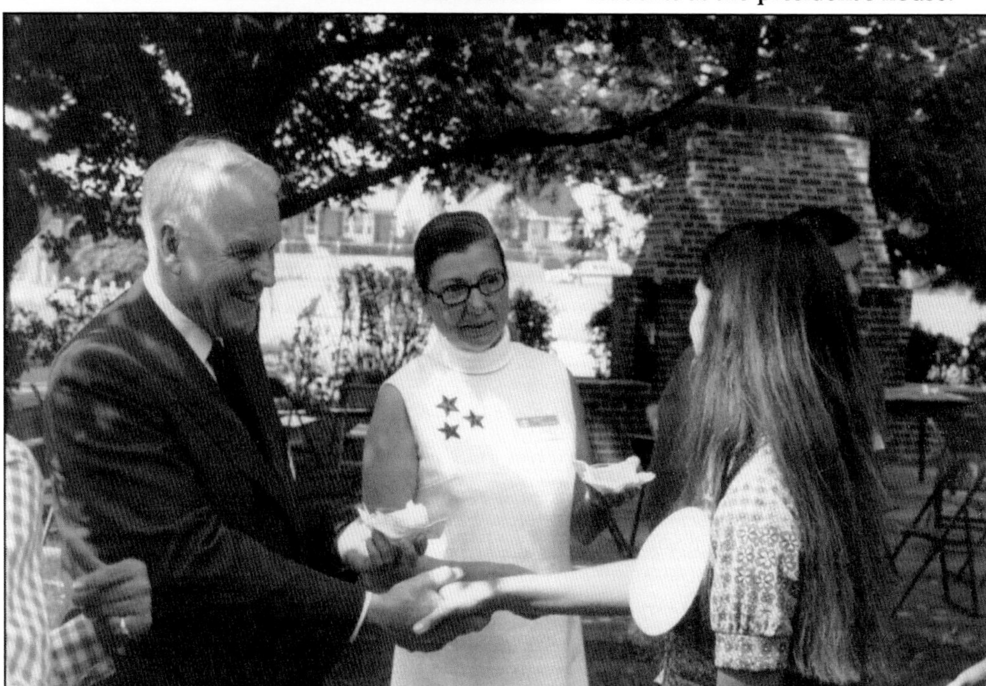

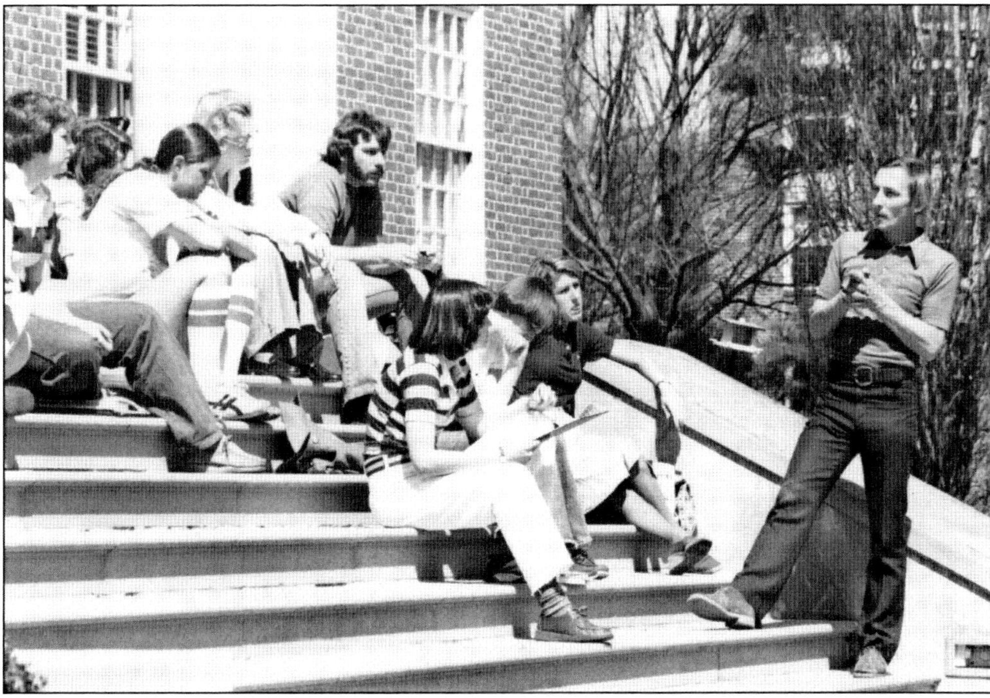

Dr. Leonard Latkovski, now professor of history, takes advantage of lovely spring weather and lectures to his class, which includes at least two men, on the steps of Rosenstock Hall in this c. 1972 photograph. "Dr. L," as he has been known by his many students, has taught at Hood for more than 40 years. His daughter Stephanie graduated from Hood in 1993.

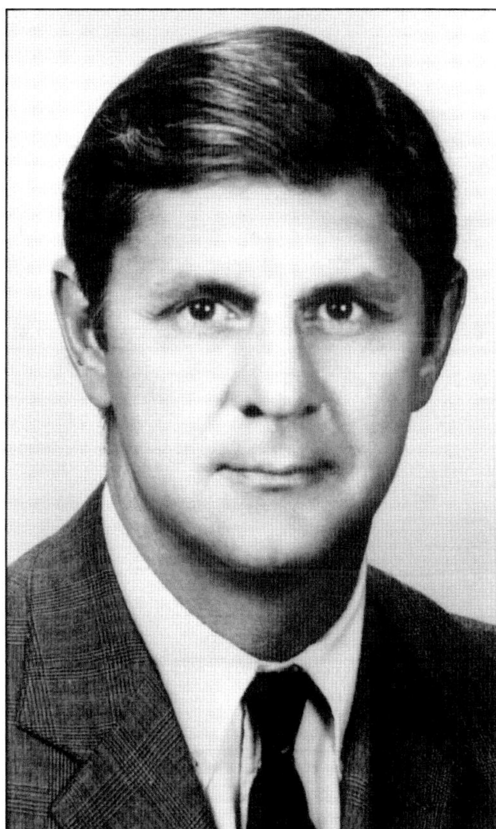

Dr. Ross Pritchard, the sixth president of Hood College, had experience not only as an academic but also as an administrator in the Peace Corps and an executive for an international development company working in Iran. He was formally invested as president at the college's fall convocation held on August 30, 1972. His inaugural speech outlined an agenda that acknowledged the college's recent problems but embraced the opportunities they presented.

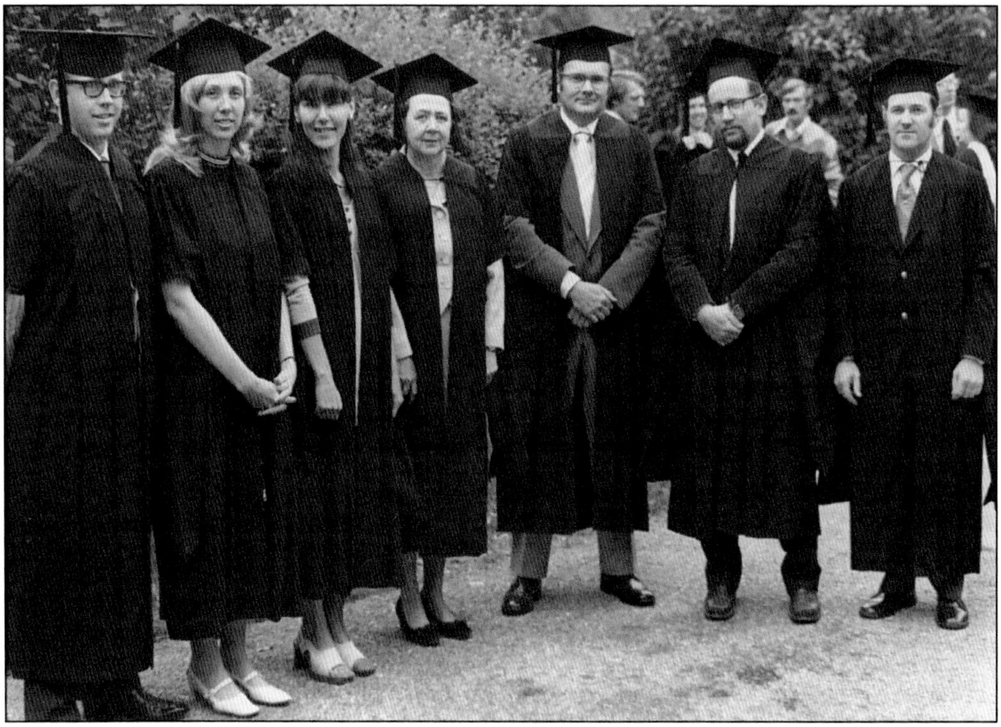

Upon his arrival at Hood, Dr. Pritchard moved forward immediately to implement the graduate program that had been approved in 1971. At the 1973 commencement, these students became recipients of Hood's first master of arts degrees. They are, from left to right, Robert Cliser, Mary Helen Cliser, Michele Kalman Siegel, Rita Marron Wagner, Michael Leftwich, Richard Henson, and Gerald Leather.

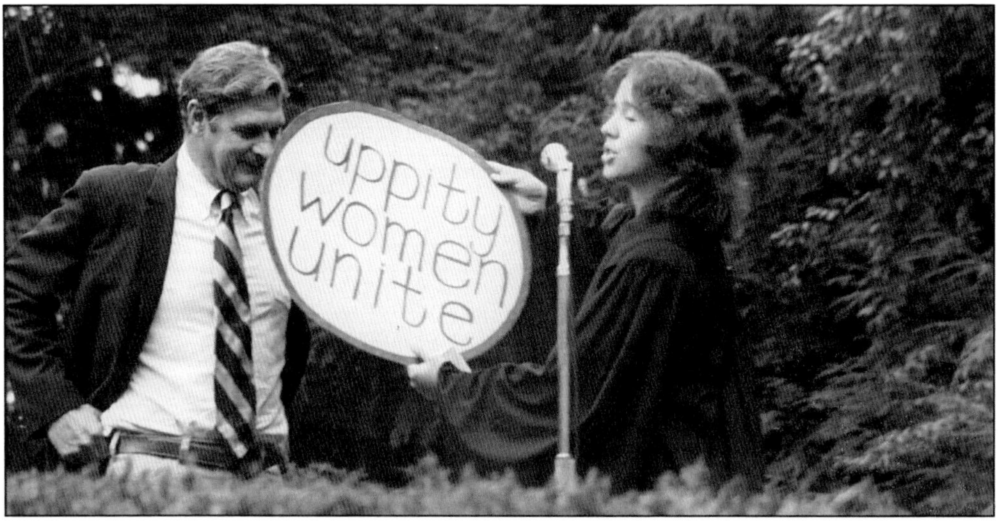

Hood women continued to push for 24-hour parietals. The trustees opted to leave that question to the students and faculty to work out, and it was resolved to the students' satisfaction in 1974. Dr. Pritchard supported women's causes and sponsored a women's task force that reaffirmed the importance of women's education. This student makes it clear that Hood women are a force to be reckoned with.

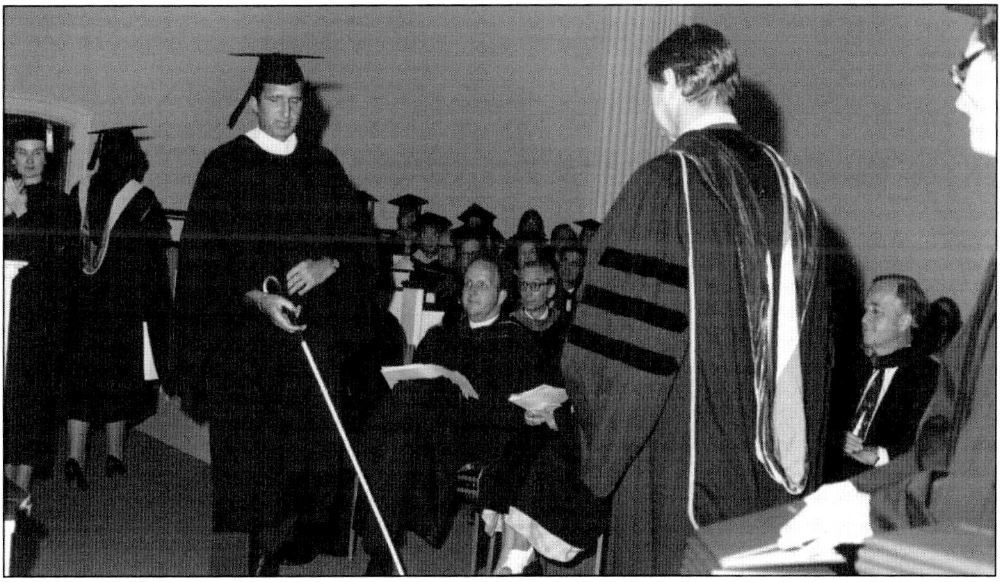

By this time, men had been attending Hood long enough that they were graduating. One of the first men to be admitted was Aldan T. Weinberg (now professor of journalism on Hood's faculty), who graduated in 1975. In this photograph from 1974, Vietnam veteran Dewey Leon Underwood is about to receive his diploma from President Pritchard. Underwood was one of the first veterans to earn a Hood degree.

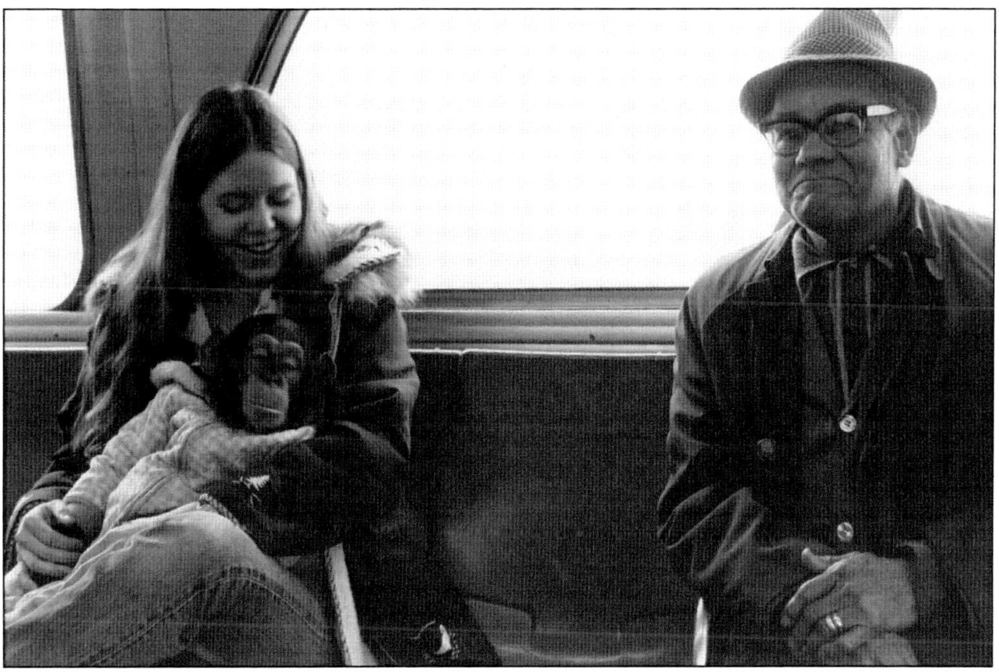

President Pritchard had instituted broad changes in the curriculum that emphasized career preparation. This affected the courses that were taught, and it resulted in the development of a wide variety of internship possibilities. In this 1975 photograph, taken on a New York City bus, Hood student Lisa Paddon (1977) holds Nim, a baby chimp. She taught Nim American Sign Language as part of her internship at Columbia University.

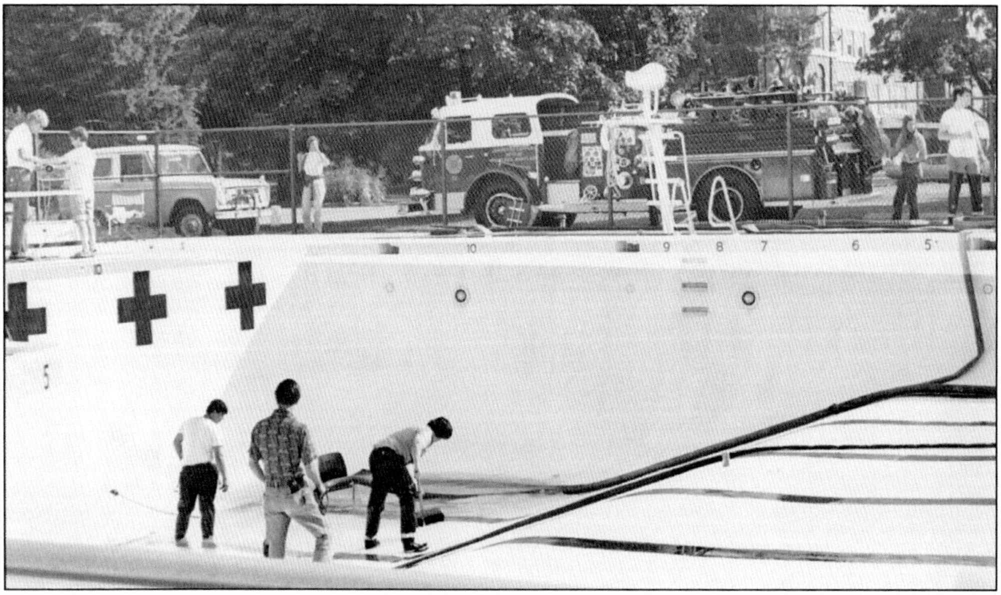

The Frederick Junior Fire Company prepares to fill the Huntsinger Aquatic Center, which opened in 1975 and was named in honor of Fritz Huntsinger Sr., who received an honorary doctor of humanities in 1977. His son Fritz Huntsinger Jr. is a former member of Hood's board of trustees. The center is a community resource, providing public swimming opportunities throughout the year.

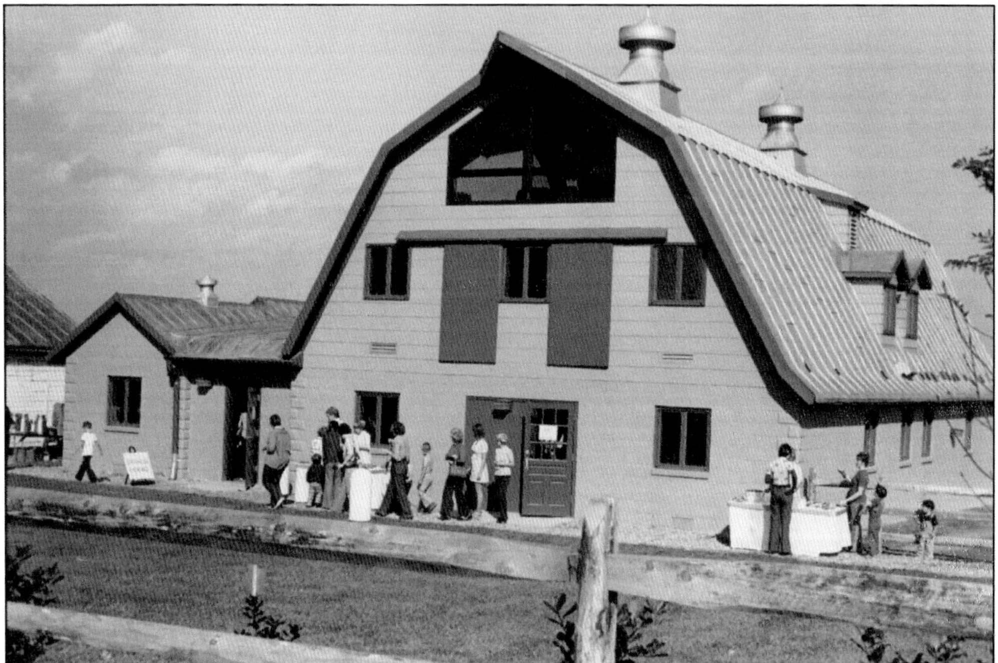

As a result of the women's movement, interest in women's colleges was on the rise, thus Hood's student population grew. The old barn on the college farm property, across from the campus on Seventh Street, was renovated in 1975 to house 33 students. A unique feature of the structure was the three-level study area that was built into the silo.

Eight

OUR FIRST WOMAN PRESIDENT
MARTHA CHURCH, 1975–1995

Excitement ran high in 1975 as Martha E. Church was installed as the first woman and seventh president of Hood College, heralding a new era of curriculum development and campus growth and culminating in a festive celebration of Hood's centennial in 1993. A graduate of Wellesley College, she earned her doctoral degree from the University of Chicago. During her tenure, the college reaffirmed is commitment to diversity, revised its curriculum and enhanced its academic reputation, instituted a nationally recognized honors program, strengthened services for adult learners, established a career center, and expanded the Hood Graduate School.

Sadly, the on-campus riding program was discontinued, and the stables were demolished; however, other facilities opened: the Huntsinger Aquatic Center, the Hodson Science Link, the Marx Center, and the Beneficial-Hodson Library and Information Technology Center. In a stellar program that continues today, Hood established a partnership with the National Cancer Institute (NCI) that enabled students to serve as interns and research assistants at NCI research laboratories at Fort Detrick in Frederick, Maryland.

After much discussion, the faculty approved a new faculty code. The board of associates awarded its first grants to faculty and staff for professional research, and the board of trustees established the Beneficial Chair in Economics, the Giles Chair in Early Childhood Education, and the Virginia E. Lewis Lecture Series. The graduate school offered new degree programs in computer science, business administration, and environmental science.

With faculty, students, staff, alumni, and friends sporting colorful T-shirts emblazoned with "Hood is #1," the campus celebrated its ranking in 1985 as the number-one small college in the East by *US News & World Report*.

Hood's centennial celebration got underway with the dedication of the new library, named in honor of the Hodson Trust, a major college benefactor since 1936. The Whitaker sisters, dedicated alumnae, announced that the Whitaker Foundation would give $2 million toward the building of the Whitaker Campus Center.

In 1995, Pres. Martha Church, recognized as one of the 100 most effective college presidents in the nation, announced her decision to retire.

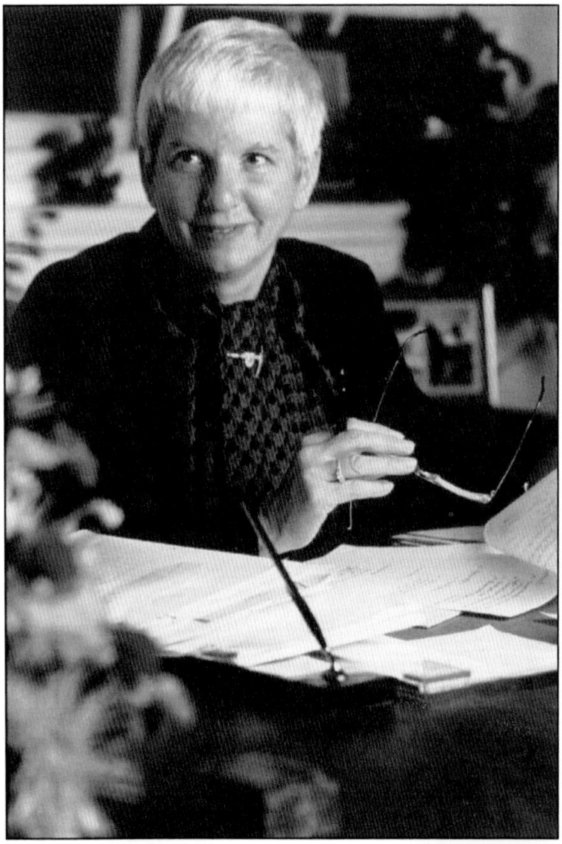

In May 1975, Martha E. Church became the college's seventh, and first woman, president. She came to Hood with a background in academia, after serving as an administrator with the Middle States Association, and was active in a number of groups of women academics. Her goal for her tenure was "to make Hood College and Frederick a center for women of all ages."

A student registers for classes during the fall 1977 orientation. At the time, registration was a process characterized by paper files, waiting in lines, and some uncertainty as to whether or not the desired classes were already full by the time one reached the head of the line. Today's computerized process takes much of the inconvenience and anxiety out of the start-of-semester activities.

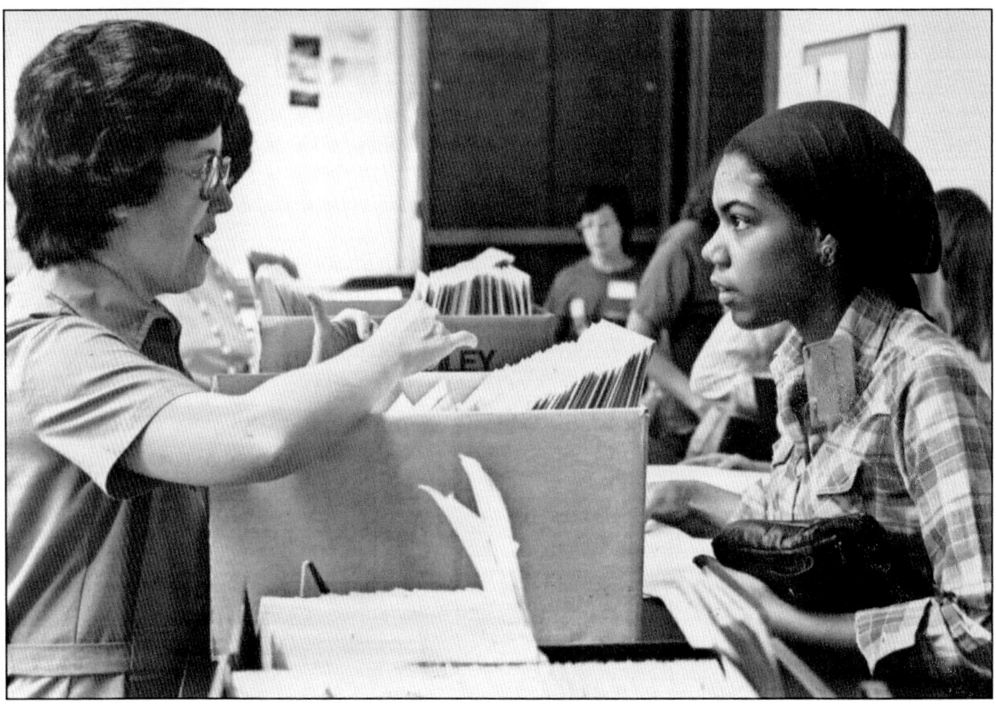

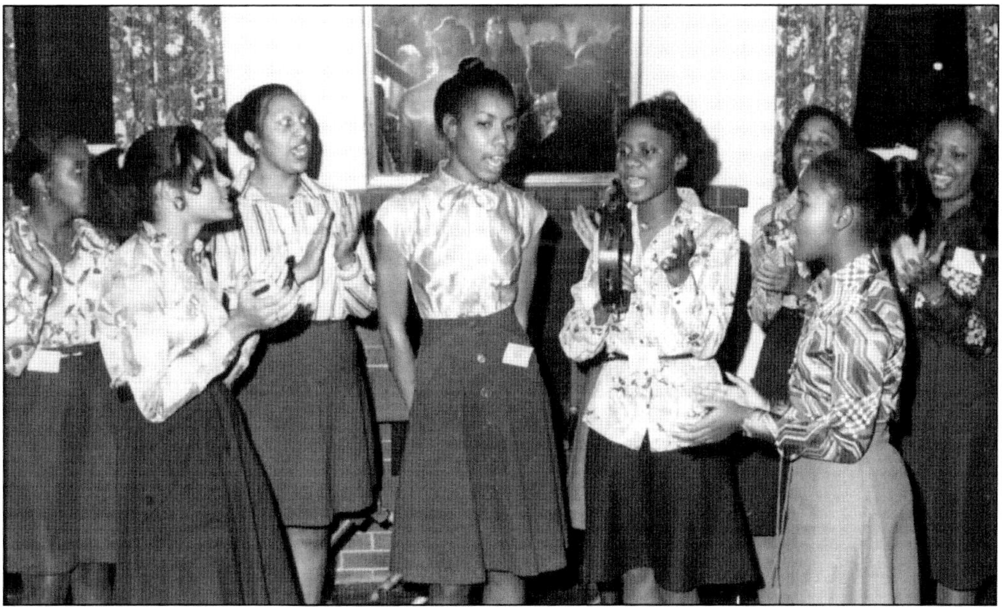

In the mid-1970s, the Campus Day tradition was running in tandem with a new tradition known as "fall parties." One of the events of the 1976 fall parties weekend was a presentation by the Hood Gospel Singers. The group has been a prized performance ensemble on the campus for nearly four decades.

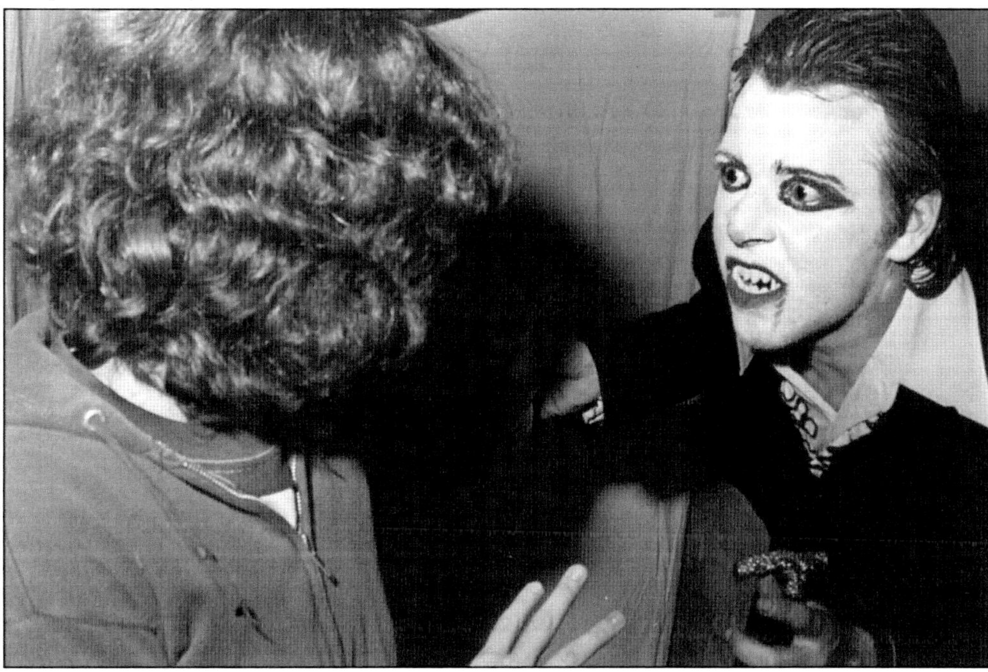

A ghoul of a student scares a visitor at the commuter council's annual haunted house in Rayford Lodge. Commuter students, once called "day students," hosted a number of events on campus, including the popular all-campus Shrove Tuesday pancake breakfast. Rayford was a home away from home for commuters until it was demolished in 1996 to make way for the Whitaker Campus Center, which now houses the commuter lounge.

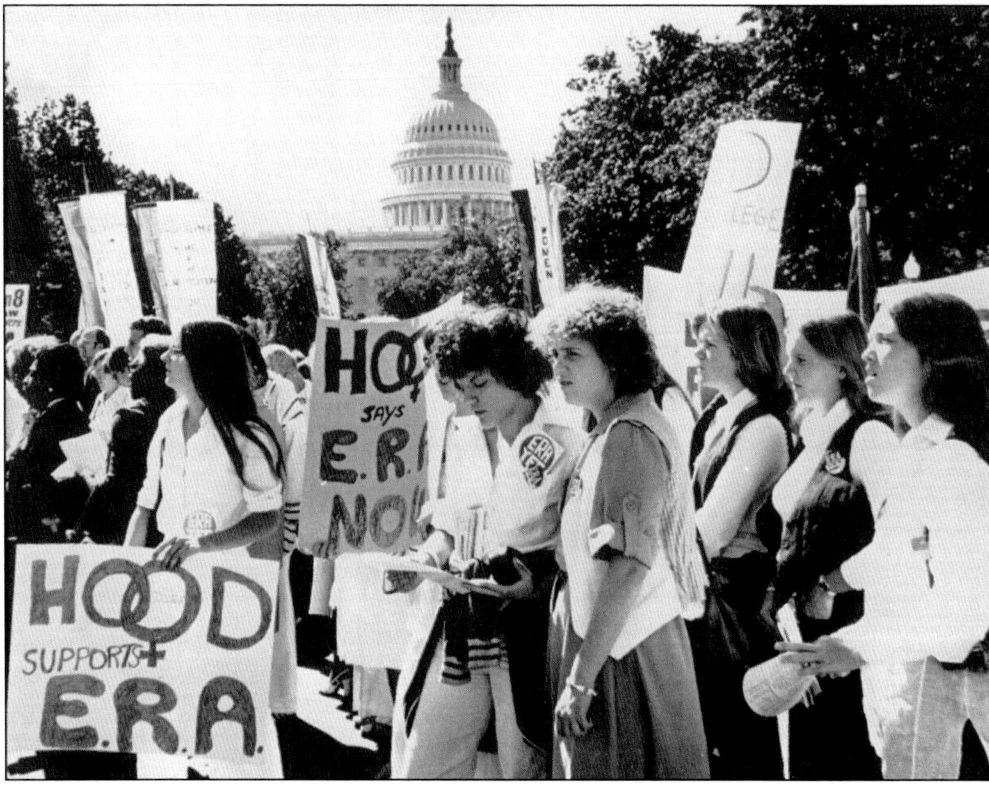

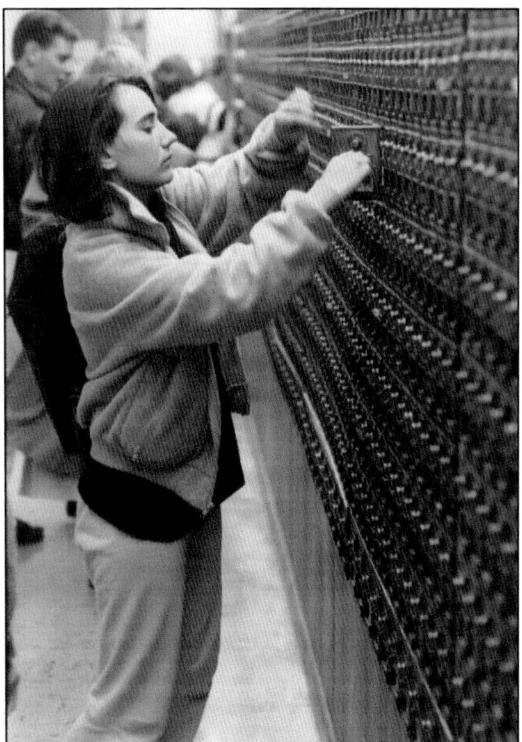

A large contingent of students from Hood was among the marchers in a July 1978 rally to show support for the Equal Rights Amendment (ERA) in Washington, DC. The ERA was passed by Congress in 1972 and sent to the states for ratification, but the states were slow to respond, and by the time the amendment expired in 1982 it was still three votes short of ratification.

A student checks her mailbox in the basement of Alumnae Hall. The post office moved down the street with the opening of the Whitaker Campus Center in 1997, where new mailboxes awaited. Shortly after the campus center opened, the Hood alumni magazine advertised piggy banks—made with the doors to the old mailboxes—for sale as souvenirs as well as to raise funds for the college.

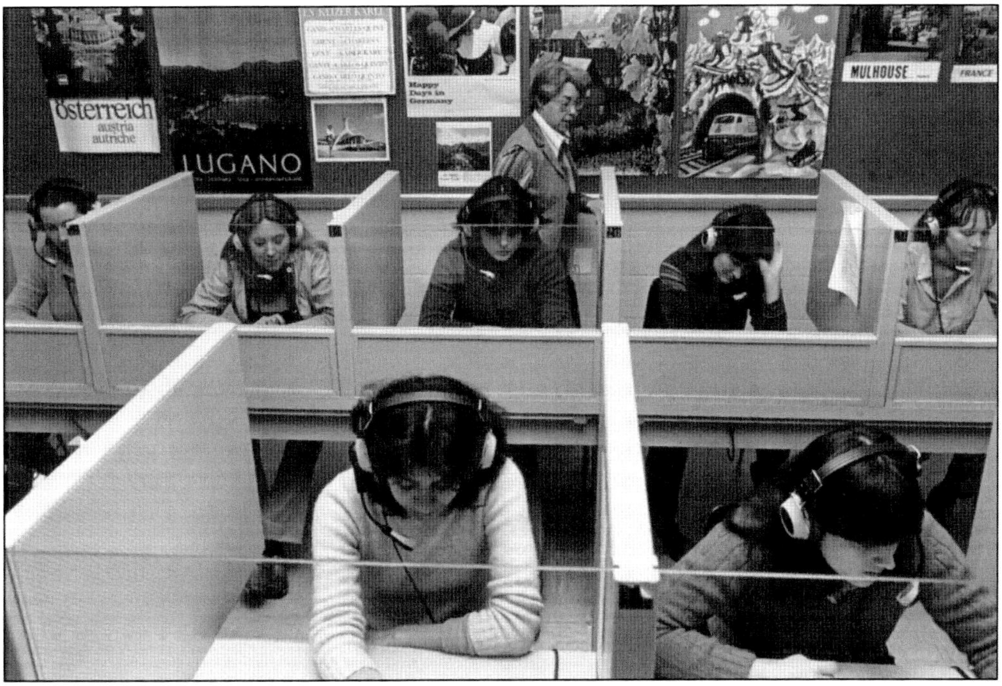

Students listen to language tapes and then record their voices in the Eddy Language Laboratory, named in honor of Frederick Eddy, professor of modern languages from 1950 to 1954. The 1981–1982 catalog describes the facility, located in Tatem Arts Center, as "an audio-active-comparative language laboratory equipped with cassette booth recorders and modular control, and simultaneous-interpretation equipment." Needless to say, language study has been changed for the better by computers.

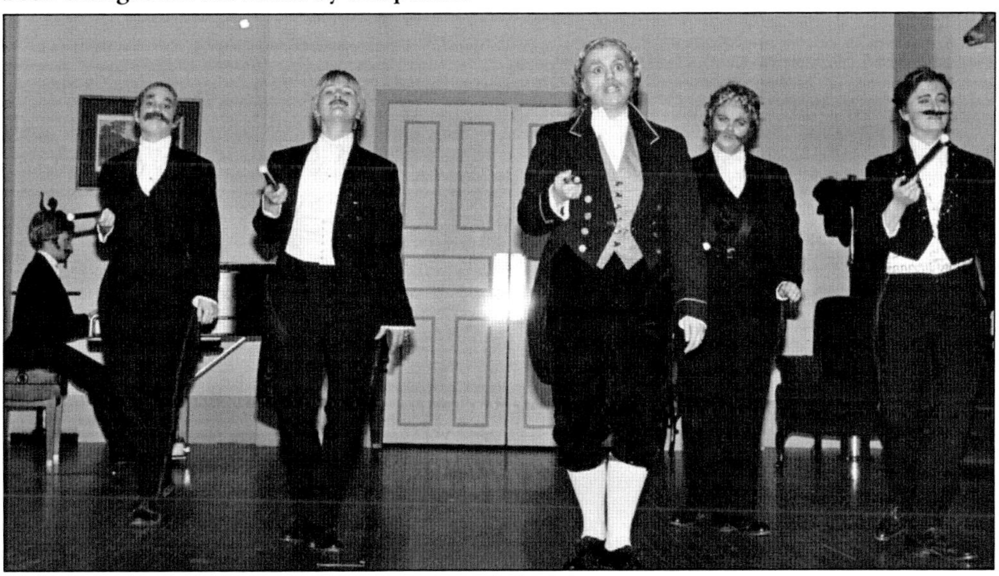

An all-female Hood Theatre cast presented the musical *The Club* in March 1980. Set in an exclusive men's club at the turn of the 20th century, it depicted a group of men having fun while out of the reach of their wives and mothers. *The Blue and Grey* reported, "Crude and chauvinistic remarks ran rampant but were presented by the actors in a manner that was not tasteless."

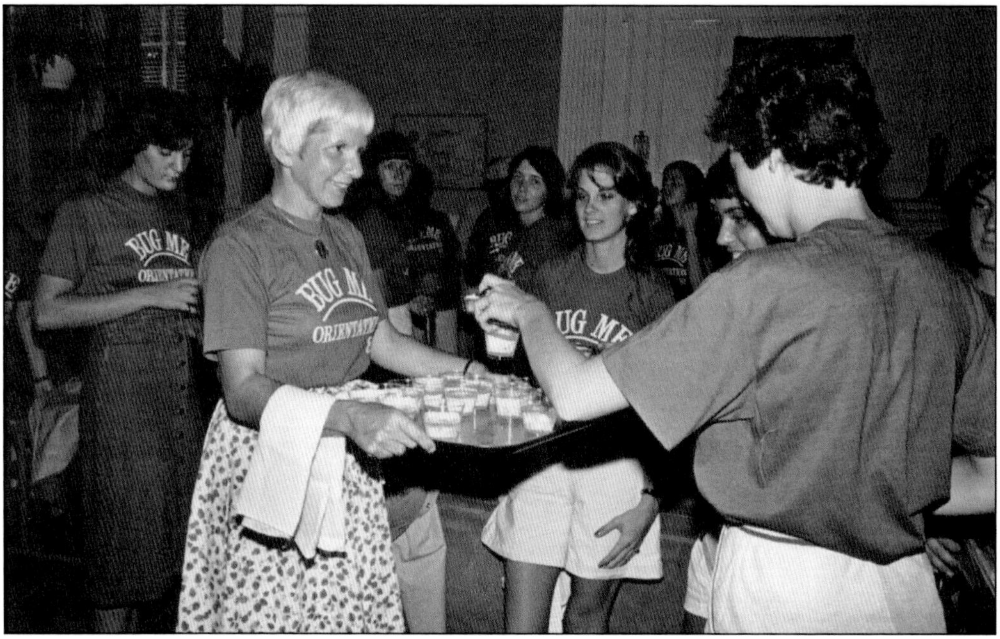

It was traditional for Hood faculty and staff to help students move into the residence halls at the beginning of the school year. President Church, sporting a "Bug Me Crew" T-shirt, offers a refreshment to a student. The Bug Me Crew was so named because the members invited students or parents with questions or problems to "bug" them for assistance and answers; the tradition continues today.

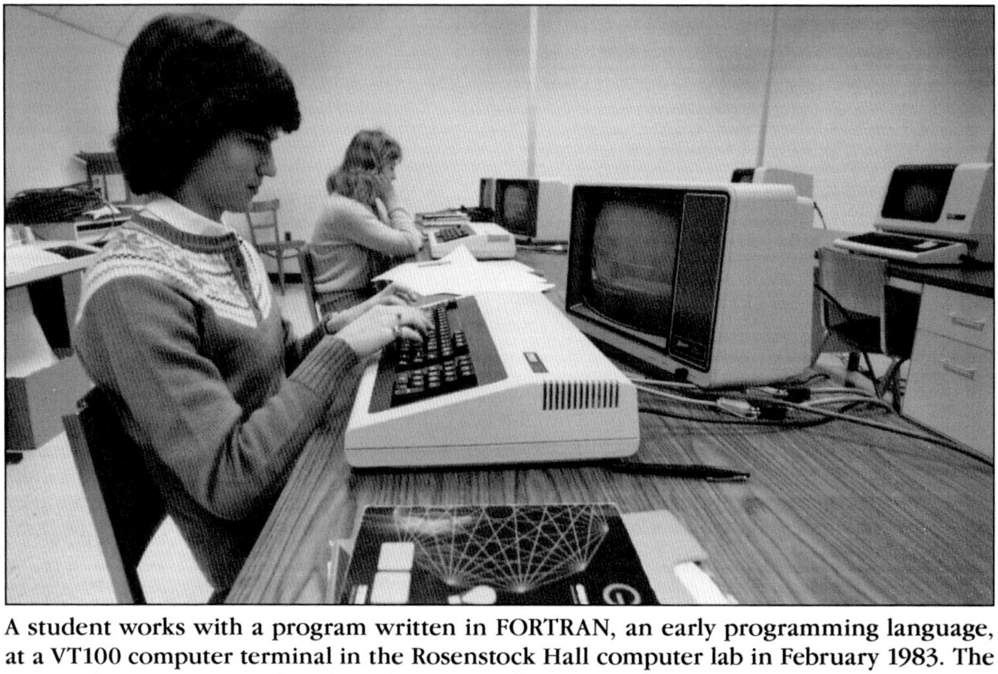

A student works with a program written in FORTRAN, an early programming language, at a VT100 computer terminal in the Rosenstock Hall computer lab in February 1983. The terminals were connected to the college's mainframe computer. In addition to the terminals in this laboratory, there were eight in the Apple Library, as well as at other campus locations. Note that the computer mouse has yet to make its appearance.

In May 1983, the dedication of the Lawrence Marx Jr. Resource Management Center ended a very successful capital campaign. Marx (with boutonniere), a trustee, smiles as Lois Smith Harrison (1945), chair of the board of trustees, makes opening remarks. The innovative facility included greenhouses, solar panels, a computing lab, offices, three student apartments of varying size and design, and the Driscoll Commons, a large reception room.

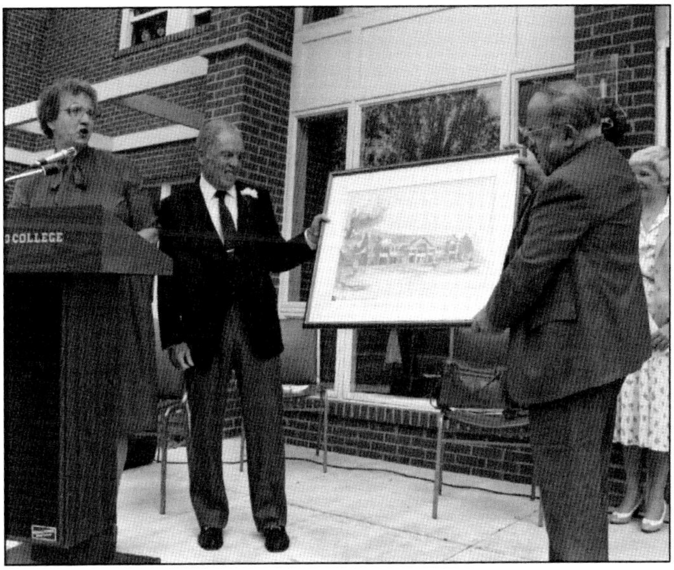

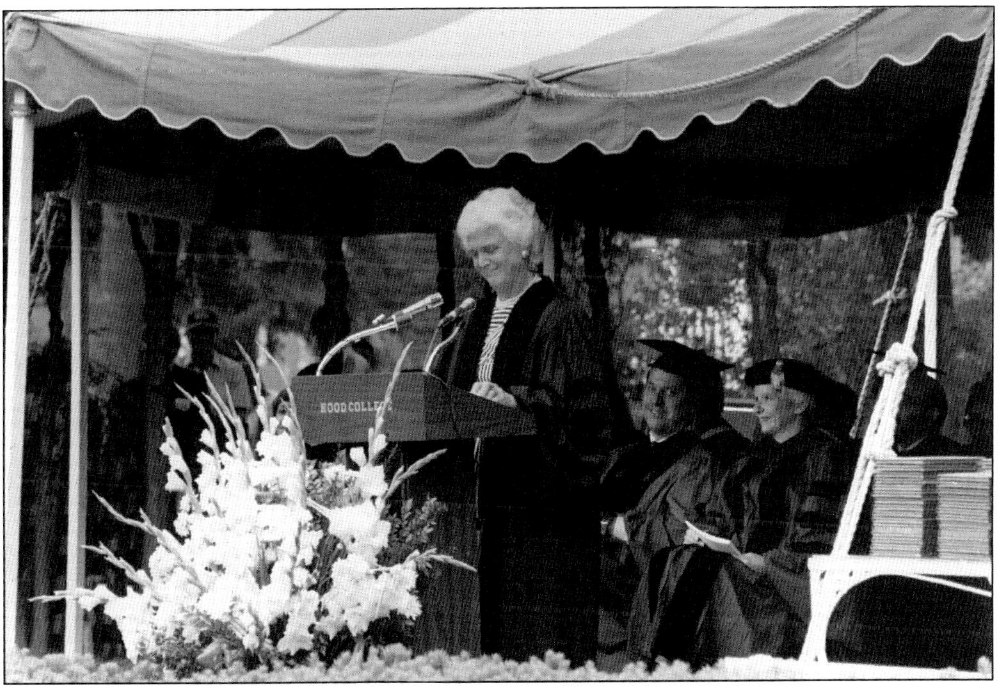

Barbara Pierce Bush was second lady of the United States, and future first lady, when she delivered the address at Hood's 90th commencement in 1983. She was awarded an honorary doctor of humanities at the ceremony in recognition of her volunteer involvement with the Reading is Fundamental program for children's literacy.

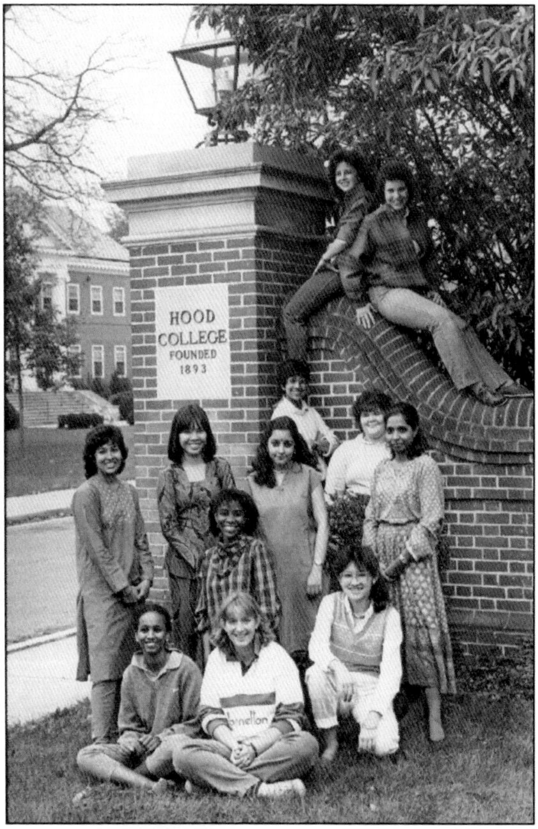

The ability to appreciate cultures other than one's own is a hallmark of an educated person. Hood's ongoing commitment to internationalize the campus was realized for the 1984 academic year when a number of international students arrived on campus. The students pictured here represented 12 countries, including the United States, Somalia, the Netherlands, Vietnam, India, Malaysia, Zambia, Pakistan, Tanzania, West Germany, Bangladesh, and Panama.

Tamara O'Rear Tartaris (1985) visits with her internship supervisor, Dr. Michael Chirigos, at Fort Detrick's National Cancer Research Facility. Hood and Fort Detrick have maintained a symbiotic relationship for a number of years. For example, Hood's master of science in biomedical sciences, the first such degree to be offered in Maryland, was developed jointly by Hood faculty members and scientists from Fort Detrick.

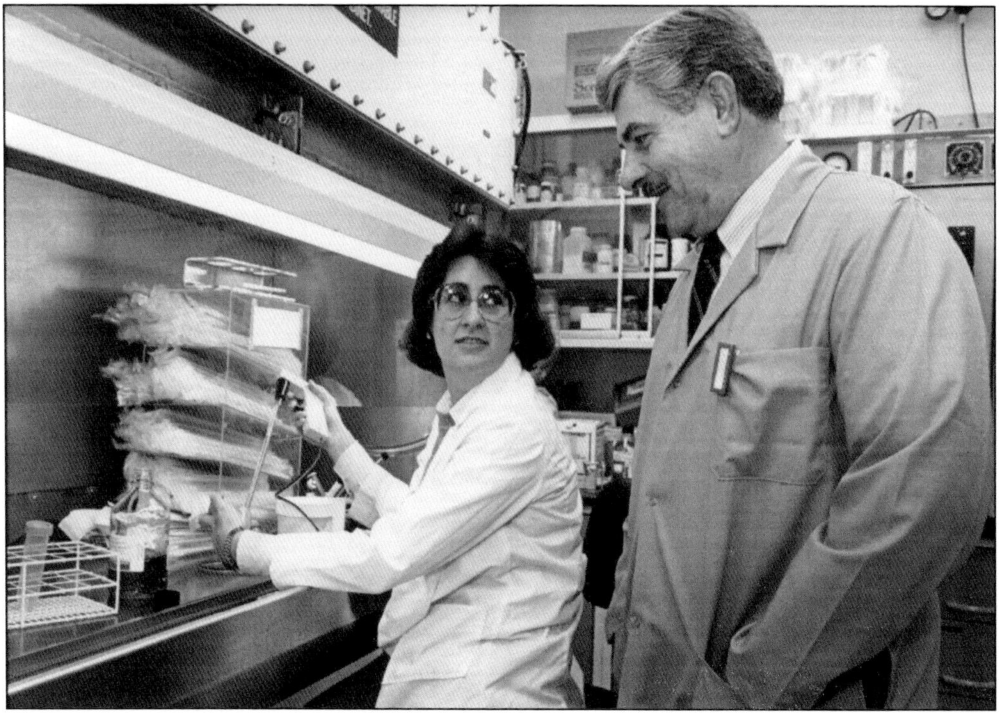

US News and World Report publishes an annual issue rating colleges from across the United States. In 1985, Hood received the number-one ranking among small colleges in the East, and the entire campus turned out to celebrate. Hood has been recognized among the top institutions in every subsequent *US News and World Report* survey.

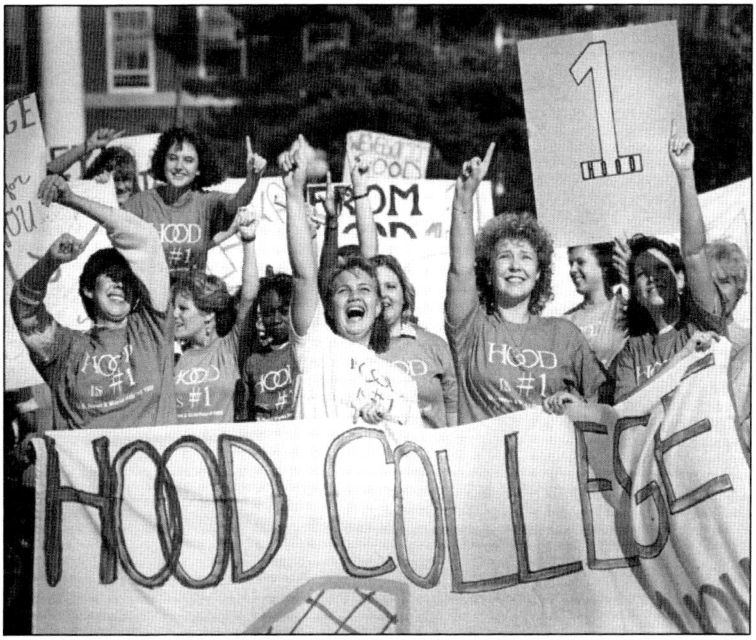

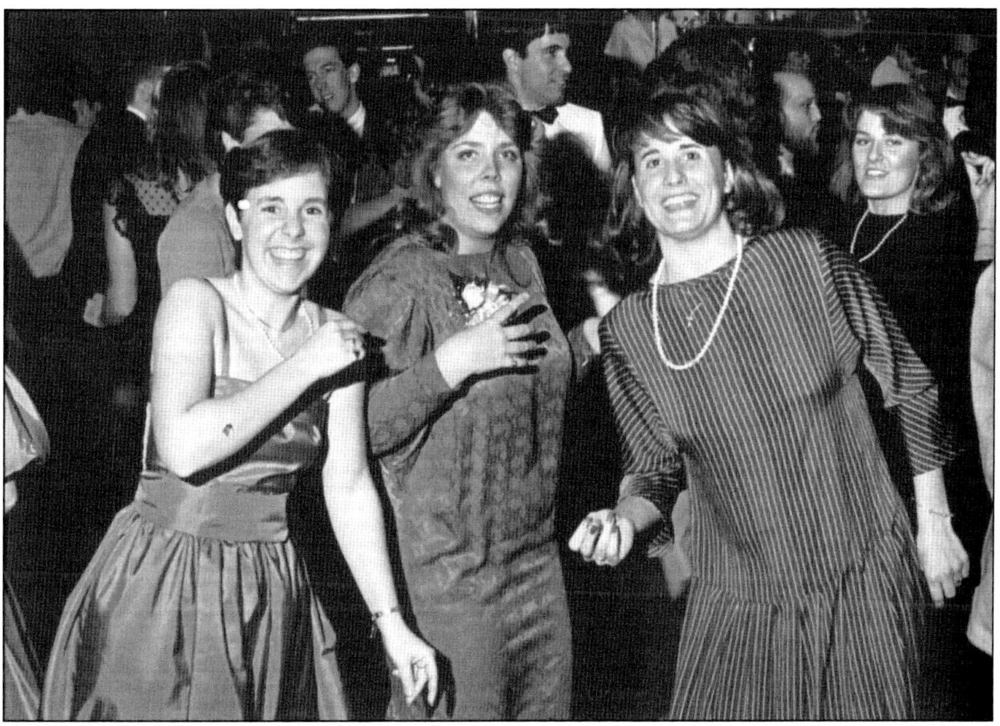

Two juniors show off their new Hood rings at the 1985 Ring Formal Dance. During the ring ceremony, which takes place in the spring of their junior year, students put their Hood rings on for the first time and, presumably, wear them—traditionally on their pinkies—for life. Stories abound of Hood alums visiting all corners of the world and encountering and identifying each other by way of rings.

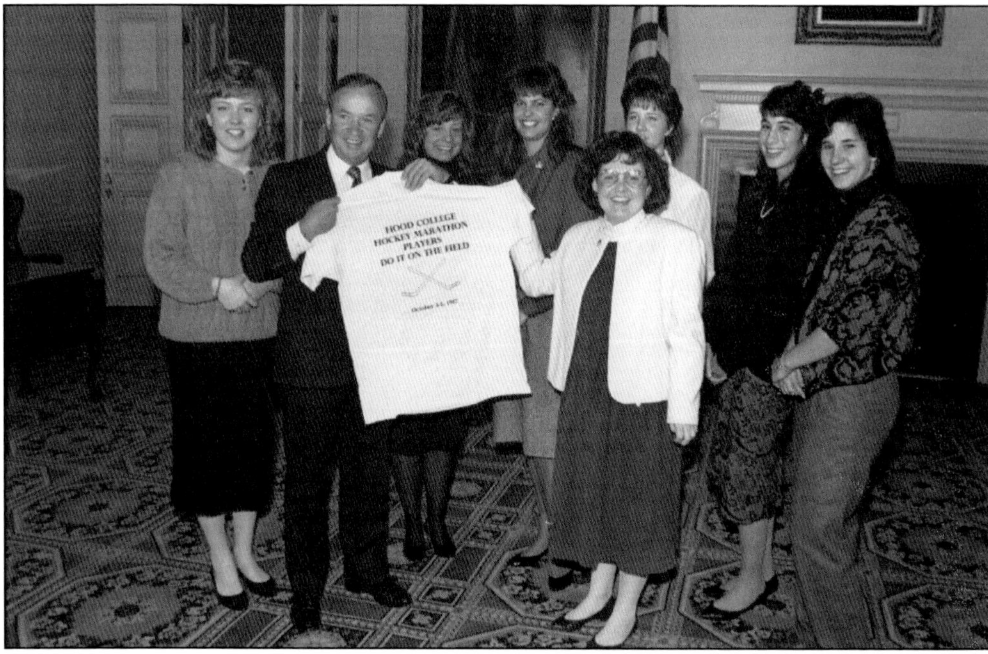

Hood students present a commemorative T-shirt to an official at the Maryland Statehouse after 22 students played 44.5 continuous hours of field hockey, a feat that was recorded in the *Guinness Book of World Records*. Play took place from October 3 to 5 in 1987. The record was broken later by a group of Canadians who played for 122 hours.

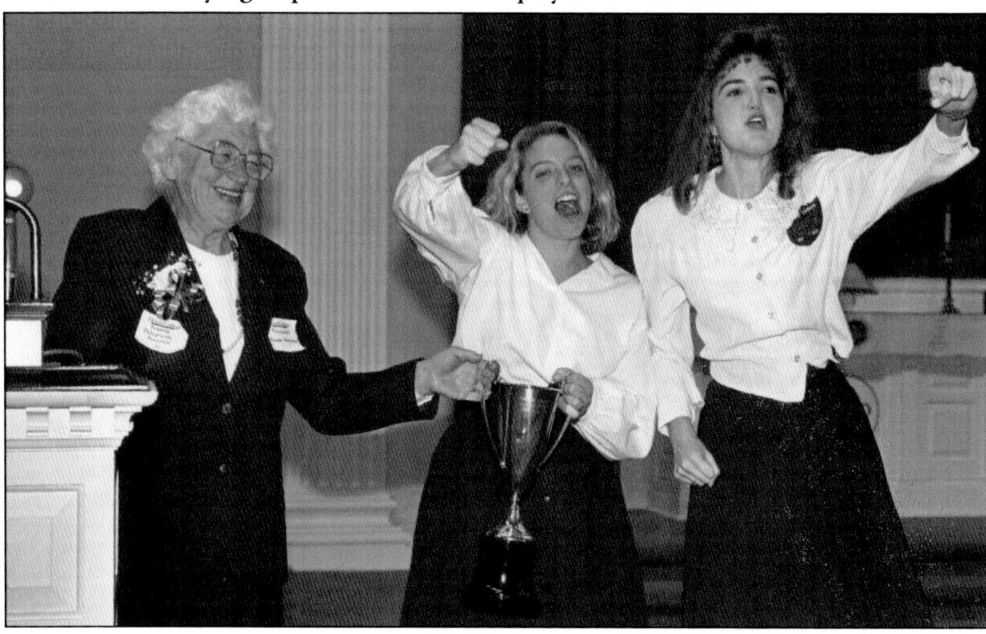

Alumna Frances Delaplaine Randall (1945) awards the Campus Day cup to the class of 1993, the overall winners of the traditional autumn competition. At the time, Randall was president of the alumnae association. She has supported Hood in multiple ways since her graduation, including serving on the board of trustees. In 2006, the college awarded her an honorary doctor of humane letters.

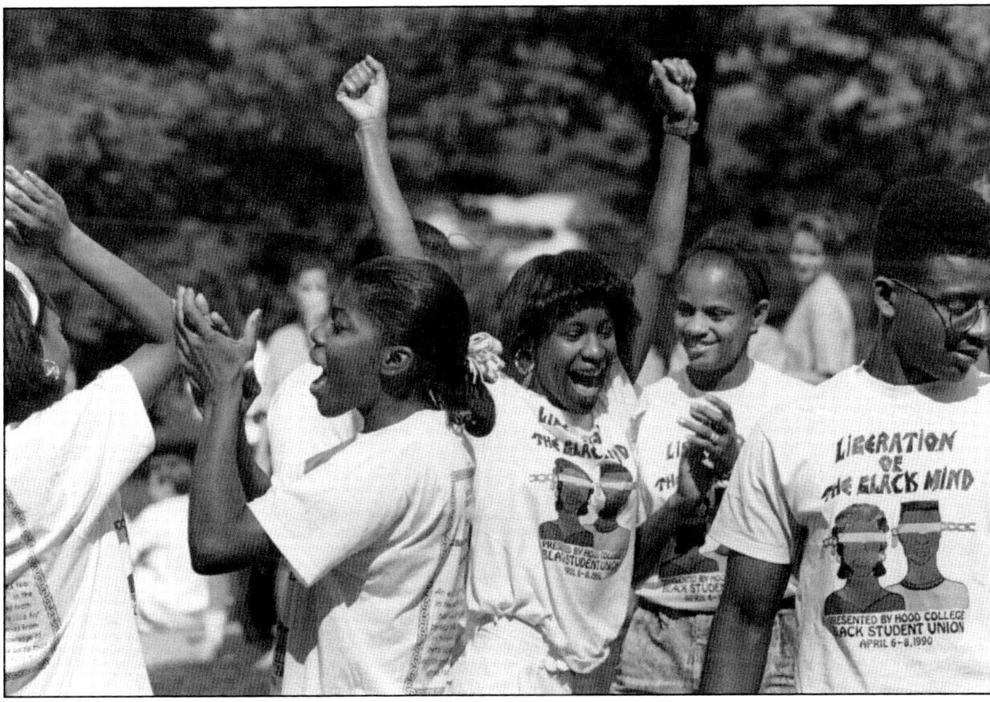

In 1994, The Hood College Black Student Union (BSU) sponsored the first conference known as the Liberation of the Black Mind, which has since become an annual event. Its purpose is to bring students and community members together, regardless of color or ethnicity, to explore topics of interest to the black community. The BSU promotes awareness of the culture and history of African Americans to the campus community as a whole.

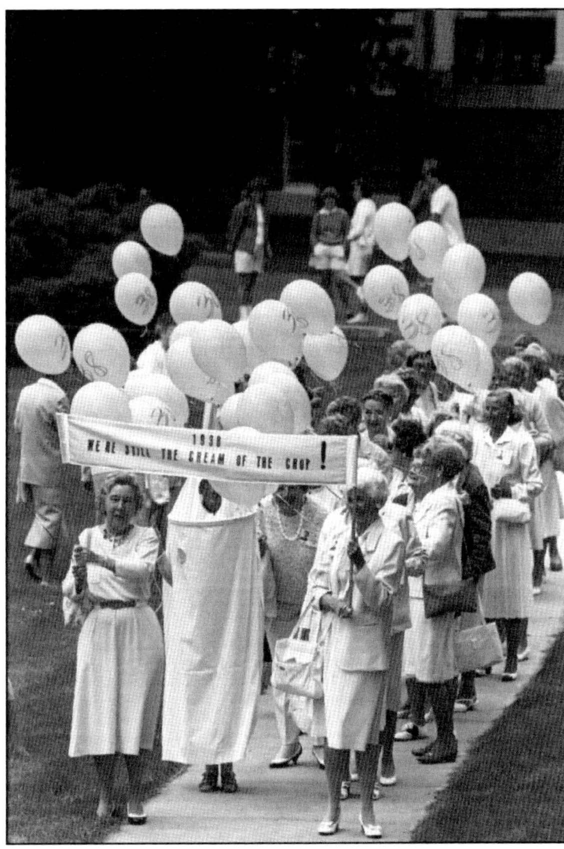

Alumnae from the class of 1938 are "still the cream of the crop" at 1988's Reunion Weekend. Carrying the banner are Doris Hannan (left) and Mary Rockwell Hovet; Janet Rath Childs is wearing the milk bottle costume. Forty-five of the eighty-five women who graduated from Hood in 1938 were in attendance at this—their 50th—class reunion.

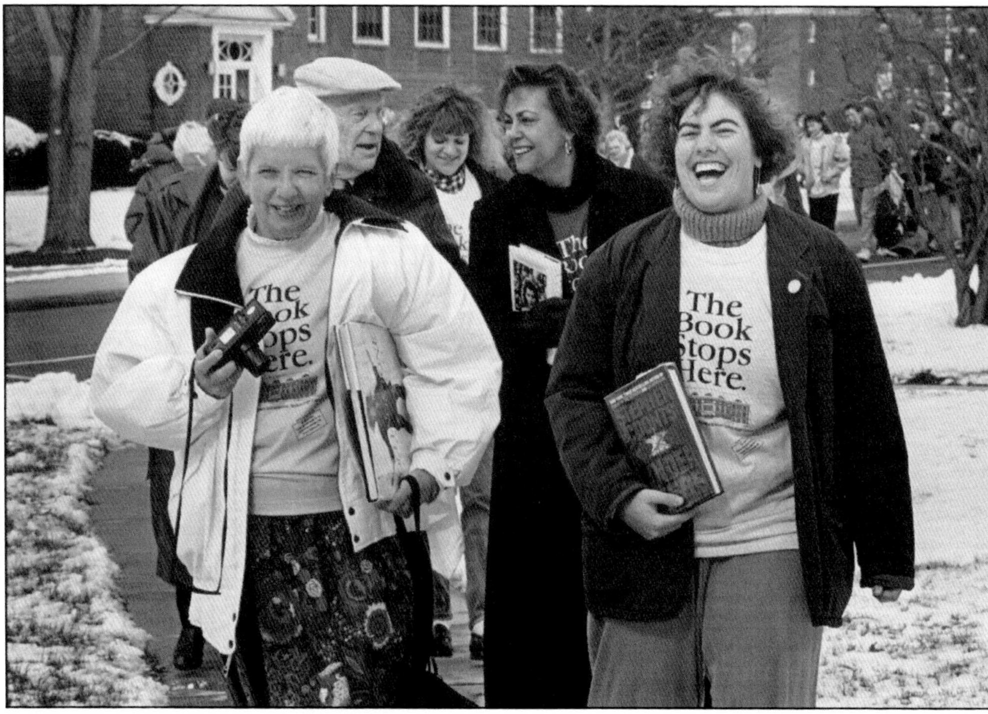

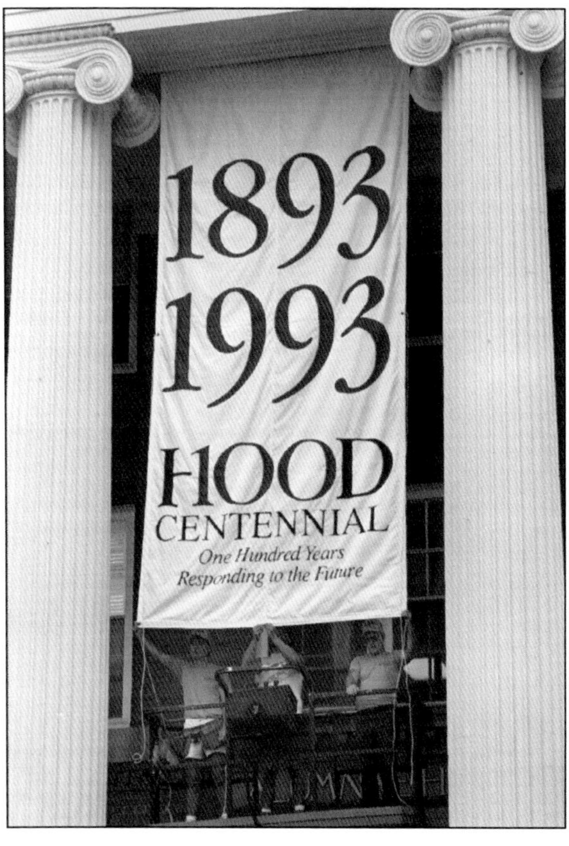

Book-mover-in-chief Martha Church (left) leads the procession of Hood faculty, staff, students, and alumni as they carry books from the Joseph Henry Apple Library to the newly completed Beneficial-Hodson Library and Information Technology Center. The 1992 T-shirt reading, "The Book Stops Here," might, in some ways, have been prophetic, as today more and more of the resources in the new library are electronic.

A colorful banner suspended from the pediment of Alumnae Hall says it all. Hood College celebrated its centennial through lectures, seminars, art exhibits, concerts, fireworks, and regional gatherings. Hood awarded its 10,000th bachelor's degree, and the graduate school awarded its 2,000th master's degree during the 1993 commencement ceremony held in a large tent on the residential quadrangle. Tuition for the 1993–1994 school year was $13,108.

The dedication of the Catherine Filene Shouse Career Center was one of a host of 1993 centennial activities. The career center provides, among other things, job search information, workshops on resume writing and interviewing, and career counseling. From left to right are student Gauri Sud (1994), Pres. Martha Church, Catherine Filene Shouse, Lois Smith Harrison (1945), and director of placement Carolyn Reynolds.

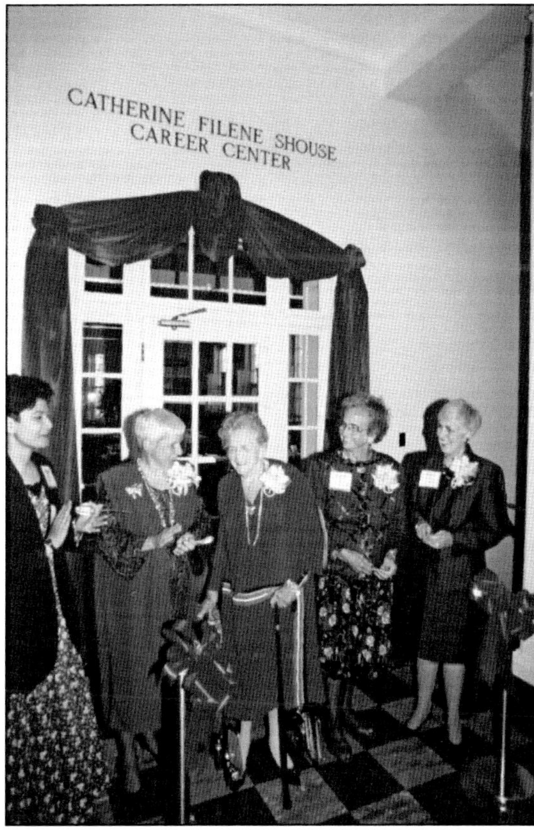

Another of the centennial activities was the preparation and sealing of a "Mailbox to the Future," a time capsule to be opened on the sesquicentennial in 2043. Members of 1993's Hood community wrote and inserted messages for the Hood community of the future. The mailbox is now padlocked and kept in the college archives. Does anyone have the combination?

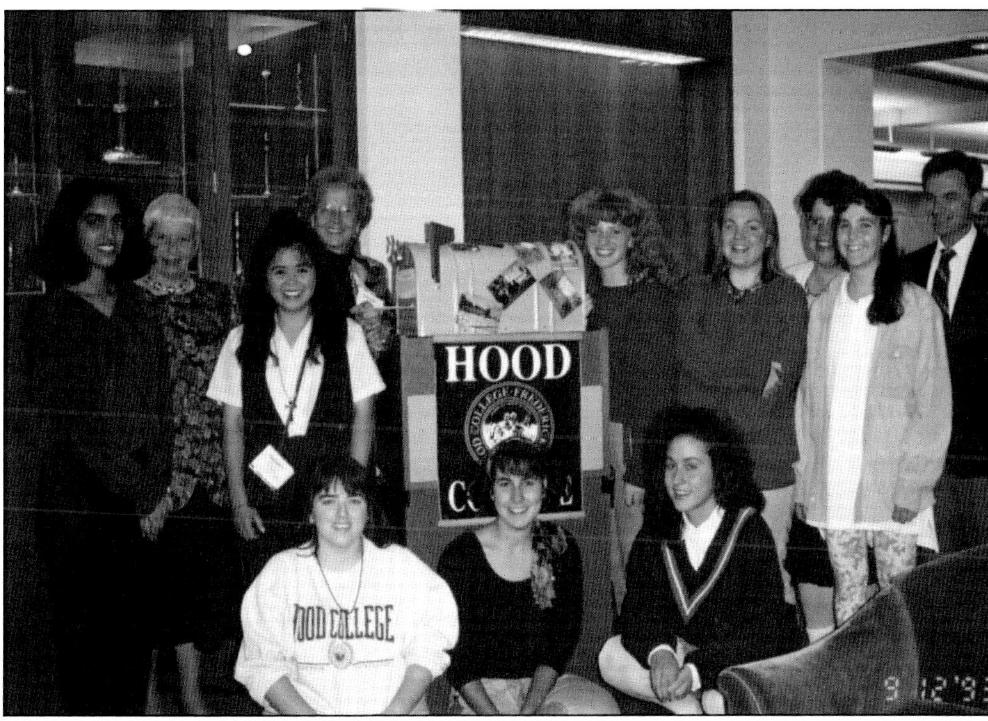

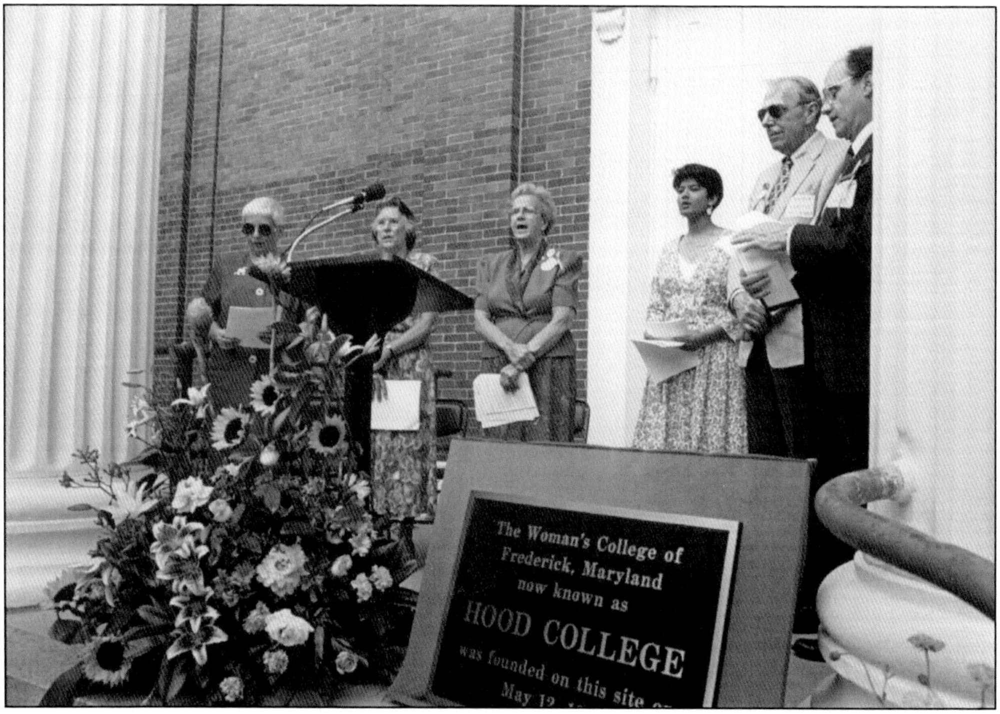

Founders Day, May 12, 1993, was the official "centennial day," marking 100 years since the Reformed Church fathers agreed to establish a women's college below the Mason-Dixon Line. In this photograph, President Church (left) and other representatives of the college dedicate a plaque memorializing the occasion. The plaque can be seen today in front of the Evangelical Reformed United Church of Christ in downtown Frederick.

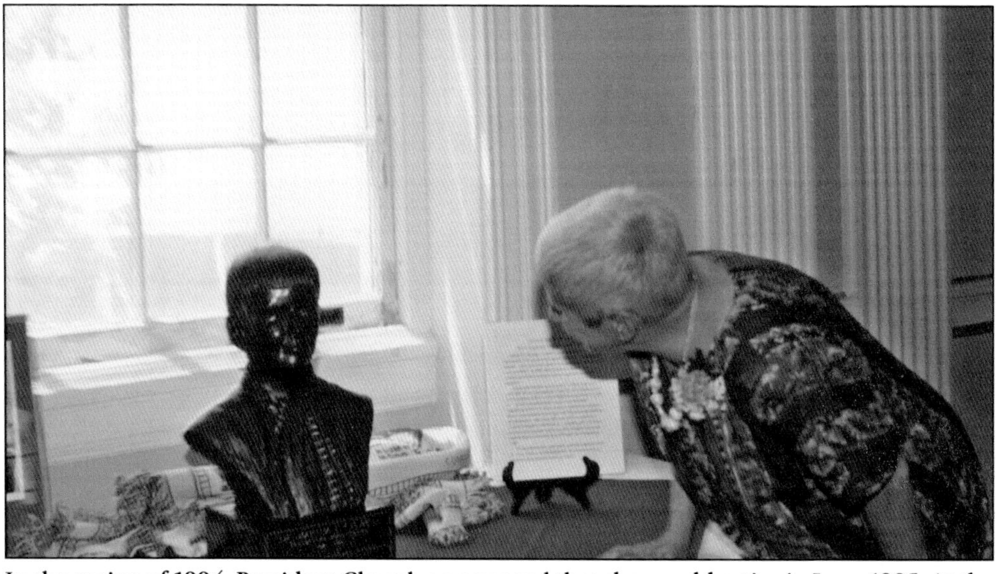

In the spring of 1994, President Church announced that she would retire in June 1995. At the staff luncheon held just before her retirement, Dr. Church inspects a newly unveiled bronze bust sculpted to honor her 20 years as Hood's president. The likeness is now on view in the lobby of the Beneficial-Hodson Library.

Nine

Our Future
Into the 21st Century, 1995–2012

Pres. Shirley Peterson led the institution from 1995 to 2000. The college had begun to reap the benefits of computer technology, which revolutionized the way Hood met the needs of its community. Fifty-four million dollars had been raised during the Second Century campaign. The Whitaker Campus Center was erected in 1997, and that year the 50th annual performance of *Messiah* was celebrated in Coffman Chapel. In 1999, the Hood College Choir appeared in concert at Lincoln Center in New York City to mark its 100th anniversary.

Upon President Peterson's resignation in 2000, Dr. Robert Funk became interim president. With the inauguration of Dr. Ronald Volpe in 2001, Hood entered the new millennium on the verge of a historical transition to coeducation. Partially in response to declining enrollment, in 2002 the board of trustees voted to admit male residential students for the next academic year and affirmed its commitment to the core mission of educating both women and men. That same year, the new Hodson Science and Technology Center was dedicated.

In 2007, the college completed a comprehensive self-study and was fully reaccredited by the Middle States Commission on Higher Education. By then, the total number of undergraduate and graduate students enrolled had reached its highest level in the history of the college. Also, in 2007, the Hood College History Museum and Archives opened in the library.

In 2009, the college dedicated an outdoor artificial turf playing field and the Nicodemus Athletic Complex. A bachelor's degree completion program in nursing was approved in 2010. The Hood College Athletic Center was dedicated in November 2011, and a year later new tennis courts, a new Huntsinger Aquatic Center, and an improved outdoor pool were ready for the Hood community to enjoy.

The college enjoys a strong "town-gown" relationship with the Frederick community. An energized faculty oversees a challenging curriculum. Alumni financial support is growing, and both undergraduate and graduate enrollment is at an all-time high. By all accounts, Hood College is thriving under the dynamic leadership of Dr. Volpe and is poised for even greater things.

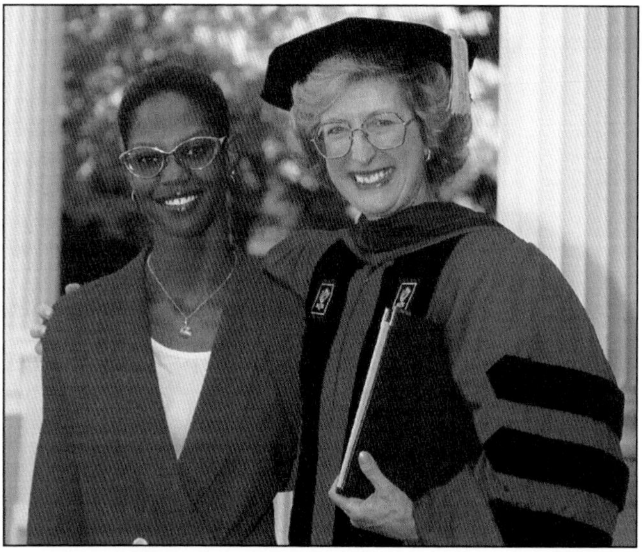

Shirley Peterson brought a unique set of experiences to Hood's presidency. She was a tax attorney and had managed one of the largest agencies in the federal government, as well as serving on numerous corporate boards. A Bryn Mawr undergraduate, she was committed to same-sex women's education. She is pictured here at her inauguration in September 1995 with student Deborah LaBoo (1996), president of the Hood College Student Government Association.

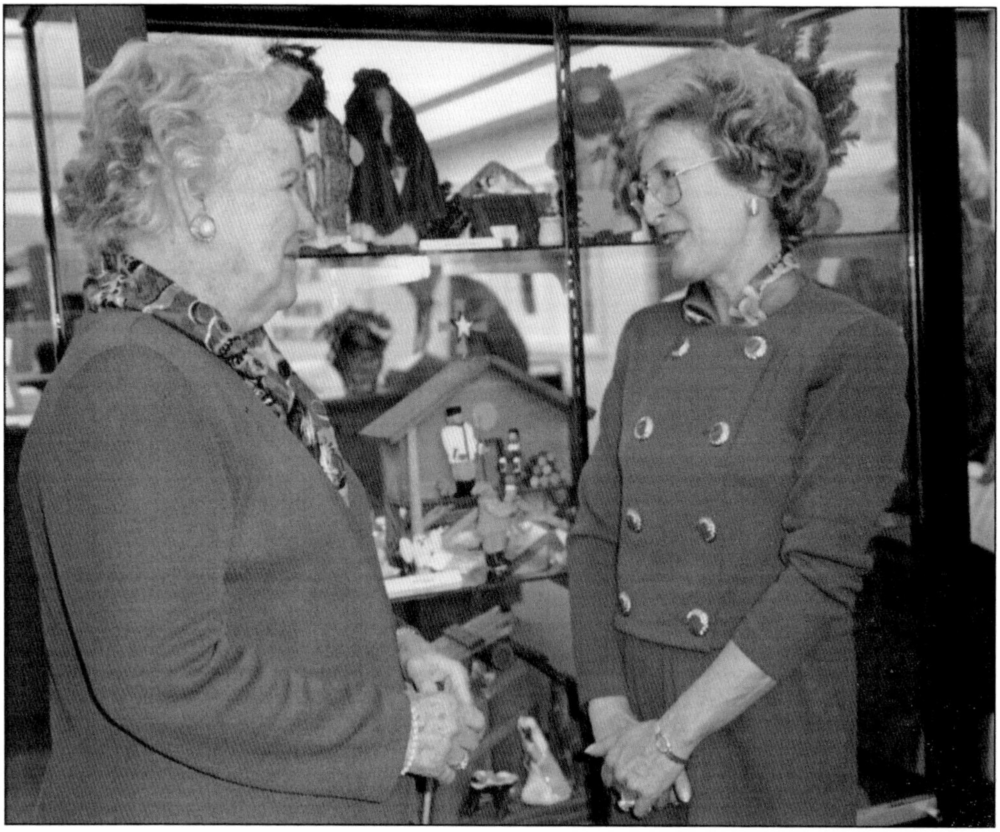

President Peterson (right) talks with Beulah Munshower Sommer (1944) about her collection of crèches on display in the Beneficial-Hodson Library. The crèches were part of a larger collection, numbering some 500 sets that Sommer gathered over many years of living abroad with her husband, who was in the US Foreign Service. The library has continued the holiday tradition and mounts an annual display of the nativity scenes.

The Whitaker Campus Center was dedicated in 1997. It was named to honor the Whitaker Foundation and recognize the Whitaker family, made up of the late Uncas and Helen Whitaker of Chambersburg, Pennsylvania, and their daughters Ruth Whitaker Holmes (1955) and Portia Whitaker Shumaker (1955). A campus gathering place, it houses the Whitaker Commons, the Blazer Express snack bar, the post office, and the bookstore, among other things.

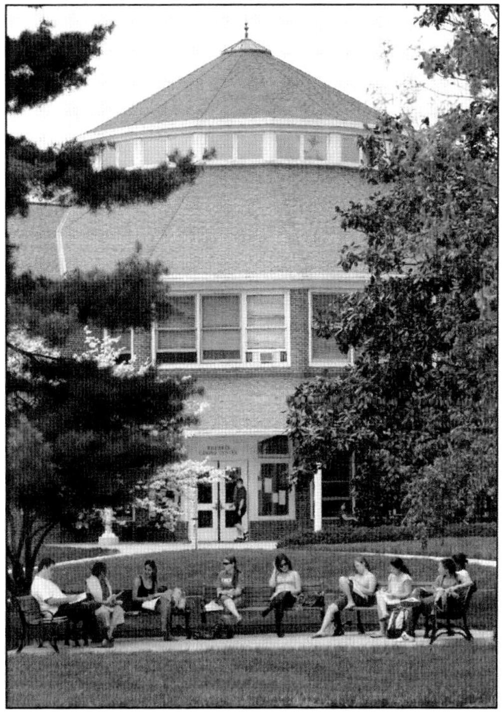

The dramatic three-story interior of the Whitaker Campus Center provides a great display space for the growing collection of class banners, a tradition begun in the early 1980s. Each freshman class creates a banner in its class color. It is divided into four quadrants, and each year the class is at Hood a design is added to one of the quadrants, completing the banner for the students' senior year.

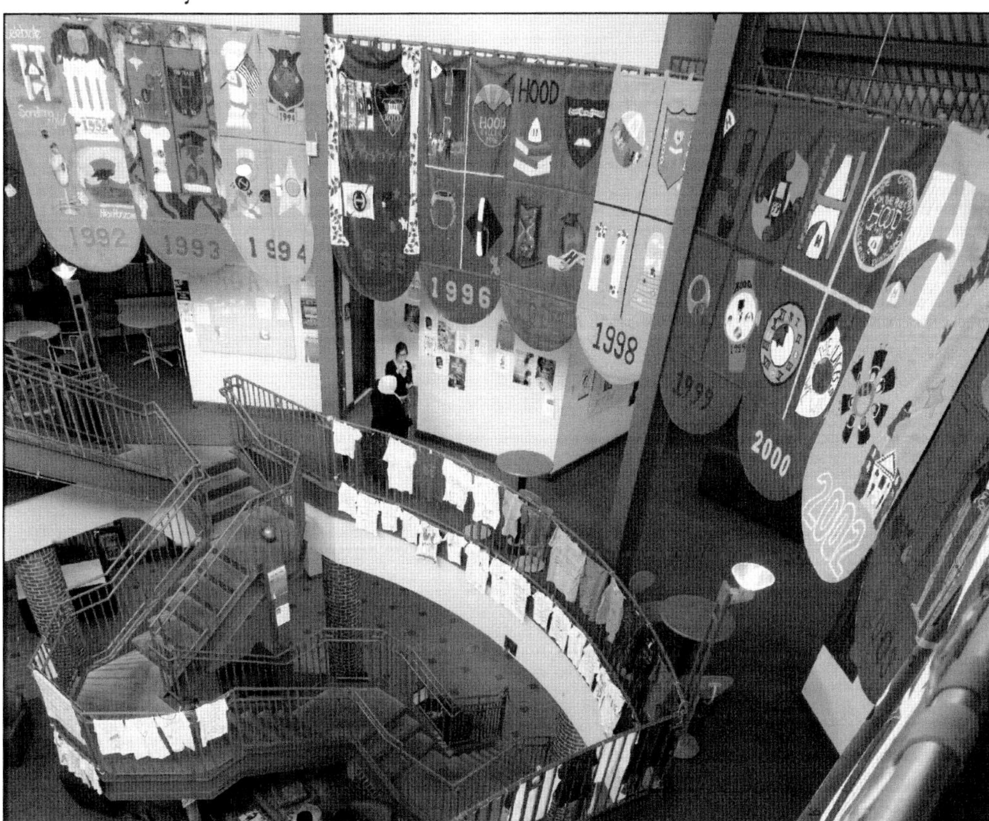

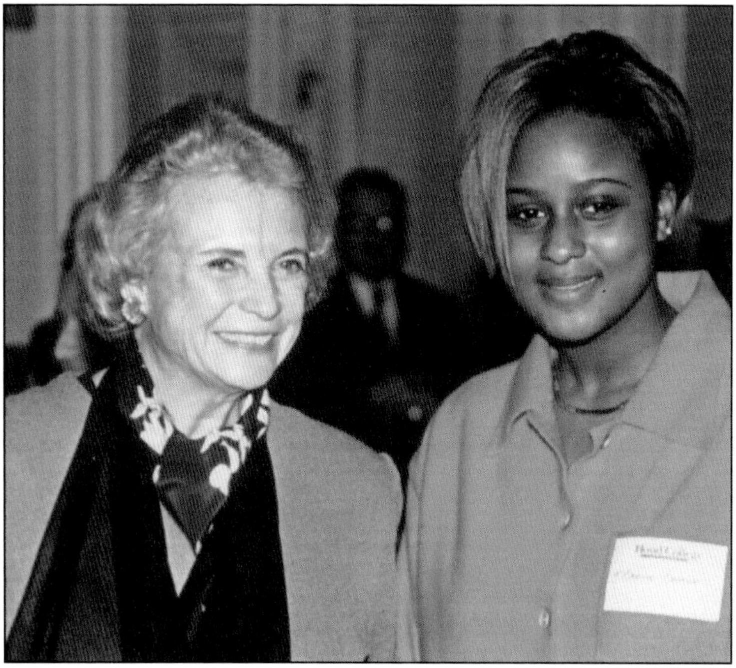

Supreme Court Justice Sandra Day O'Connor, the first woman appointed to the high court, was welcomed in March 1996 as part of Hood's yearlong colloquium exploring the topic of justice. O'Connor spoke of her efforts to establish a working justice system in war-torn Bosnia, and she stated that she was "in awe of the Bill of Rights." She is pictured here with student Marnie Cromwell (1997).

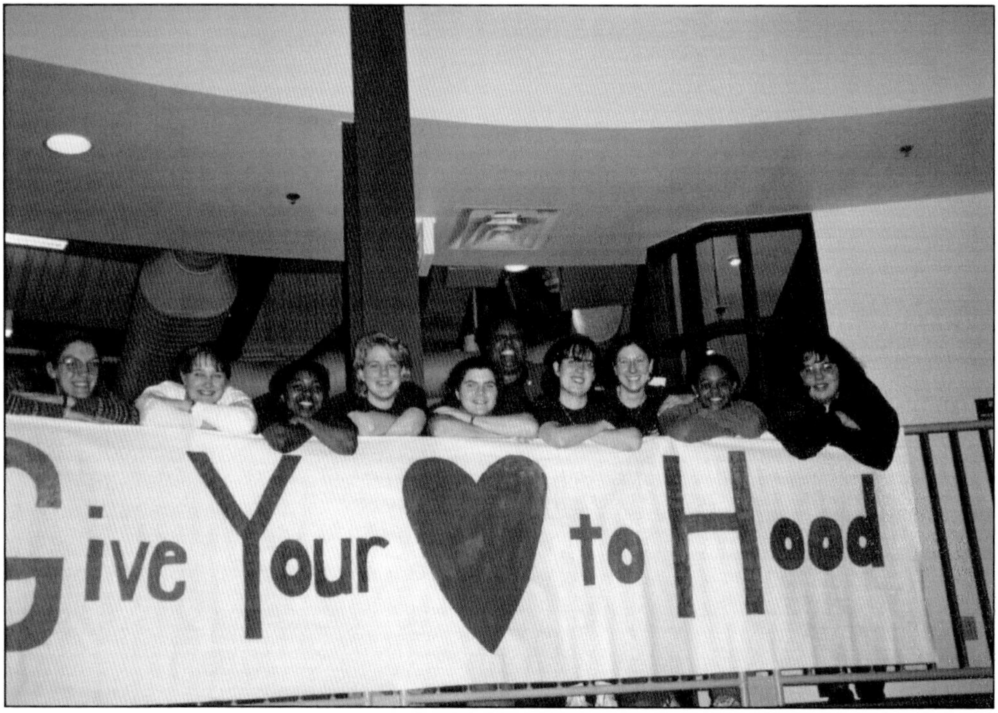

"Give Your Heart to Hood Day" began in 1998 as an opportunity for the entire Hood community to exemplify the college's motto, *Corde et Mente et Manu* (Heart and Mind and Hand), by offering a day of volunteering to the college. Classes were canceled, and students picked up paintbrushes alongside faculty and staff who also were lending their hands—and their hearts—to help make Hood a better place.

Two students work with Profs. Eric Annis (left) and Eric Kindahl as part of their fieldwork for a Summer Science Institute research project. Students collaborate directly with faculty for eight weeks in this highly sought-after summer program that began in 1997. Some of the projects have involved studying the ecology of chestnut trees, investigating the causes of cancer, and studying sea anemones as indicators of coral reef health.

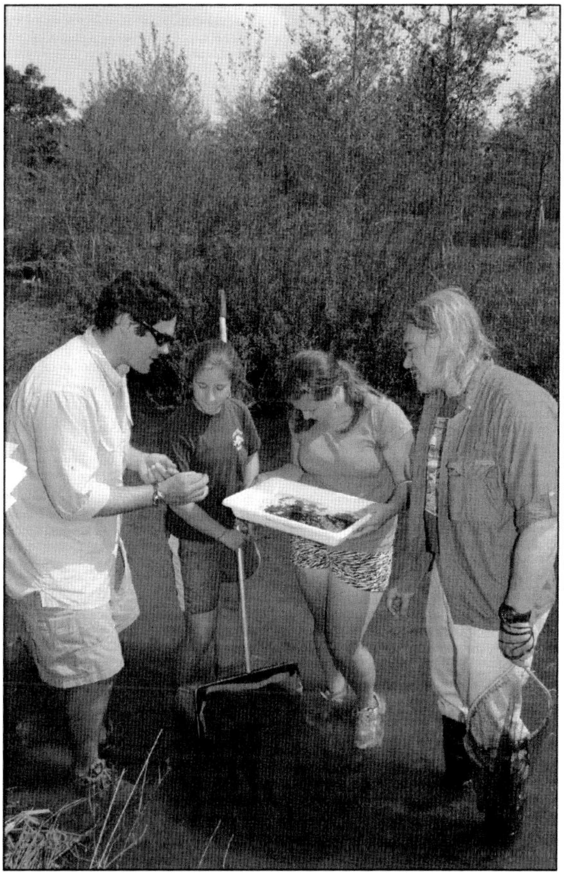

Midnight Breakfast is Hood's way of fortifying students for final exams, as well as wishing them good luck. Faculty and staff serve a hearty breakfast to students on the eve of finals. In this c. 1998 photograph, Dr. Oney Smith of the biology department hands a heaping plate to a hungry student who is taking a study break.

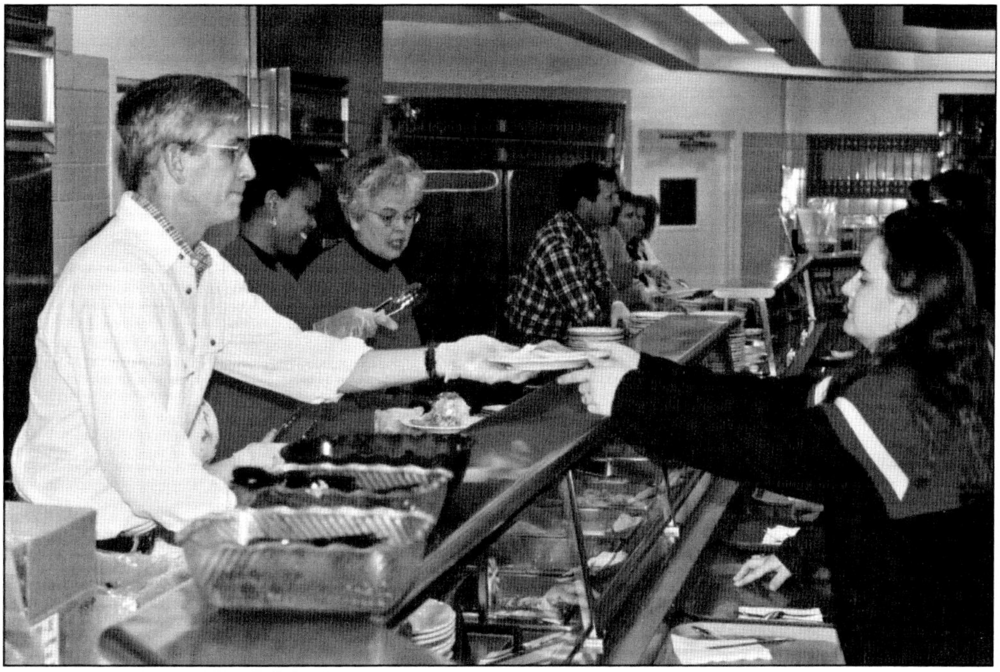

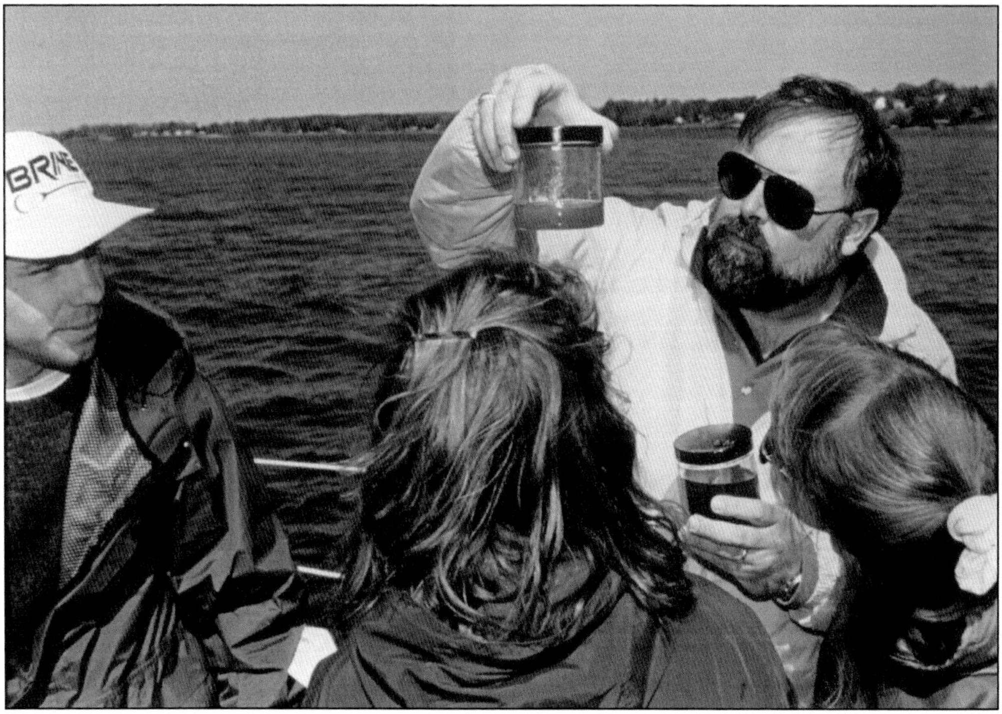

Hood's Coastal Studies Semester is a cross-disciplinary program based in the biology department but open to all students. Faculty and students travel for about a month to field laboratories along the East Coast, exploring unique coastal environments from a variety of perspectives. In this mid-1990s image, Prof. Drew Ferrier helps some coastal studies students observe aquatic life.

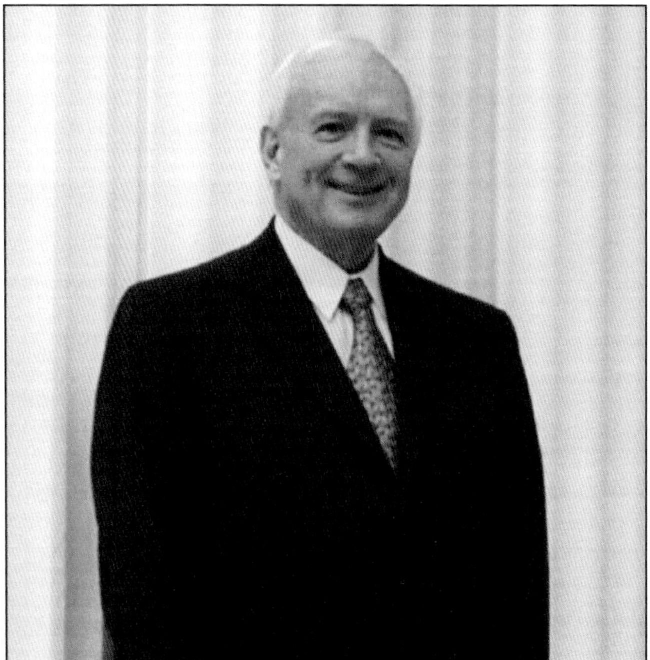

Shirley Peterson resigned as president of the college in 2000, and Dr. Robert Funk was appointed interim president. Dr. Funk, a man of rare and dry wit, guided the college as it transitioned into a new presidency. When Dr. Ronald Volpe assumed the presidency in 2001, Dr. Funk was named vice president for academic affairs and provost, remaining in that position until 2010.

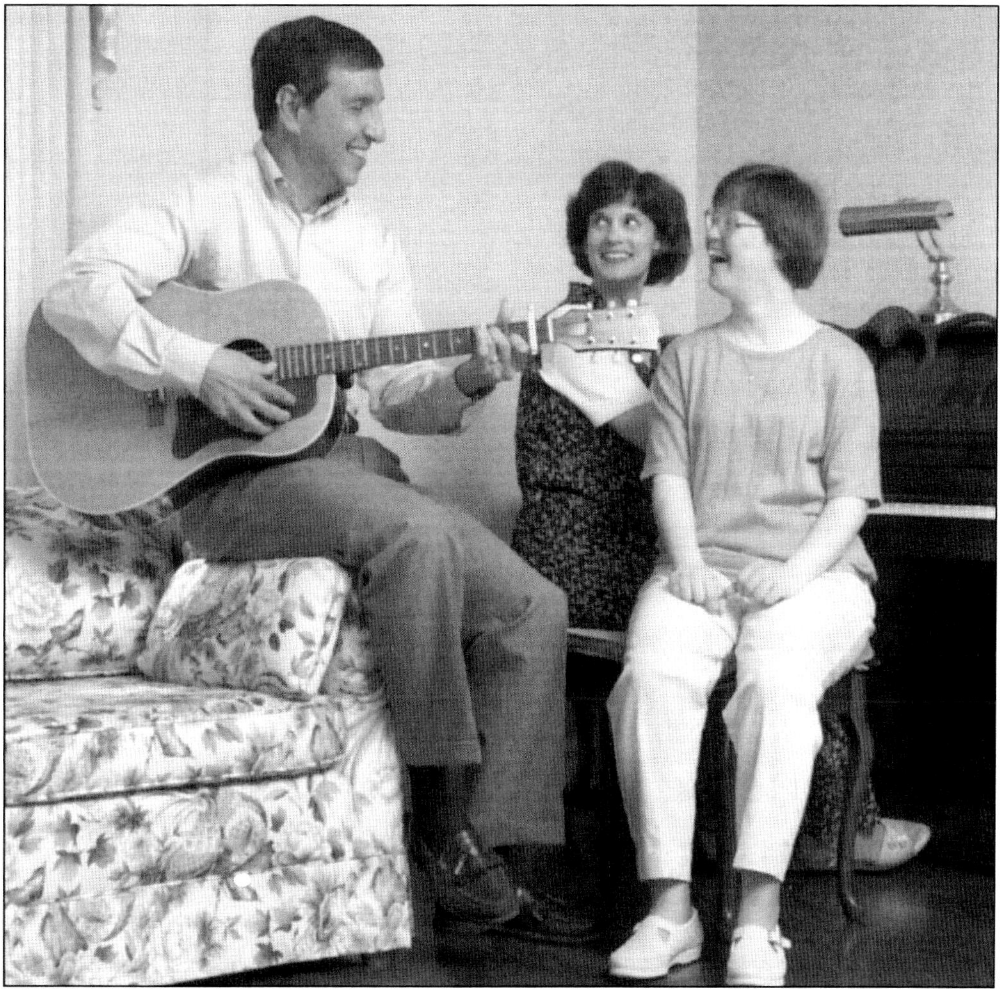

Dr. Volpe, with wife Lin and their daughter Stephanie, settled into life at Hood. The new president brought a background in business, management, and economics at a time when enrollment was down and Hood was in need of an innovative vision for the future. A tireless cheerleader for the college, he attends as many campus events as possible while finding time to visit alumni across the nation. His wife and daughter are energetic Hood supporters as well, taking the time to be involved in various campus activities and events, getting to know students, faculty, and staff, and exemplifying family life for students who are living away from their families.

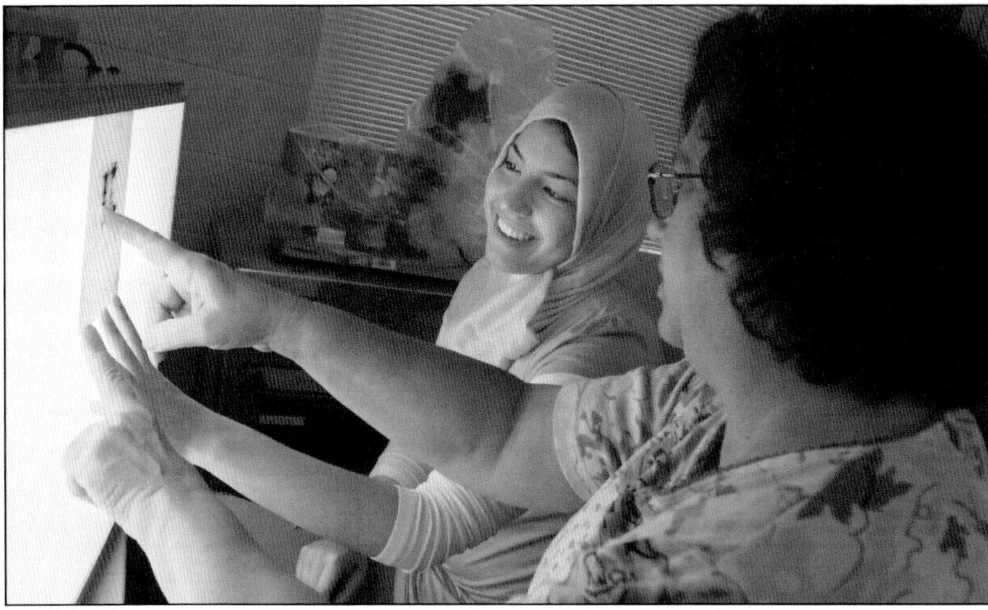

An anonymous alumna of Hood College provided funds in 2001 to initiate the Summer Research Institute, enabling students to work one on one with faculty in a summer-long collaborative research project. The institute is now funded by the Hodson Trust. Projects can encompass a wide variety of disciplines. Here, Dr. Ricky Hirschhorn, professor of biology, works with a student in the laboratory.

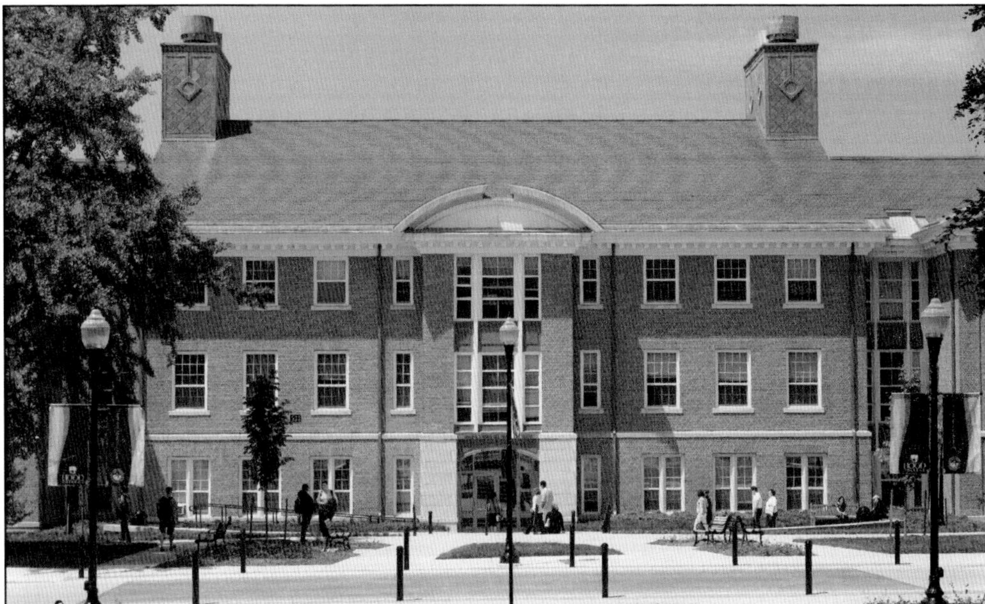

Another structure that had been feeling its age was the Hodson Science Building. After an expansion of the building that more than doubled its size, the new Hodson Science and Technology Center was dedicated in October 2002. Dr. Rita Colwell, director of the National Science Foundation, was the keynote speaker at the dedication, presenting an address entitled "Bridging the Cultures: Celebrating Science and the Liberal Arts."

In the fall of 2002, the board of trustees approved admitting men as residential students, beginning in 2003. Hood became a college in transition, a transition that had been carefully planned and that went smoothly. Eighty male students, nearly half of whom were freshmen, and most of whom moved into the dormitories, enrolled in 2003. Applications from women increased substantially, and enrollment began to grow again.

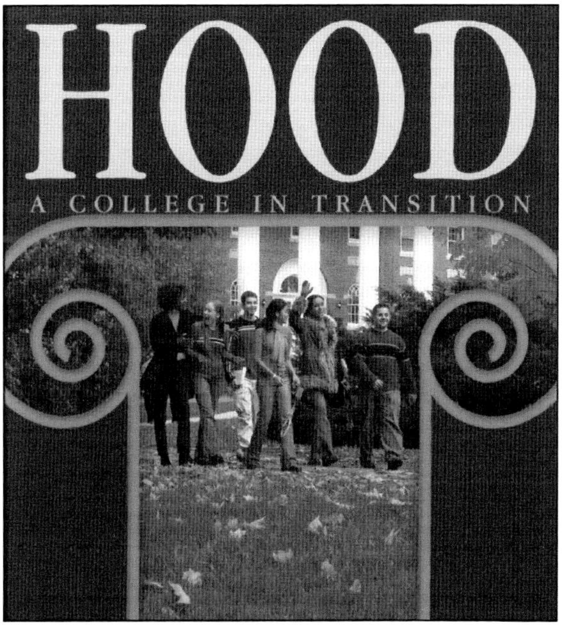

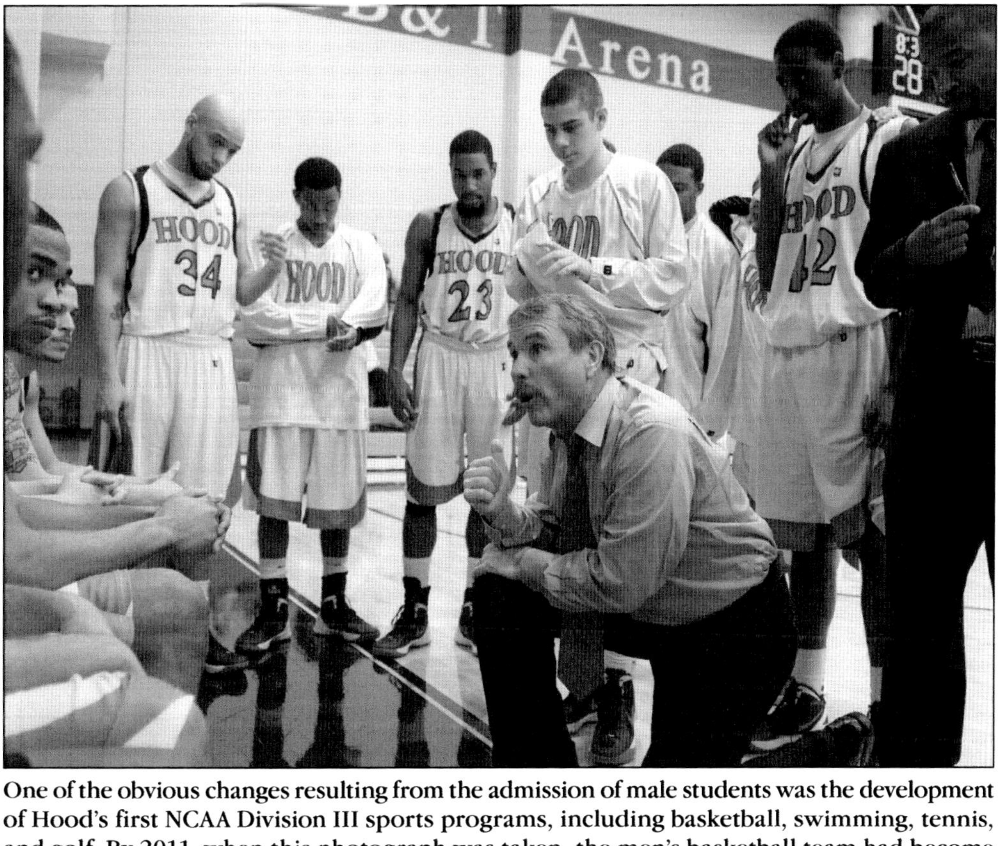

One of the obvious changes resulting from the admission of male students was the development of Hood's first NCAA Division III sports programs, including basketball, swimming, tennis, and golf. By 2011, when this photograph was taken, the men's basketball team had become an accepted part of campus life, and Tom Dickman (center), Hood's first men's basketball coach, had entered his ninth year at the college.

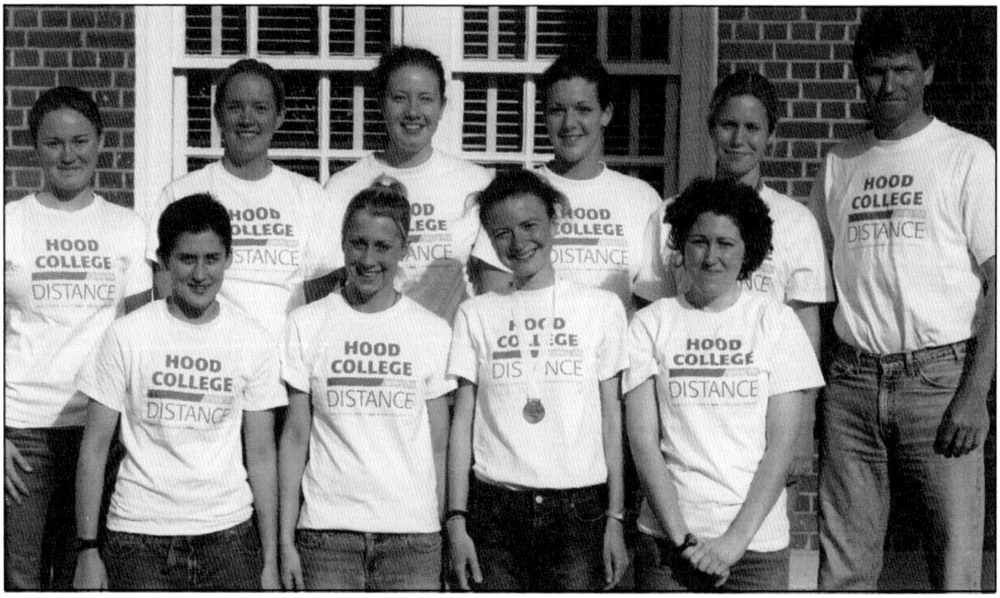

The arrival of male students not only meant there would be men's sports, but also that there would be changes to women's sports. Today both genders have a chance to participate in basketball, cross country, lacrosse, soccer, swimming, tennis, and track teams, while men have a golf team and women field hockey, volleyball, and softball teams. The women's cross country team poses with coach Brent Ayer at their first-ever meet in 2004.

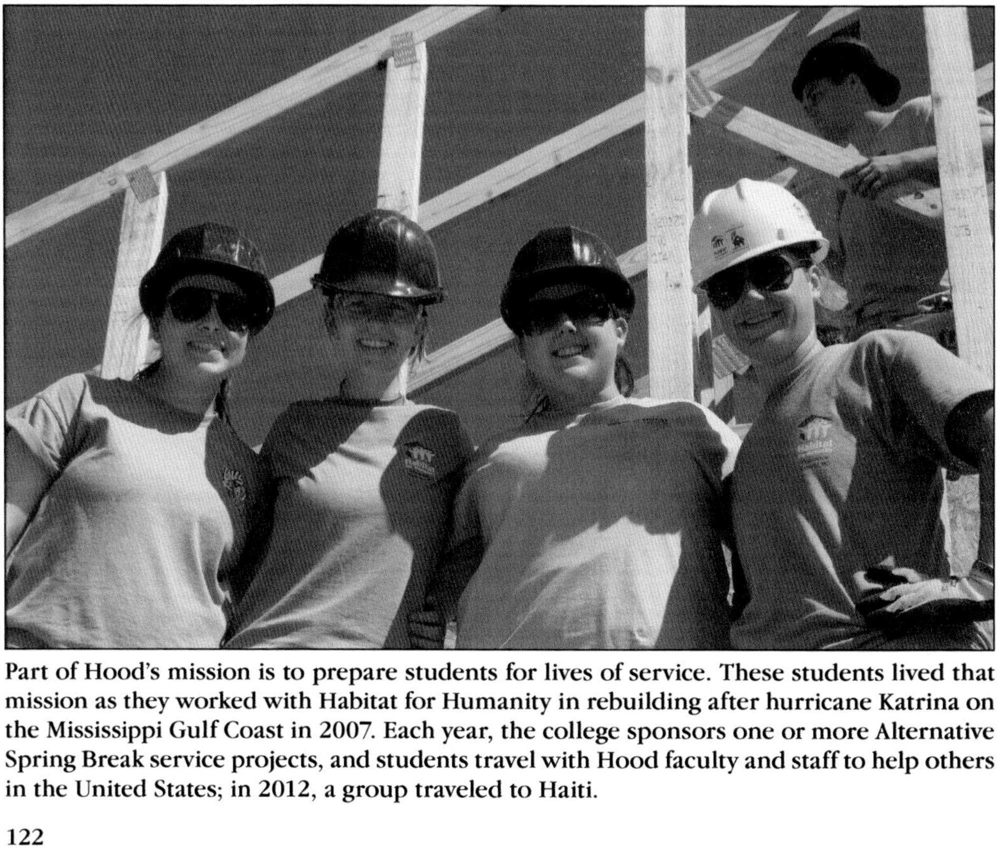

Part of Hood's mission is to prepare students for lives of service. These students lived that mission as they worked with Habitat for Humanity in rebuilding after hurricane Katrina on the Mississippi Gulf Coast in 2007. Each year, the college sponsors one or more Alternative Spring Break service projects, and students travel with Hood faculty and staff to help others in the United States; in 2012, a group traveled to Haiti.

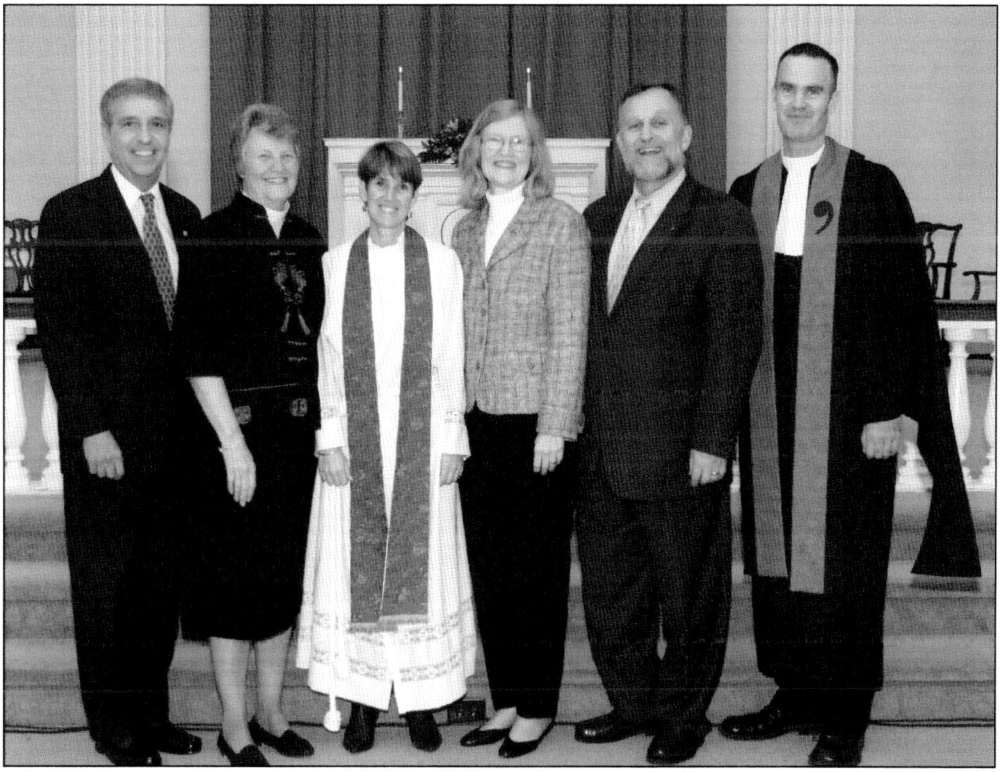

Rev. Beth O'Malley (third from left) was invested as the McHenry Dean of the Chapel in 2008. Emerita Hood trustee and alumna Dr. Christine L. McHenry (1973, third from right) endowed the position in memory of her parents, Thomas McHenry III, M.D., and Gloria Schmitt McHenry (19[illegible]2). With them are, from left to right, President Volpe, the Reverend Dr. Ann Boyd, Rev. David Flaherty, and Rev. Dr. John Deckenback.

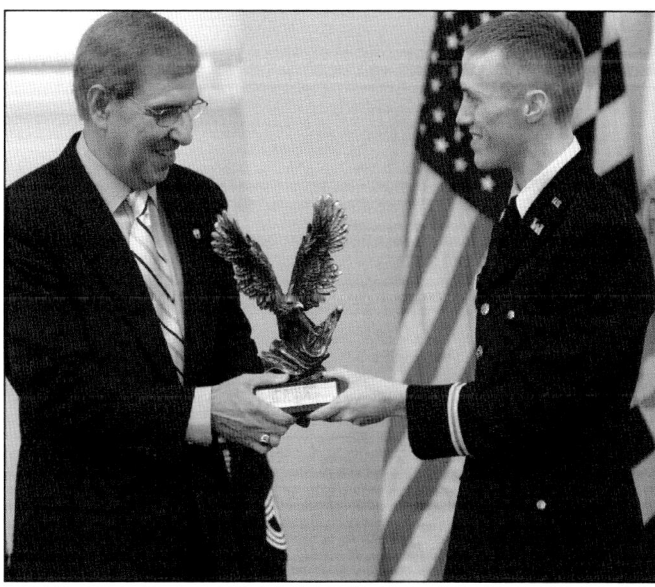

Hood established a US Army Reserve Officers' Training program in association with the military science department at McDaniel College in 2008. Upon graduation from Hood, students in the program receive commissions as second lieutenants in the Army. Newly commissioned Lt. Ian Sparks (2011) presents President Volpe with an American eagle statue in thanks for his remarks to the new officers during Hood's commissioning ceremony.

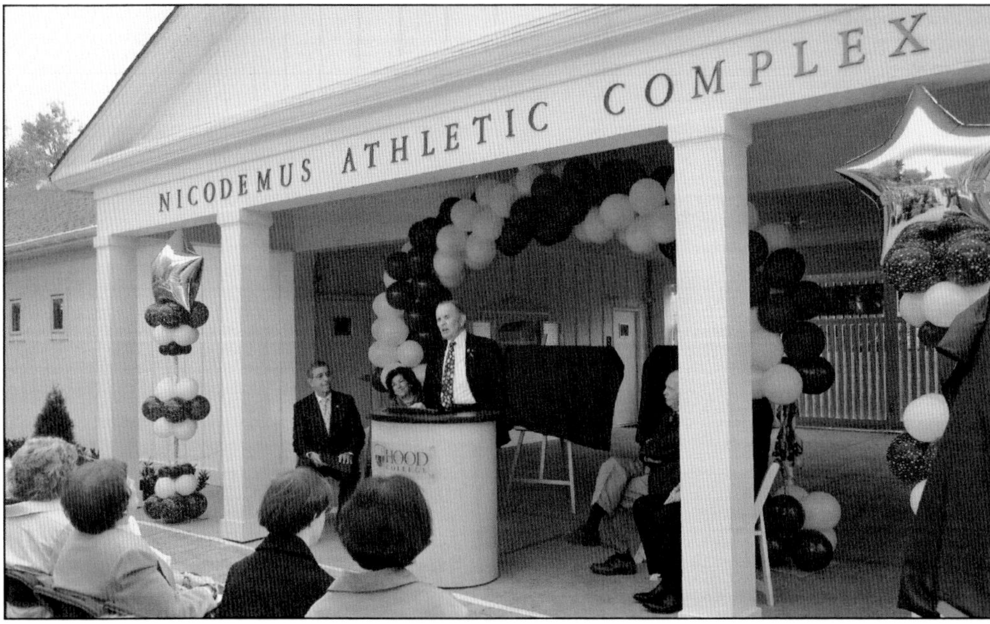

Charles Nicodemus, Hood trustee emeritus, addresses the crowd that came to witness the dedication of the new artificial turf playing field and locker room facilities in 2009. The new athletic complex was named for Nicodemus and his wife, Kathryn Zimmerman Nicodemus, in recognition of their ardent and generous support of Hood athletics. The two were recipients of honorary doctorates of humane letters from Hood in 2005.

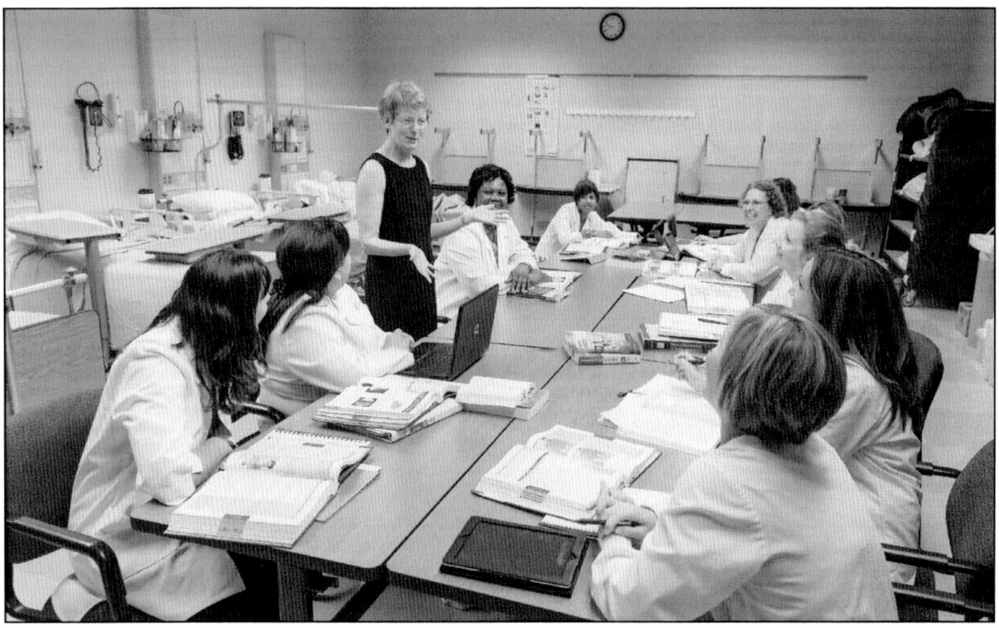

In 2010, Hood initiated its bachelor of science in nursing (BSN) completion program in collaboration with Frederick Community College and Frederick Memorial Hospital. Registered nurses with an associate's degree are able to receive the BSN after completing Hood's two-year program. Dr. Carol Snapp, standing and addressing a group of students in this photograph, was named Hodson Professor of Nursing and is the program's director.

Carlie Colella (2012) of Hagerstown, Maryland, decided to participate in the 2012 Miss Maryland competition in the simple hope of finishing in the top 10 so she could win some scholarship money—she ended up taking the crown. Her platform issue in the Miss America Pageant was the empowerment of women. President Volpe was no doubt pleased that Hood was so well represented in the competition.

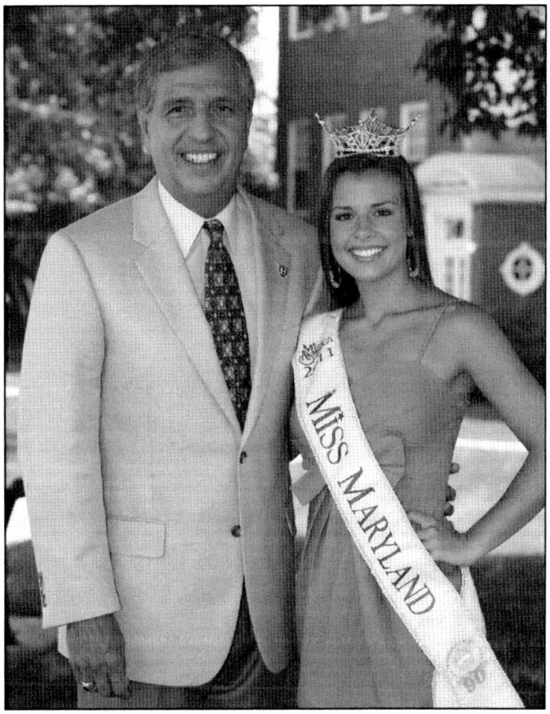

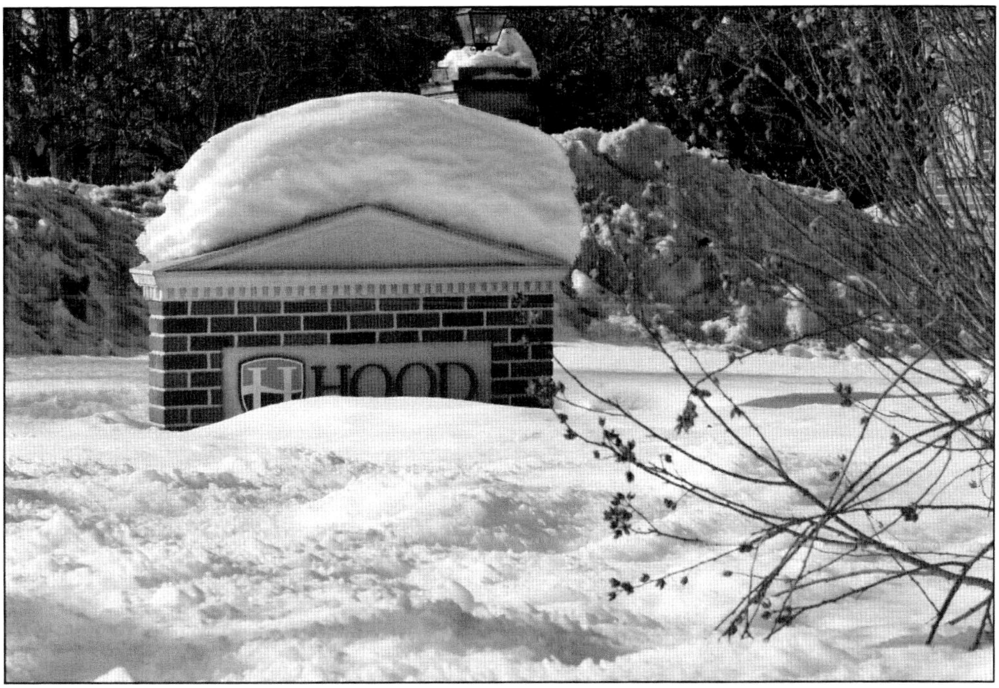

Between February 5 and 10 in 2010, Hood was hit with two nor'easters that brought nearly five feet of snow to Frederick County in what was dubbed "Snowmageddon." Classes at Hood were canceled for a week, but there were still students in the dormitories. Hood's student life division, facilities folks, security officers, and dining service kept several hundred students well fed, entertained, and safe for the duration of the storm cleanup.

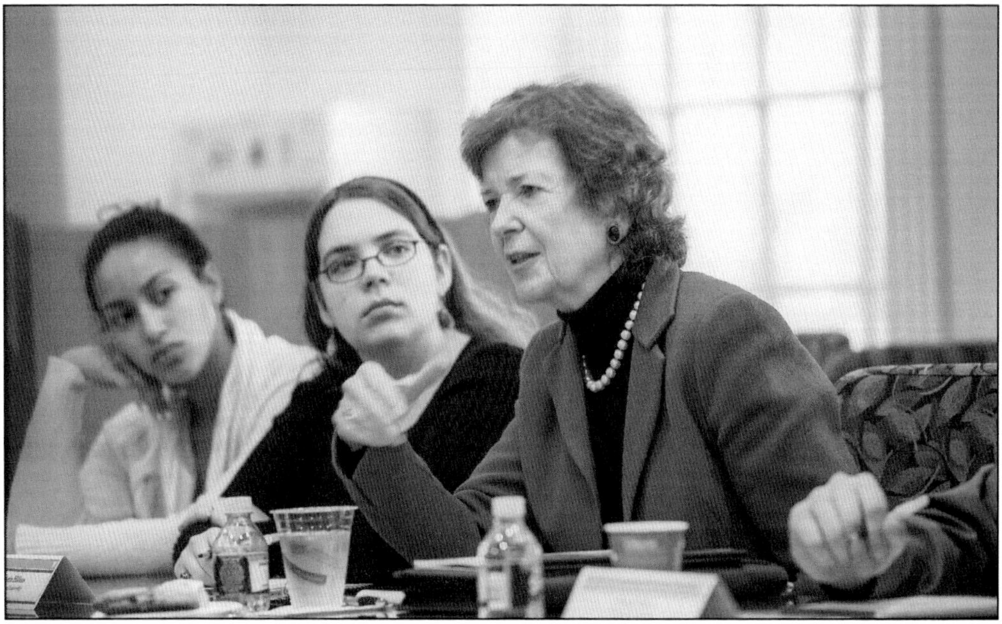

Mary Robinson was the first woman president of Ireland, serving from 1990 to 1997, and she then served as the United Nations high commissioner on human rights from 1997 to 2002. In March 2012, she spent a day at Hood talking with faculty and students and leading a panel discussion entitled, "Connecting the Local and the Global: Social Justice Issues in the Twenty-first Century."

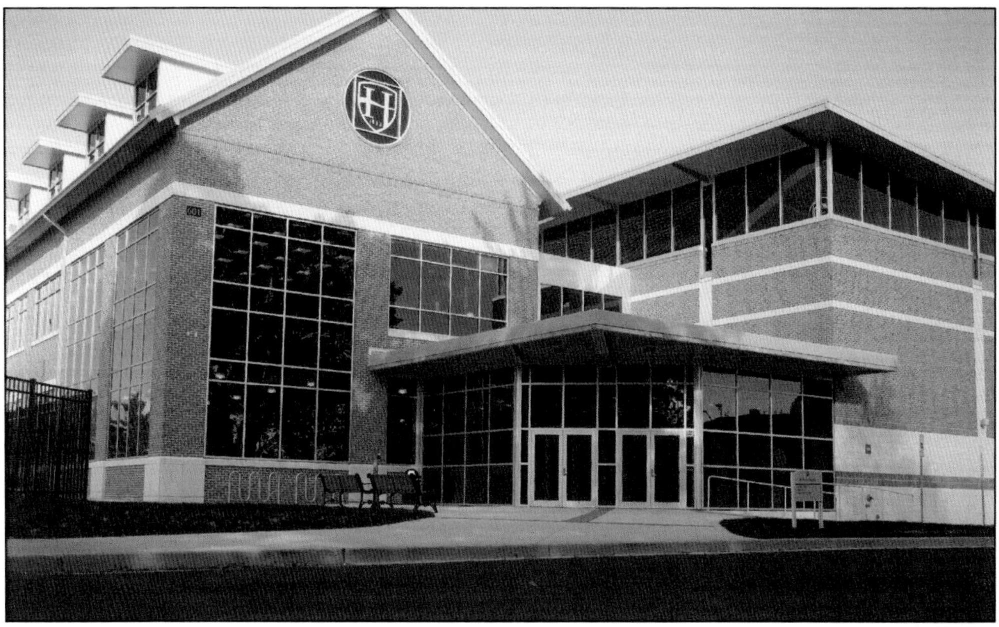

There had long been a need for a space for very large gatherings on campus, and it was apparent that with the growth of Hood's student body Gambrill Gymnasium was no longer adequate. The new Hood College Athletic Center, dedicated in 2011, addresses those needs in fine style. The facility houses an arena, a fitness center, training rooms, offices, and the Hood College Athletic Hall of Fame.

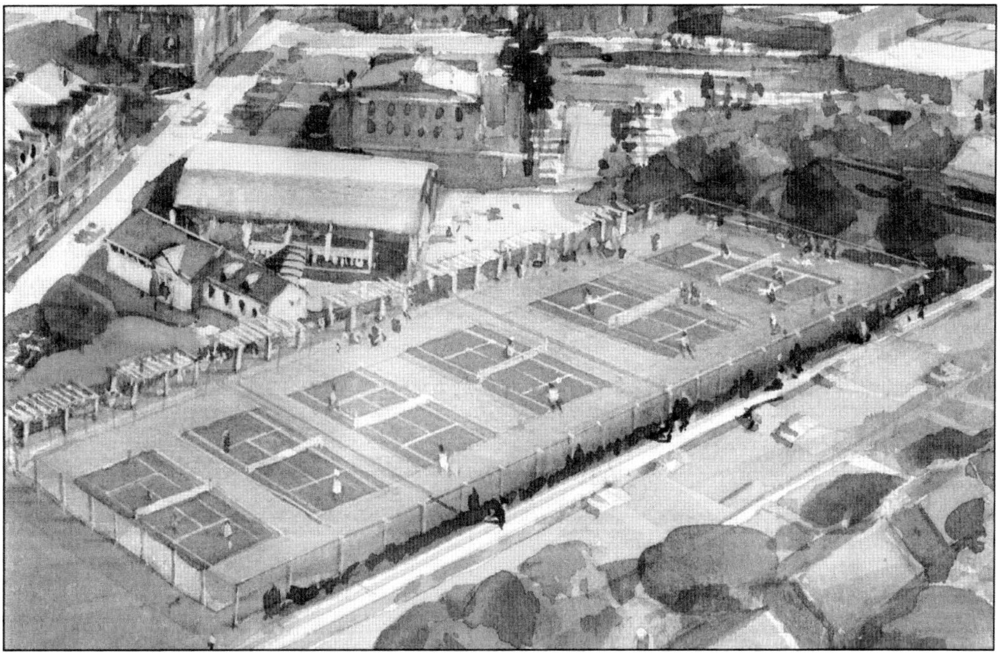

The summer of 2012 saw major changes taking place on the west side of campus. The old Huntsinger Aquatic Center building was torn down so a modern facility could be constructed in its place, and the pool was widened. A new pool enclosure replaced the old "bubble." Six new Blazer blue tennis courts are ready for play beside the refurbished aquatic complex.

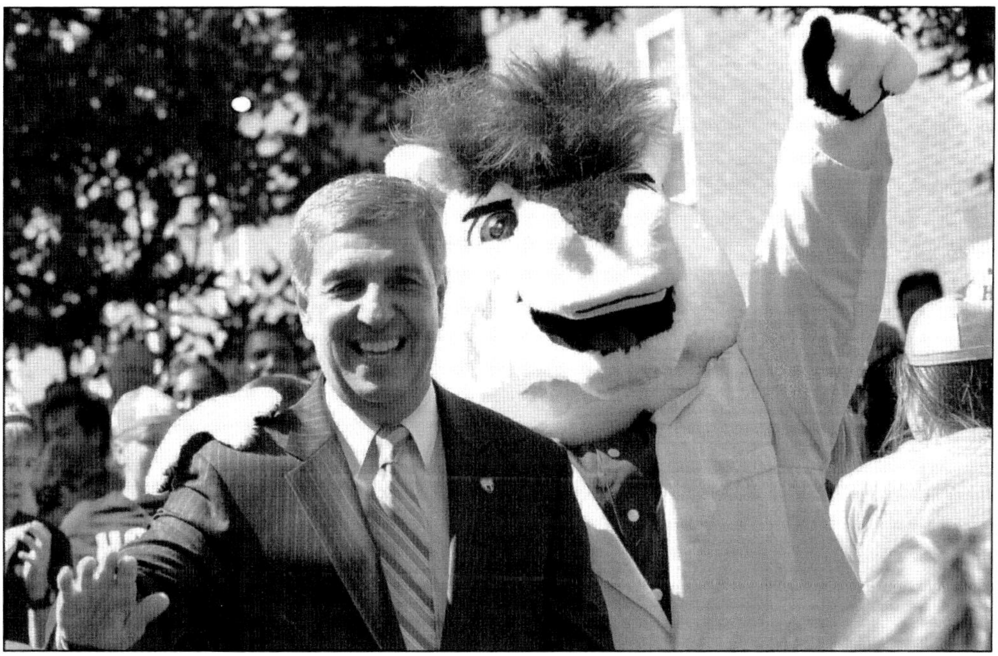

President Volpe and Blaze, Hood's mascot, greet students at Hood's fall convocation, the first day of the academic year. For Hood's students, convocation is a time full of promise. For the president, seeing that promise being nurtured by the people and traditions that epitomize Hood College is what makes each day at Hood a wonderful one.

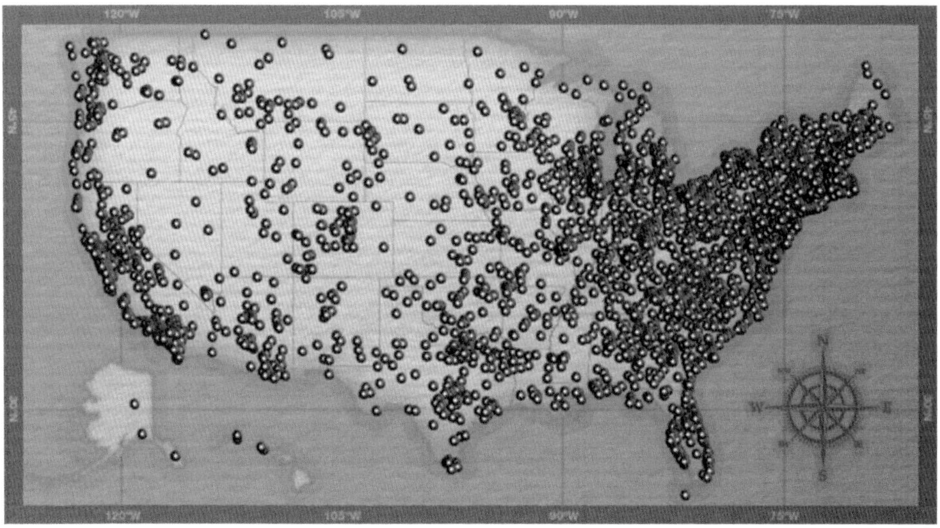

Consistent with our mission to preserve history on a local level, this book was printed in South Carolina on American-made paper and manufactured entirely in the United States. Products carrying the accredited Forest Stewardship Council (FSC) label are printed on 100 percent FSC-certified paper.

MADE IN THE USA